Curious Annals

Curious Annals

NEW DOCUMENTS

RELATING TO BROWNING'S ROMAN

MURDER STORY

Translated, edited,

and with an Introduction by

BEATRICE CORRIGAN

University of Toronto Press

SCHOLARLY REPRINT SERIES
ISBN 0-8020-7007-8
LC 56-3780

TO MY PARENTS

A pretty piece of narrative enough,
Which scarce ought so to drop out, one would think,
From the more curious annals of our kind.

BROWNING, *The Ring and the Book*, I, 448–50

Preface

One night at the end of December, 1697, a certain Guido Franceschini of Arezzo, maddened by his real or supposed wrongs, gained admittance to the house in Rome where his estranged seventeen-year-old wife was living with her parents, and, aided by four confederates, brutally slew all three of them. His wife survived long enough to identify her assassins, who were promptly pursued, arrested, and brought back to Rome to be tried for their crime. The case was long and involved: the evidence and the pleas for and against the principal defendant reached voluminous proportions: anonymous pamphlets were written, and public feeling rose high. Then the murderers were executed; and Guido Franceschini and his victims were forgotten for a hundred and fifty years, until Robert Browning bought in Florence a volume containing their unhappy story, and turned it into one of the greatest narrative poems in English, *The Ring and the Book*.

The antecedents and consequences of this violent deed of revenge are the subject of the documents which form the major portion of this book. It was my good fortune to discover their existence almost by accident, and the opportunity to transcribe, translate, and comment on them gave me a twofold pleasure. In the first place, *The Ring and the Book* had been dear to me for many years, and without question the primary importance of these records is their relation, remote though it may be, to Browning's poem. I say remote, because they were unknown to him; but they fill in so much of the background against which his characters acted out the tragedy consequent on an ill-advised marriage that they are valuable in increasing our understanding of the story. Because the poet breathed immortal life into a series of characters, the long-dead persons on whom they were based have assumed an importance which was never theirs while they were alive: and the details of their relations, of their financial transactions, of their ambitions and disappointments, cannot seem entirely trivial.

In the second place, the seventeenth century in Italy is such an obscure period that any research done upon it is both difficult and highly instructive. Of all the epochs in Italian history, it is the most neglected. In the nineteenth century both the English historians, for the most part Protestants, and the Italians, almost without exception anticlerical and nationalist, were fascinated by the Renaissance but were repelled by a period which was unswervingly Catholic, and apparently quite content to be deprived of political autonomy. Moreover, it was an era without great literature, and the baroque art and architecture in which it was supreme were, until recently, decried as decadent and in ludicrously bad taste. As a result, almost the only works which can be drawn on for information about Italian life and interests during the seventeenth century are the numerous travel journals and letters which I have constantly used to illustrate details of my story. And, in their turn, the documents of the story reveal much about the customs and psychology of the Seicento, which, owing to a marked revival of interest in its art and history, is now at last experiencing the sympathetic re-evaluation denied it for so long.

My acknowledgments are due to the Microfilm Committee of the Modern Language Association for making available to me microfilms (now in the Library of Congress) of manuscripts in the Biblioteca del Comune in Cortona, the Biblioteca Giovardiana in Veroli, the Biblioteca Universitaria in Bologna, and the Biblioteca Angelica and the Biblioteca Casanatense in Rome; to the librarian of the Biblioteca Oliveriana in Pesaro, through whose good offices I obtained a copy of a manuscript there; to Professor W. O. Raymond who kindly enabled me to transcribe a microfilm owned by the library of Bishop's University, Lennoxville; to the librarians of the Vatican library; to the librarian of the Biblioteca dei Laici in Arezzo; to Dr. Renato Rubrichi of the Archivio di Stato in Florence; to Signor Alessandro de Gregori, secretary of the Confraternita della Misericordia in Rome; to the staffs of the University Library and of the Reference Library in Toronto; to Dr. Annamaria Belcredi of Rome for assistance in obtaining illustrations; and to Miss Elsa Amadio for finding and transcribing for me a poem by Paolo Franceschini.

I should like to express my appreciation of financial assistance from the Humanities Research Council of Canada and the Publication Fund of the University of Toronto Press.

I am indebted to Miss Francess Halpenny, Associate Editor of the University of Toronto Press, for her careful and able editing of the text and notes of my manuscript.

I am greatly indebted to Professor W. O. Raymond, not only for his help in obtaining the transcription, but also for his continued interest and for his many valuable suggestions, bibliographical as well as critical.

My debt to Professor J. E. Shaw of the University of Toronto cannot be adequately acknowledged. He has checked all my translation with unwearying thoroughness, has supplied my many deficiencies in Latin, and has been an inexhaustible source of encouragement and wisdom.

B. C.

Contents

Illustrations

Introduction

I

For many years it was taken for granted that the Old Yellow Book, that collection of printed and manuscript documents which Browning bought in Florence, and on which he based the tale told in *The Ring and the Book*, was unique. From time to time another narrative, or version of a narrative, was discovered, but no other collection of material on the famous Roman Murder Case had ever come to light. Then in 1940, nearly eighty years after Browning's purchase, I ascertained that a codex in the Biblioteca del Comune in Cortona,[1] very like the Old Yellow Book in form but nearly twice its size, consisted entirely of documents dealing with the personages and events of the Comparini-Franceschini relationship, and that about half these documents contained material which had hitherto been unknown.

The papers in the Old Yellow Book are not arranged in any logical order, as Judge Gest has demonstrated,[2] but those in the Cortona codex are presented in three groups arranged chronologically, and preceded by a general narrative. The contents of the codex are as follows (the titles of documents which appear in the Old Yellow Book are in italics; the new documents which are in Latin are indicated by (L), otherwise they are in Italian; printed documents are indicated by *).

TABLE OF CONTENTS OF THE CORTONA CODEX

Part One

Deplorable / and impious homicide / committed in Rome / by Guido son of the late To / maso Franceschini / and 4 other Companions / on the Persons of Pietro / Comparini / and Violante Peruzzo Spouses / and Francesca Pompilia / believed the daughter of the same / and wife of the above-mentioned Fran / ceschini.

Part Two

[This second part is preceded by a title-page printed by hand within a double margin. The general title is:]

DOCUMENTS / Concerning the three legal cases of / Guido Franceschini of Arezzo / that is / Concerning the claim to daughterhood and the / surrender of the bonds / Concerning the alleged abduction at Arezzo and / Concerning the murders at Rome. / With the addition of the / Account of the Execution.

In the lawsuit brought by Guido Franceschini against Pietro Comparini.

1. A case tried at Rome concerning a claim of daughterhood and a transfer of bonds.

2. Summary of the documents supporting this argument.

i. Note of the assets and income of Signor Guido Franceschini, the opponent, written by his own hand.

ii. Sworn testimony of the mediating agent, deposing how the marriage in question was arranged.

iii. The first matrimonial contracts drawn up between Signor Pietro Comparini and Signor Guido Franceschini, in which the said Comparini cedes to Signor Guido Franceschini, the bridegroom, free administration of two houses and three bonds, with the obligation of taking Signor Pietro and his wife with him to the city of Arezzo, and of providing them with food, clothes, and a suitable dwelling-place.

iv. Second matrimonial contracts, in which are assigned 24 21/100 bonds of different loans, together with another 10 bonds held in trust by Signor Pietro Comparini for his lifetime, and another 3 bonds resigned to the late Pietro Zacconi; and in which another obligation concerning maintenance is assumed.

v. Dower settlement drawn up between the said parties, in which both Abate Paolo Franceschini and Signor Guido, the bridegroom, promised solemnly to have it ratified by Signori Girolamo and Antonio Franceschini, their brothers.

vi. *The sworn deposition of a witness concerning the poverty of the said Signor Guido Franceschini, and the miseries endured by the said Comparino while he was living at the former's house in the city of Arezzo.*

vii. Order to put into effect the granted maintenance as in the position of a daughter, and the transfer of the bonds assigned as a dowry; with the decision.

viii. Production and repetition of the various arguments for the reconsideration of the said decree.

ix. Repetition of the said arguments.

x. Sentence of the Reverend Father D. Tomati, absolving from the exceptions taken against the order for maintenance in the position of a daughter and for the transfer of the bonds.

xi. The deposition of Signora Violante Peruzzi, asserted mother of Francesca Pompilia, concerning the substitution at birth.

xii. Baptism certificate of the same Signora Violante, from which it is apparent that at the time of the feigned birth she was 48 years old.

xiii. Testimony of Signora Caterina Fiori, aunt of Francesca Pompilia.

xiv. Another deposition by Signora Cristina Paperozzi, sister of the said Signora Francesca Pompilia.

xv. Another deposition by Signora Anna Maria Amadei: all these witnesses were present when Corona gave birth to the said Signora Francesca Pompilia.

xvi. Testimony of Signora Anna Maria Bobba, who was present at the substitution of the said child.

xvii. Another deposition by Signora Petronilla Feure.

xviii. Another deposition for the permanent record by Signora Agnese Santa Olivieri.

xix. Repudiation of his paternal inheritance made by Signor Guido Franceschini. (L)

xx. Testimony of the Chancellor of the city of Arezzo. (L)

In the lawsuit brought by Guido Franceschini against Giuseppe Caponsacchi.

1. A trial for abduction and theft at Arezzo. (L)
2. A trial on the charge of abduction at Arezzo.* (L)

In the trial of Guido Franceschini and his confederates for murder.

1. *Argument of Signor Giacinto Arcangeli in favour of Biagio Agostinelli.*
2. *Argument of Signor Arcangeli in defence of Guido Franceschini.**
3. *Argument of Signor Desiderio Spreti in defence of Franceschini.*
4. *Argument of Signor G. B. Bottini against the defendants.**
5. *Another argument of G. B. Bottini.**
6. *Summary of fact made on behalf of the Fisc.**
7. *Argument of Signor Francesco Gambi against Guido Franceschini.**
8. *Another argument of Arcangeli in defence of Franceschini.**
9. *Argument of Signor Spreti in favour of Franceschini.**
10. *Argument of Signor Gambi against Franceschini.**
11. *Another argument of Signor G. B. Bottini.**
12. *Another summary made on behalf of the Fisc.**
13. An argument by Signor Dionisio Pignatelli on behalf of Guido Franceschini.
14. *An account of the facts and grounds, by an anonymous author.**
15. *A response to the account of the facts.**
16. Description of the death of Guido Franceschini.
17. *Argument of Signor Antonio Lamparelli.**
18. *Sentence of Signor Marco Antonio Venturini, restoring to her original fame the memory of Francesca Pompilia Comparini.**

Part One of the Cortona codex, preceding the legal documents and giving, as it were, a narrative of the events which they might serve to illustrate, is a longer version of the account generally known as the Secondary Source of *The Ring and the Book*, which was sent to Browning from Florence by Mrs. Baker in 1862. The Cortona version is for the most part identical with that of the Baylor MS., which has been translated by Professor E. H. Yarrill in the *Baylor Bulletin*,[3] and whose relation to the Secondary Source has been analysed by Professor W. O. Raymond.[4] For this reason I do not propose to publish the whole of it, but only to present in the Appendix a summary of its variations and additional material.

Part Two of the codex is divided into three groups. The first group concerns the suit brought by Guido Franceschini and his wife against Pietro Comparini to force him to acknowledge Francesca Pompilia as his daughter and to complete the payment of her dowry. It is particularly interesting, for it includes the summary of the evidence given on behalf of Pietro in his attempt to prove that Pompilia was not his own child. It presents as well a list of the assets of the Franceschini family, and summaries of the three marriage contracts. The second group is connected with the trial of Giuseppe Caponsacchi on the charge of theft and abduction after his flight with Pompilia to Rome, and contains only two documents, the counsels' arguments for and against Caponsacchi. In the third group are the documents already familiar through the Old Yellow Book dealing with the trial for murder and the rehabilitation of Francesca Pompilia, with two additions, a plea by Dionisio Pignatelli which is presumably the summing up for the defence,[5] and a lengthy description of Guido Franceschini's last hours.

I am publishing here in translation and unabridged all the documents from the first group of Part Two (section A, pp. 3–65), both documents from the second group (section B, pp. 66–81), and the two documents of the third group which do not apear in the Old Yellow Book (section C, pp. 82–103).

Some of the documents in the codex are printed, but most of them are in manuscript, and it is evident that many of these have been copied hastily with frequent omissions and abbreviations. This is particularly unfortunate in the case of the marriage contracts, because it is still impossible to have any exact knowledge of Pietro Comparini's fortune, or of how it was entailed. It is to be regretted that most of the printed documents are those which are already known, whereas the fresh material is, with one exception (the plea on behalf of Caponsacchi in the trial for adultery), in the less reliable, often indeed obviously corrupt, form of manuscript copies.

Two documents in the Old Yellow Book which are not to be found in the Cortona codex are the series of letters written to Monsignor Francesco Cencini, and the sentence of the Criminal Court of Florence in the suit against Gregorio Guillichini, Francesca Pompilia Comparini, and the driver of the carriage in which Pompilia fled from Arezzo. The original of this sentence is in the Archivio di Stato of Florence.[6] As only the first part of it appears in the Old Yellow Book I am publishing a translation of the remainder at the end of the Cortona documents (pp. 107–111), though chronologically it should be inserted after section B.[7]

Besides the documents already mentioned, I have examined several other manuscripts relating to the Franceschini story belonging to various libraries in Italy: two (apart from the codex) in the Biblioteca del Comune in Cortona: 233 (316), item 12,[8] and 245 (328), item 8; one in the Biblioteca Angelica in Rome: 618, item 8; one in the Biblioteca Casanatense, also in Rome: Misc. MS. 2037;[9] one in the Biblioteca Oliveriana in Pesaro: 1188, item 3;[10] one belonging to Baylor University, Texas;[11] and three in the Vatican library: Urb. lat. 1692, Urb. lat. 1696, and Vat. lat. 13658 (S. XVIII).[12]

It is evident from an examination of all the material just described that there are two independent narrative accounts of the Franceschini-Comparini story, which, as they are represented by the Secondary Source and the Casanatense MS., I shall refer to as S and C respectively. They belong to a minor literary genre which was extremely popular in Italy in the seventeenth century in manuscript though not, as far as I am aware, in printed form: a genre closely akin to the tragic or cautionary *novella* dealing with historical personages, such as Bandello's stories of the Countess of Cellant and the Duchess of Amalfi.[13] Favourite subjects for similar narratives are Beatrice Cenci and Vittoria Accoramboni, and innumerable collections still exist in Italian libraries of these accounts of famous criminal cases, written with a certain amount of literary skill in the florid style of the period.

Two such collections in the Vatican Library, already cited above, have general titles which indicate the circumstances in which the accounts were written. One, Vat. lat. 13658, S. XVIII, whose elaborately arranged title-page is framed in pen and ink decorations, is called "Various executions which took place in Rome under several Pontiffs," a title which is rather misleading as one or two of the twenty-four cases described in its 374 pages occurred in Vienna. The other, Urb. lat. 1696, is entitled, "Relation of the method followed in the capture, abjuration, and other events concerning the accomplices mentioned below in crimes affecting this Holy Office," and here too the title is misleading, for not all the cases it contains, the Franceschini trial being one of the exceptions, are of offences against the Inquisition. The stories were, however, probably written and collected by members of that Office. All but two of the narratives in these two collections are anonymous; the first in the collection "Various executions" was written by Cardinal Pallavicino,[14] and another by a Marchesa, the wife of a Vicecastellano, who had actually known the prisoners whose last days she describes. This indicates that some at least of the narratives were composed by people who had first-hand knowledge of the events. The style and form suggest that many of the authors were clerics.

The popularity of this form of literature may be inferred from the fact that six versions of S are now known to exist, after what has been far from an exhaustive investigation of manuscript collections in Italy. Version is possibly a misleading word, for they are all copies, more or less complete, of some original narrative.[15] The original version of S may be Part One of the Cortona codex, though this is by no means certain. It is one of the most elaborately composed of all these accounts, its title hand-printed like a title-page, and the story divided into chapters, each with its own heading. The Pesaro manuscript preserves much of the elaborate form of the Cortona version, and is more closely related to it than any of the others, though it omits some of the material. Two Vatican accounts are also versions of S: that in Urb. lat. 1696 is very similar, though a little shorter still; the other, much briefer, in Urb. lat. 1692 (which is a miscellany of letters, sonnets, narratives, etc.), contains some of the mistakes (though generally scored through, as though someone had undertaken to correct them) which Professor Raymond has pointed out in the Baylor MS., an even more abbreviated form of S, with no general introduction and no division into chapters. The Secondary Source is the shortest version of all, with much material omitted, as well as the divisions and general reflections.

Versions of C, the independent account of the Franceschini case, unrelated to S, appear in the Casanatense MS., which was discovered in 1900, after Browning's death; in a very much abridged form in the manuscript in the Biblioteca Angelica; and in still another form in the Vatican collection, Vat. lat. 13658, S. XVIII. There are so few additional details in any of the variants of C that I am not dealing with them separately in an appendix. It would be pleasant to be able to state that the Vatican MS. is the original from which the others are copied, but though it is slightly longer it does not contain the testimony of the witnesses who attended the dying Pompilia, nor a detail concerning the youngest accomplice, Biagio Agostinelli,[16] which appears only in the Angelica MS., so it must be supposed that the original version of C has not yet been discovered (see n. 14 for comment on a possible author). What the Vatican MS. adds is some tantalizing information about much printed material in the case which has still not come to light, including four volumes of lawyers' pleas in the trial for abduction, and a "celebrated argument" in favour of Guido by Monsignor Lancetta, which reached the hands of the Pope, though it did not succeed in changing his decision to have the murderers executed. As Ciriaco Lancetta was an Auditor of the Sacra Rota Romana whose *Decisiones* were published 1731–5, this work may still be discovered. In no version of C is the presentation as elaborate as that of S in its fullest form; and though there is a general conclusion there is no introduction and no division into chapters.

It is evident that the writer of S has produced a more accurate narrative than the author of C, and that he has, as he says himself, had access to the legal documents in the case he describes, as well as to a third narrative, a description of Guido's last hours and death, which appears in the Cortona codex as well as in the two other items from the

Cortona library, and which was probably written by a member of the Confraternita della Misericordia in Rome. It is to be regretted that in 1891 the records of this society were transferred from its headquarters, the church of S. Giovanni Decollato, to the Archivio di Stato in Rome, and that volume 33 of the Order's *Giornale*, which according to the index[17] contained the account of Guido's execution, has been mislaid or lost.

II

The story of Guido Franceschini's ill-fated marriage, his crime, and his death, has often been told, but the new material which has come to light during the past few years may serve as an excuse for my attempt to tell it once more. I shall endeavour to make my account as factual and objective as possible, and to support my occasional conjectures by references to the documents now available. It should be noted that the general narrative accounts (S and C, and particularly the anonymous pamphlets) are less reliable than the legal documents, and can often be proved inaccurate. The depositions of the witnesses, too, are not wholly reliable. I shall also attempt to relate the events of my narrative to the social background of the period.

The story really begins more than fifty years before the execution which ends it, and thirteen years before the eldest of the protagonists, Guido Franceschini himself, was born. In 1645 the will of Francesco Comparini,[18] father of Pietro Comparini, was probated. Some time before his death Francesco and his brother-in-law, Domenico Canzi,[19] had arranged to leave their estates to Pietro, but to subject them to the terms of a *fedecommesso*. This was a form of entail[20] which dated back to classical times, and had in the sixteenth and seventeenth centuries become very popular in Italy as a means of enabling a prosperous member of the middle class to prevent the dissipation of his property after his death. The provisions of the entail in question are not clear: it seems probable that both estates were tied up in some way until a son was born to Pietro Comparini, or until a daughter of his was married;[21] after that, apparently, he could dispose of them freely.[22]

According to the marriage contracts, the property was of two kinds: real estate, consisting of two houses in Rome, one in the Piazza Lombarda, the other, Pietro's own home, with shops beneath it, in the Strada Paolina;[23] and forty bonds in various public loans, called *luoghi di Monti*. The first of these Roman public loans[24] had been floated in 1526 by Clement VII,[25] at the rate of 10 per cent, each bond (there were 2,000) having a value of 100 scudi. The idea was so popular that there were many other issues in the sixteenth century, with rates of interest ranging from 4 to 12 per cent. In the seventeenth century there were still more loans with a generally lower rate of interest as the papal financiers learned that much of the sum realized by a new loan went to pay the interest on the old ones. Most of these bonds reached maturity after a certain number of years, and for some of them the interest was not annual but cumulative. Pietro was evidently obliged by the terms of the entail to reinvest the proceeds from any bond that fell due. Part of his fortune in 1693 was in various series of the Monti di San Pietro, nine of which had been floated under Innocent XI, with interest at 3 per cent; another part was in bonds of the Novennale secondo,[26] which had been floated in 1640 at 4 per cent to refund an earlier issue at 10 per cent,[27] and which was the only loan to survive the refunding of 1685. Almost certainly the dower documents as we possess them are incomplete, and there was probably attached to them originally some more specific inventory which would have shown the value of the real estate, the rents derived from the shops under the Comparini home and from the other house, and the exact income from the bonds.

Although the *fedecommesso* made it so important to Pietro to have children, he did not marry until 1666, and then chose a wife, Violante Peruzzi, who was already 33. For fourteen years no living child was born to them.[28] Pietro acquired debts, and, unable to touch his capital or even that part of the interest which was cumulative, he was forced to turn over some of his interest-bearing bonds, apparently as security to a creditor.[29] By this time Violante was 47, her husband was 50, and she was beginning to fear that his death would leave her destitute. If the story which she told in her deposition is to be believed, she decided to take matters into her own hands and feign the birth of a child. This would be more difficult to accomplish than it might seem at first glance, because such an event was, as Italian paintings of the birth of the Virgin prove, a social and semi-public occasion. The ingenious means by which she hoped to convince her husband, her neighbours, her servants, and her friends of the genuineness of her motherhood are most graphically described in her own narrative.[30]

She claimed that in November 1679 she sent for a certain midwife, Angela Biondi, swore her to secrecy, and asked her to find a poor woman who was going to bear a child but who would not be able to keep it. Angela replied that she already knew such a woman, a widow called Corona Paperozzi, who had recently come to Rome from Canapina, a village in the hills southeast of Viterbo, and who was living with her sister, Caterina Fiori. Corona was expecting a child in the following

July, and was persuaded without too much difficulty (probably by the promise of a gift of money) to surrender the child at birth to an unknown lady of means, who would give it great advantages.

Immediately Violante began her impersonation of an expectant mother, modelling her symptoms on those of Corona, and forestalling all suspicion on her husband's part by promptly banishing him to a remote bedroom.

On the evening of July 16, 1680, the child was born, unfortunately a girl instead of the boy for whom Violante had hoped. It was an inconvenient hour, but the midwife took the baby to her own home for the night, and the next day Violante waited until her husband had left the house, sent her servant for the midwife (giving him other errands to do as well, so that he might not return too soon), and then played out with Angela's help the comedy which they had arranged. It ended with the presumed mother, outwardly languid, inwardly exultant, watching the baby being bathed in a copper basin, receiving the congratulations of her female friends, and preparing to eat the chicken which one of them had considerately brought and killed, and was cooking before the fire for her refreshment.

A few days later the daughter who was to save her from penury was baptized with names that may have had for Violante some secret significance—Francesca for the grandfather whose inheritance she had made secure; Angela for the midwife to whom she owed her new home; Vittoria, possibly for the street near which she lived, possibly as an expression of Violante's private triumph; Pompilia, the name by which an English poet was to make her famous nearly two centuries later; and Camilla.[31] She is almost always spoken of in the documents as Francesca Pompilia, she signs a letter to her brother-in-law Francesca,[32] and apparently her nickname was Checca.[33]

The child was put out to nurse, and twice her life and the inheritance were in danger: once because the wet-nurse's grief over the death of her son affected the health of her foster-child; once because this nurse's successor gave to her own baby a share of the food which she was paid to reserve for her nurseling. In both emergencies the jealously vigilant Violante intervened, and fortune and baby were saved.

When the child was four she was sent to a day school a few doors from her own home,[34] where she was immediately seen and identified by her own elder sister, Cristina. She attended this school for four years, and it was probably there that she learned to read and write, though she later neglected these accomplishments so much that she was forced to relearn them as a married woman in Arezzo.[35]

Both Pietro and Violante took great care of their daughter. The school mistress called for the child every day, and brought her home again if the Comparini servant could not be spared. Sometimes Pietro himself would take the little girl for a walk down the Strada Paolina and into the Piazza del Popolo,[36] where there was the obelisk to be seen, and the fountain, and where sometimes public executions were held, though they were no fit spectacle for innocent eyes.

For a short time after Francesca Pompilia's birth the family fortunes seemed secure, but in 1685 Innocent XI, anxious to stabilize the papal finances, called in all the Monti at their par value of 100 scudi, not at the market price of 116, and refunded them at 3 per cent, regardless of the rate of interest which they had originally carried.[37] This was a serious blow to Pietro Comparini.[38] As we have seen, he was obliged to reinvest his capital at once, and he had already incurred debts which he could not repay from his diminished income; although, ironically enough, his capital soon increased again, for the new bonds were regarded as so sound that their market value rose to 127 scudi.

In 1681, the year after Francesca Pompilia was born, Tomaso Franceschini died intestate in Arezzo, leaving an impoverished estate and five children: one daughter, Porzia, and four sons, Paolo, Girolamo, Guido, and Antonio Maria.[39] The Franceschini family was extremely old, and its degree of nobility seems to have risen steadily during the seventeenth century. In 1658 it was listed as in the fourth of the eight grades.[40] In 1693 it stood in the second rank.[41] At the end of the century or the beginning of the next Porzia Franceschini obtained a certificate admitting it to the highest standing.[42] Despite the age and dignity of his lineage, Tomaso Franceschini died so impoverished that Guido and Antonio Maria, the two sons who were still minors at the time of his death, made a formal repudiation of their inheritance. The document which records this repudiation (printed below from the codex) is so abridged that no precise estimate of the situation can be formed, but it appears that the two minors renounced all claim to the estate so that they might not be held responsible by its creditors. They also asked the court to appoint a guardian for them in the person of their maternal uncle, Tomaso dei Romani. All this was done with the consent of their elder brothers, Paolo and Girolamo.

There was, however, a brighter side to the picture. Tomaso Franceschini's wife, Beatrice dei Romani, was a member of one of the oldest and most noble houses in Arezzo,[43] and so could exert a certain amount of influence. Moreover, at least two earlier members of the Franceschini family had had distinguished careers in the Church, one in the service of Cardinal Chigi,[44] the other, Felice Franceschini, who flourished in the middle of the seventeenth century, as a celebrated preacher and theologian.[45] Consequently, though Tomaso's children were not wealthy they had powerful friends who could help them to establish themselves in the world. Porzia made a good match, by marrying a nobleman of Arezzo, Count Conti. All four brothers took holy orders, and Girolamo and Antonio Maria remained in Arezzo, where they received a number of benefices under the patronage of Cardinal Cibo,[46] Innocent XI, and the Grand Duke of Tuscany.

Paolo also enjoyed benefices in Arezzo, one of them under the patronage of Cardinal Chigi, but his real career was made in Rome. There he became, as early as 1683, when he dedicated a poem to his patron,[47] the secretary of Cardinal Lauria, an appointment which carried with it much prestige, as the cardinal was one of the most distinguished prelates of his day, and was favoured as a candidate for the papacy.

Paolo's younger brother, Guido, had also come to Rome, and had obtained a position with another distinguished prelate, Cardinal Nerli.[48] Browning and many Browning scholars, Sir Frederick Treves in particular, have attributed to Guido great cunning and skill in intrigue, but the truth seems rather to be that he was a stupid man, lacking in native talent, devoted to his elder brother, whose success he admired and whose advice he followed unquestioningly, and cursed with the faculty of doing everything at the wrong time and in the wrong way. He had been fortunate enough to secure a good position, but he had not the ability to keep it, and when he left or was dismissed from the Cardinal's service it was evident that his hope of a career in Rome was over, and that he would have to seek his fortune in the marriage market, his value somewhat enhanced by his brother's excellent prospects. In accordance with a custom common in noble Italian families of that era (a custom which, like the *fedecommesso*, was designed to preserve a family fortune undivided) Guido alone of the four Franceschini brothers was free to marry, for he had taken minor holy orders only. But it was not until 1693 that, unemployed and desperate, he tried this final expedient.

While ordering a wig for a lady in Florence[49] (who a few years later may have shown it to her friends as a memento of an interesting acquaintance) he suggested that the wig-maker, Antonia Scarduelli, should find a wife for him. He specified the dowry he demanded, and offered a commission for a successful negotiation. Antonia's shop was in the Corso, not far from the Comparini home. She did not know the family,[50] but her daughter Ursula began to make inquiries about possible heiresses, and in a backstairs way heard that Pietro Comparini had a marriageable daughter and would pay a suitable dowry.[51] Inventories of property were exchanged, and the match between Guido and Francesca Pompilia was made. Characteristic of Guido are his anxiety over the arrangements, evinced in his daily visits to the shop, and his apparent attempt to break his bargain by assuming charge of the negotiations himself and abruptly ceasing his acquaintance with Antonia,[52] thus making himself an enemy for the sake of 40 doppie.

Pietro's readiness to accept as a suitor for his daughter this middle-aged man who had failed in his career may be explained in two ways. First, his creditors were impatient, and if his daughter married, his fortune, inaccessible until then, would be at his own disposal. At the same time he would secure a son-in-law whose rank was higher than his own, so achieving one of the purposes for which entails were often founded. The exact station of the Comparini is never defined in the documents. Pietro is three times called *dottore*,[53] which indicates a certain education. Violante's closest friend seems to have been the wife of Cardinal Maidalchini's steward,[54] which probably gives some clue to the class of society in which they moved. In 1680 their household consisted of two men-servants, Ventura and Domenico, but no maid-servant, though Ventura's wife assisted with the housework when she was needed.[55] This may be an indication of the poverty of the Comparini rather than of their social position. The harpischord covered with yellow leather and the gilded four-poster bed mentioned in the evidence of Anna Maria Bobba, a neighbour,[56] testify to some degree of luxury and taste. Almost certainly, social consideration influenced the ambitious Violante, who together with Paolo urged on the marriage.[57]

However, Pietro was shrewd enough not to be satisfied with the inventory drawn up by Guido, in which every item of the Franceschini property was described in the glowing terms of a real-estate advertisement, and where even pending lawsuits figured as assets.[58] He insisted on some verbal confirmation of this wealth from persons whom he knew and trusted, and the reports he succeeded in obtaining were not reassuring.

In the first place, he discovered that Guido belonged to the second class of nobles and not to the first, as he had claimed. Much more disillusioning was the revelation that the house at Arezzo did not belong to Guido at all, but to his two elder brothers, Paolo and Girolamo, their mother, of course, also possessing a dower right in it. That Pietro had discovered this early is evident from the wording of the first marriage contract,[59] yet despite his knowledge he proceeded with arrangements for the wedding, which may indicate that his financial situation was indeed desperate.

In this first contract,[60] drawn up as was the second on June 24, 1693, Pietro gives Guido free administration during Pietro's life of the property left by Francesco Comparini and Domenico Canzi, mentioning particularly the income from the two houses and three bonds. This property by the terms of the entail was to revert to Francesca Pompilia on Pietro's death without male issue. He assigns it to her as a dowry as well as all his other property present or future, but reserves the right of making a will to the value of 100 scudi. Despite the sweeping declaration of complete surrender with which the contract begins, he also reserves for himself ten bonds which cannot be touched until after his death, the three bonds which he had had to pledge with a creditor, and some other unspecified property. The income from these thirteen bonds (or possibly eight, for he seems uncertain about the availability of five of them) is to form Francesca Pompilia's pin-money, and half the capital from them is to be hers when it is available.

Guido on his part agrees to take Pietro and Violante to Arezzo, to provide for them completely there, to pay Pietro 20 scudi a year in cash, and in the case of Pietro's death to provide maintenance for Violante and pay the 20 scudi a year to her. If both Pietro and Violante should die, the 20 scudi are to be paid to Francesca Pompilia as pin-money. If Pietro and Violante should desire to return to Rome Guido pledges himself to pay the costs of the journey, and either to restore to Pietro the income of the property assigned for his administration, or to return to Rome himself and there establish a household where the couple can live with him at his expense.

The other contract, drawn up on the same date,[61] enables Guido to sell five of the twenty-four 21/100[62] bonds of various loans which formed part of the dowry, and to use the proceeds for the expenses of the marriage, a provision which shows that the Comparini must have been well aware how poor the future bridegroom was. The remaining bonds also might be sold, but the proceeds were to be reinvested at once in Arezzo in certain specified ways which had to be satisfactory to Pietro; such investments had to be acknowledged as proceeding from the dowry.

The final dower settlement is dated August 27,[63] and apparently in the meantime Pietro had learned something more about Guido's repudiation of his inheritance, and knew that Paolo's signature was not sufficient guarantee for the contract of maintenance in the Franceschini household.[64] By the terms of this third contract, Guido is to have immediately the proceeds from seven 82½/100 bonds instead of five.[65] He may realize the remainder of the dowry one year after the marriage, but must reinvest it at once, to Pietro's satisfaction, in either Arezzo or Rome. And this time Paolo signs not only for himself but for his brothers, Girolamo and Antonio Maria, having received their power of attorney for this purpose. At the same time, he and Guido pledge themselves to have the other two brothers ratify the contract in person within two months.

It is evident that Guido had given some sort of guarantee and pledged his own property in some way, but what he had to pledge and what his assurance was cannot be ascertained from the documents available to us. Pietro had every reason to demand some such guarantee, for the dowry he was giving his daughter, estimated by his lawyer at 8,000 scudi,[66] was a large one for that day, even in Rome, very large for one of the smaller Tuscan cities. Beckford says that in Pisa the usual portion in the eighteenth century was 4 or 5 thousand scudi.[67] In 1689 Cristina Paleotti's daughter was married to a noble of Milan with a dowry of 3,000 scudi, and at about the same time the Conestabile Lorenzo Onofrio Colonna provided a dowry of 10,000 scudi for an illegitimate daughter who had been brought up in princely luxury.[68] The 20 scudi a year which Guido promised to pay first to Pietro, and after his death successively to Violante and Francesca Pompilia as pin-money, seems pitifully small in comparison, particularly as Beckford says that 4 or 5 scudi a month was the usual pin-money in Pisa, and implies that it was a meagre allowance.[69] It is possible that there was some secret agreement between the two men. Typical of both of them is the admission that the contracts were drawn up in Rome to avoid paying a tax in Arezzo.[70]

The date of the third marriage contract, late in August, makes it very unlikely that Francesca Pompilia's marriage on September 6 took place without her father's consent as the anonymous pamphleteers claimed,[71] nor is there any suggestion of this in the lawsuit, though if it had been true it might well have been used as an argument to defame the Franceschini brothers. In any case the marriage did take place, and on November 30, 1693, a day so rainy that heaven itself seemed already to be weeping for the disaster which it foresaw,[72] the two couples left Rome for Arezzo. On the same day Paolo's patron, Cardinal Lauria, died, so depriving his secretary of his sound advice and his skill in dealing with difficult situations.

Although the Comparini had learned before they went to Arezzo that Guido had been untruthful in his statements about his family, they found that the mode of life there was very different from what they had expected. Quarrels broke out almost at once between Violante and Guido's mother, Beatrice dei Romani. Each was used to ruling her own household without interference, and in birth and training they were very different. Pietro's taste for low company angered the Franceschini brothers who were living in Arezzo, Girolamo and Antonio Maria,[73] who now refused to ratify the dower contract as Guido and Paolo had pledged that they would do.[74] According to the stories of Angelica,[75] the servant dismissed by the Franceschini and persuaded later by the Comparini to give evidence on their behalf, the Franceschini family behaved with shocking violence and pettiness, Beatrice and Girolamo in particular proving so intolerable that Pietro tried to insist that they should be forced to leave the house,[76] which however was their property rather than Guido's.

Letters from both parties to the dispute, containing angry accusations and counter-charges, soon began to rain upon Paolo Franceschini in Rome,[77] and he employed fruitlessly all the diplomatic talents which he had acquired in the service of his cardinal. At first he refrained from taking sides, pointing out to Violante that as he and she had been equally responsible for the marriage it was the duty of both to endeavour to make it successful. He rejected most positively the suggestion which she seems to have made that she and Pietro should return to Rome and live with him.[78]

The violence of the quarrels increased instead of abating, and the Comparini actually seized some of their daughter's jewels and had to be forced to restore them by the Governor of Arezzo, who threatened to imprison them if they did not behave more quietly.[79]

Francesca Pompilia's appeals to the Bishop and the Governor of Arezzo must have been made at the end of February, 1694, for Paolo has heard of them at the beginning of March,[80] and begs Pietro to consider the scandal they are causing in Arezzo and Rome, adding that already for fear of mockery he is shunning all who know the story, particularly his fellow townsmen. This is the first mention we have of the motive which undoubtedly was to play so large a part in the coming tragedy. In the next letter, dated March 6, also addressed to Pietro, Paolo refers to Comparini's threat "that the papers shall be turned into waste-paper."[81] Evidently the "papers" are the dower contracts, and Pietro and Violante were already planning a way out of their dilemma.

Violante's explanation of her startling revelation was that after the Jubilee was declared on December 3, 1693,[82] she began to search her conscience most scrupulously lest any unconfessed sin should be the cause of her present sufferings, and that then for the first time it occurred to her that perhaps her pretence of having borne a child had not been morally justifiable.[83] Her confessor confirmed her doubts, and made her reveal the truth to her husband, who after saying, "I forgive you," refused to speak to her again for several days.[84] If this conversation actually took place it would explain Pietro's veiled threats to Paolo at the beginning of March. At the end of March the Comparini returned to Rome, Guido keeping his bargain to pay the expenses of the return journey, but so sparingly that Pietro was forced to borrow money before he could leave Arezzo.[85]

Once more there is ambiguity in the financial record. By the terms of the marriage settlement Guido was to have had full administration of both the Comparini houses, yet Pietro returned to his old home in the Strada Paolina, and had evidently not yet transferred the dower bonds to Guido's possession. By his own admission he had handed over to Guido only the five 3/100 bonds of the original contract,[86] not the seven and a fraction bonds agreed on in the third settlement. It may be conjectured that Paolo had persuaded his brothers before the marriage to agree to settle the Franceschini property on Guido and his heirs despite his repudiation of inheritance, and that their refusal to sign the final documents accounts for Pietro's delay in making over to Guido the remainder of the dowry. However this may be, immediately after his return to Rome Pietro issued a judicial notice, denying his paternity and repudiating the dower contract. He produced in support of his statement the evidence of six witnesses, as well as various certificates. His search for the witnesses seems to have begun in May or June, 1694.[87] The only dated depositions were made on June 24, 1694, and August 2, 1695.[88] He also alleged misrepresentation by the Franceschini at the time of the marriage, a charge which can have had little foundation as it had been plain from Guido's inventory that much of the Franceschini income was from benefices belonging to Girolamo and Antonio Maria.

On August 20, 1695, Francesca Pompilia and her husband brought suit for the implementation of the dower settlement.[89] The judge decided in their favour, and Pietro appealed the case on August 31. A second decision was given against him on September 17, and he appealed once more, this time to the Supreme Court. It is to the second appeal that the Summary in the Cortona codex belongs,[90] and it contains the abbreviated testimony of the six witnesses, as well as abridgments of the certificates.

It is still impossible to know how truthful the story of the feigned birth may be considered. The six witnesses whose testimony, together with Violante's deposition, gives such a curious and circumstantial account of a seventeenth-century lying-in, were Caterina Fiori, the aunt, and Cristina Paperozzi, the sister (so Violante claimed) of Francesca Pompilia; Anna Maria Amadei, the aunt's gossip, who had witnessed the birth of the child and had seen it taken away by the midwife; two neighbours, Anna Maria Bobba and Petronilla Feure, who had worked in the Comparini household; and Agnese Santa Olivieri, who had actually seen the midwife and her husband carrying the child to Pietro Comparini's house. The two persons whose testimony would have carried the most weight, Corona (the alleged mother) and the midwife, were both dead, and all the witnesses examined were poor women who might have been bribed without too much difficulty. However their evidence is extremely circumstantial, and it is apparent even from the abridged form of it which we possess that the examiner had been careful to ask them questions framed to test their agreement on certain important points. Even so, it is quite possible that they may have been drilled in their stories, and every account is cautious in accepting the tale as true. But if it is true, what a strange story it reveals! a story of an intrigue exclusively among women, with the unconscious Pietro in the midst of them, proud of his paternity, and walking forth with his handsomely dressed little daughter under the mocking sceptical eyes not only of his neighbours but of the child's true relatives.[91] And the child herself, another puppet in the hands of the plotters, probably encountering many quizzical glances which were inexplicable to her, faced on her first day at school with the knowing smiles and jeering questions of a girl twelve years her senior, and later perplexed by the tearful embraces of a strange woman.[92] If Cristina Paperozzi's story is to be believed it seems almost incredible that Pompilia should not have had from childhood some knowledge of her true parentage, or at least some suspicion that Violante and Pietro were not her mother and father.

The details in these depositions[93] are so unsavoury that the rage and shame of the Franceschini family must have been intense. They secured letters from the Governor and the Bishop of Arezzo supporting their cause, and all Pietro's appeals against the judgment in their favour seem to have failed. But he persisted in his refusal to pay the rest of the dowry, and still Francesca Pompilia remained childless, a constant grievance to the Franceschini, since the continuance of their house and their greatest hope of securing the dower both rested on the birth of an heir.

And here there must still occur a long gap in the story, for our last dated document before the elopement in 1697 is the deposition of Agnese Olivieri in 1695: a gap of nearly two years, during which Francesca Pompilia was growing from a child of fifteen to a woman of seventeen, pretty even in her mother-in-law's malignant eyes,[94] romantic, as her letters show, and all the more attractive because her husband and his mother and brothers were so unkind to her. She gained without difficulty the sympathy of Canon Conti, the brother-in-law of Guido's sister, and also of Gregorio Guillichini, a young noble of Arezzo related to both the Caponsacchi and Franceschini families, whose role in the story is a puzzling one. Francesca Pompilia makes no mention of him in her deposition,[95] but speaks of him in a letter to her parents as though his name would be familiar to them.[96] According to the evidence brought before the court of Arezzo he was on excellent terms with her, actually assisted at her flight with Caponsacchi, and was accused of being her lover.[97] As this latter accusation seems to have been based on his throwing snowballs up at the window where she was standing it should perhaps not be taken too seriously, but it is evident that such a gesture was a valid cause for jealousy in the seventeenth century. Guido had also objected to confetti being thrown at Francesca Pompilia after a play, he said by Caponsacchi, she said by Conti, who as a connection by marriage had greater privileges.

With Giuseppe Caponsacchi, a young man seven years older than herself, a sub-deacon and Canon of the Pieve di Santa Maria in Arezzo, she formed one of those half-literary half-emotional relationships which are so pleasantly dangerous, and in consequence she experienced the sudden flowering of heart and mind which results when a young girl, little more than an adolescent, becomes the eager pupil of a charming and gallant man who assumes over her the authority given him by his superior years and knowledge. Under his guidance she read such poems as Marino's sensuous *Adone*, such novels as Morandi's *Rosalinda*, in which the stirring adventures and amorous episodes are excused by a religious ending;[98] and though she reproved him for sending her also a copy of indecent verses she did not attempt to put an end to their friendship. Apparently at her suggestion, she and Caponsacchi soon adopted for their secret correspondence the names of Mirtillo and Amarilli, the hero and heroine of Guarini's pastoral play, *Il pastor fido*. Francesca Pompilia probably saw some resemblance between her own position and that of Amarilli, who loving and loved by Mirtillo is solemnly betrothed to Silvio. The claims of spontaneous love as superior to the bonds imposed by an artificial society are reiterated throughout the play, with all the eloquence and sensual allurement that the poet can lend them. Amarilli preserves what she herself considers an inhumanly icy chastity, but a sadly prophetic episode occurs in the fourth act when she is surprised with Mirtillo in a compromising situation, is arrested, accused of adultery, and condemned to death.

The letters were exchanged by various means, sometimes by the hand of Canon Conti, against his better judgment, sometimes through Maria, a maid in the Franceschini household, sometimes by being lowered from Francesca Pompilia's window to Caponsacchi waiting in the street below. Often too the lovers talked to each other through the window, and Guido became angrily and justifiably suspicious of his wife's behaviour.

The melodramatic episode which brought this unhappy situation to a close is, like so much else in the story, subject to more than one interpretation, and whether Francesca Pompilia's departure from Arezzo was an elopement with a lover or an escape from a tyrannical husband to whom she did not dare to confess her newly discovered pregnancy has been the subject of much argument. It is a fact that on the night of April 28–9, 1697, Guido and his brother Girolamo were drugged, and Francesca Pompilia accompanied by Caponsacchi climbed over the city wall, got into one of the new caleches which had recently made night travelling possible, and started out towards Rome. She took with her a very complete wardrobe and some jewels which were not, according to the Franceschini who later accused her of theft, all her own property. She also carried off a suit of Guido's clothes, possibly as a trophy, possibly as an amusing present for her father.

The details of the departure from Arezzo are described in many different ways. The longer versions of S say that Guillichini was sorry for Francesca Pompilia and thought that she was in danger from Guido. He consequently decided to help her to escape, and discussed the matter with her parents in Rome. When he heard that Canon Caponsacchi was going to Rome he sent a message to the Comparini asking them if they would receive their daughter. It was their affirmative reply, according to this story, that determined the flight. This would explain Francesca Pompilia's otherwise ambiguous letter to her parents, in which she says that she had planned to go to Rome with Guillichini, but that as he was ill Caponsacchi had decided to take his place.[99]

In her deposition, however, Francesca Pompilia tells quite a different story, for she mentions neither Guillichini nor Canon Conti, and says that she approached Caponsacchi directly by calling him into her house.[100] Lamparelli, the Procurator of Charity, in a defence of her character made after her death, evidently feels that this admission would be damaging to his case, for he says that Caponsacchi was suggested to her by Conti and Guillichini.[101]

Caponsacchi in his deposition tells a story which agrees with none of the others. He says that Francesca Pompilia had heard through Canon Conti of his projected journey to Rome, and that she wrote him several letters urging him to take her with him.[102] And he makes an admission which would provide a very convincing motive for the flight when he says that Guido had learned about the letters because one fell into the hands of a woman who lived opposite his house, and who took it to him. He was also warned of the intrigue by his sister.[103]. Here Caponsacchi contradicts his own story, for he says that Guido's consequent threats against himself and Francesca Pompilia made him decide to go to Rome and take her with him, though he had begun his story by saying that it was after his journey to Rome had been planned that she had first written to him.

It may be conjectured that Porzia knew of the intrigue through confidences made to her husband by his brother, Canon Conti, and that she warned Guido to guard his honour, and Caponsacchi to avoid Guido's wrath. It may also be supposed that the woman who took the incriminating letter to Guido was Maria Margherita Contenti, whose windows are described as overlooking the Franceschini house. It is probable that she is one of the women of whom Francesca Pompilia speaks in her deposition, when she says that Caponsacchi used to linger in the street talking to "certain insignificant women who live opposite."[104] If this identification is correct, jealousy may have played a part in the woman's accusations both at this time and during the trial in Arezzo.

Whether the departure from Arezzo was flight or elopement, it seems certain that Canon Conti connived at it, and that Guillichini went with the escaping pair as far as the carriage; perhaps, as both he and Caponsacchi were armed, to help to ward off any attack or attempt to detain the fugitives. Caponsacchi provided the carriage, and helped to carry the stolen goods. He and Francesca Pompilia left the city at 1 A.M. on April 29, and Guido later claimed that they halted for a time at Foligno and shared a room there.[105] In any case it is known that they stopped at 7.30 P.M. at Castelnuovo, fifteen miles from Rome, and were overtaken there the next morning by Guido. He was armed with a light sword, but by his own admission he was afraid of Caponsacchi's superior strength and reputation for boldness, and had heard that he was carrying fire-arms.[106] Consequently he made no attempt to avenge himself (an omission which he was to regret bitterly later) but went to the governor of the place and asked for help. When he returned to the inn with constables, Francesca Pompilia, desperate as she saw her hopes of escape destroyed, snatched up Caponsacchi's sword and attacked her husband. She was at once disarmed,[107] and the two fugitives were arrested and taken to Rome. An inventory of the stolen goods was made before they left Castelnuovo.[108]

A complaint was apparently laid immediately by the Franceschini before the episcopal court of Arezzo,[109] where several witnesses were examined, among them Maria Margherita Contenti, who testified that she had seen Francesca Pompilia with a light in her hand stealthily letting Caponsacchi out of a door. The date of this hearing is not known, but the evidence presented during it was used at Caponsacchi's trial for abduction and theft, which took place in the court of the Governor of Rome late in September.

Two documents survive in the Cortona codex dealing with the latter trial, and they are the first to be known concerning this phase of the case. They are a plea on behalf of the plaintiff, Guido Franceschini, by Giovanni Maria Serbuceri, and a counter-plea on behalf of the defendant, Giuseppe Caponsacchi, by Antonio Lamparelli, the Procurator of Charity. The arguments of the latter are at times extremely specious, being based on legal quibbles rather than on fact or evidence,[110] and surely his contention that Caponsacchi was obliged to share Francesca Pompilia's room at the inn because it was his duty to protect her must have caused a certain amusement in a seventeenth-century court of justice. He appears to have realized himself that his client's case, eloquent and detailed though his defence of it is, was weak, for he ends by suggesting exile rather than death as a penalty for the offence which he thus tacitly admits. His suggestion was adopted, and Caponsacchi was banished to Civita Vecchia for three years.[111] No decision was reached, however, in the separate case against Francesca Pompilia, who was relegated while it was pending to a convent.[112]

This situation not unnaturally did not satisfy the Franceschini family. Guido and Paolo had been clamouring for a decision which would have secured the dowry for them;[113] instead they were left with their thirst for revenge unquenched, and with a multiplicity of lawsuits on their hands, including Francesca Pompilia's unexpected suit for divorce, the success of which would be a death-blow to their hopes.[114] Moreover Pietro was boasting all over Rome of his daughter's skill in tricking both the Franceschini and the judge.[115]

Guido now began to find the ridicule of his position intolerable.

According to the prevailing code of honour he should have killed at least his wife and if possible her lover too when he had come on them at Castelnuovo. Instead he had feebly summoned the constables and invoked the processes of the law as though he were a meek bourgeois rather than a noble. And he still seemed helpless against the wife who had been a target for snowballs, confetti, and gossip, who had drugged and robbed him, who had taken up arms against him, who had persuaded the courts that she was a persecuted heroine, and who had found inviolable sanctuary from his wrath in a convent. He could endure no longer the city which had seen the failure of his career and now witnessed his shame as a deceived husband.

For a time he went to Florence, probably to lay his case before Cosimo III who, a devout moralist at all times, had so many causes for complaint against his own wife that he held rigid views on female conjugal fidelity, and who had long been a patron of the Franceschini family. Then Guido returned to Arezzo where his mother had assumed charge of his interests by bringing suit in the criminal court of Florence against Francesca Pompilia, Gregorio Guillichini, and the coachman who had driven the eloping pair. Beatrice Franceschini had collected thirty witnesses at least to prove a variety of matters, from the prosperity of the Franceschini[116] to Caponsacchi's predilection for walking past their house.[117] The purpose of the suit was probably less revenge (for the two important defendants were out of reach) than anxiety to secure in a Tuscan court, where the Franceschini family had more influence, a positive decision which might hasten and even affect the notoriously slow course of justice in Rome,[118] where Pietro Comparini had not yet been forced to comply with the decision of the judge in the suit to recover the dowry brought against him in 1695. If Guido could obtain an outright conviction for adultery he could repudiate Francesca Pompilia and yet secure the dowry, thus ridding himself of a most embarrassing wife, obtaining a substantial sum of money (the need for which must have been ever more pressing with the mounting legal costs), and triumphing over his jeering opponent, who would be left with the burden of heavy debts and an unmarriageable daughter.

The Florentine judges (probably assize judges who heard the case in Arezzo) do not seem to have taken the case too seriously, and their eagerness to know whether the wife was young and pretty and where the husband was hiding his shame[119] strikes the reader as curiously frivolous. The strongest circumstances against the accused were Guillichini's flight after an attempt to intimidate a witness,[120] and his apparent readiness to accept such a severe penalty rather than return and testify on his own behalf. The Guillichini, like the Conti and the Dei Romani, belonged to the first rank of nobility in Arezzo, and must be supposed to have had as much influence at least as Guido and his mother.

The verdict of the court was that Guillichini should be sent to the galleys for five years and that Francesca Pompilia should be imprisoned for life. The latter part of the sentence was suspended, as she was already confined to a convent, which shows that the trial in Arezzo must have taken place before October 12 when she was released in her parents' custody. The decision was reviewed and confirmed by Francesco Panciatichi, apparently the highest authority in the court of Florence.

But positive though it was, this verdict made little difference in Guido's position, and he returned to Florence,[121] unable to bear the mockery of his fellow citizens. Paolo in Rome had suffered even more: his health had been infirm for some time,[122] he had been ignominiously forced to resign from his position with the Knights of Malta, and he heard himself accused on all sides of avarice and mocked with his brother's pusillanimity. Nearly on the point of suicide,[123] he resolved to sell all his possessions and leave the city of which he considered himself almost a native, and where for a time he had enjoyed a career which in its own range was brilliant. He went to Venice[124] some time after he had made arrangements for Francesca Pompilia to be transferred from the convent to the home of her putative parents, a move which, like almost every other event in the story, was accompanied by a wrangle over the financial details. It was suggested even by the defence in the murder trial that this arrangement might have been consented to by the brothers so that Guido might have an opportunity to wreak his vengeance,[125] impossible of course while his wife was safe in the convent. There seems general agreement among the anonymous narrators that before Paolo left Rome his parting instructions to his brother were to wash the family name clean from its dishonour in blood; and the verdict from the Tuscan court possibly encouraged Guido to believe that he might now do so with impunity.

Francesca Pompilia was released in her parents' custody on October 12, 1697, on the plea of illness, though the truth was that she was pregnant and the convent would keep her no longer. Why Guido waited so long before he struck is still unknown. It is possible that his sluggish nature needed not only Paolo's letters urging him to act but also the more violent sting of the birth of his wife's child, which he refused to believe was his own. In any event, it was not until December 24, a week after Francesca Pompilia had become the mother of a son,[126] that he and his fellow assassins assembled at Paolo's Villa Quadrata at Ponte Milvio, on the outskirts of Rome.

There followed a week of spying on the doomed family in the Strada Paolina, and here a minor problem arises for which no solution has yet been found. The longer versions of S say that the assassins watched the Comparini house closely, hoping to trap and slay there other persons as well, and that though they had seen those persons go in they did not find them there when they themselves gained admission. Who was it who had the good fortune to escape that shambles? It cannot have been Caponsacchi, for he was in exile and his name was used as a password by the murderers. The probability is that it was the unnamed benefactor of the Comparini who is referred to several times in the Old Yellow Book. The anti-Comparini pamphleteer says that during the protracted lawsuit Pietro "was supplied with plenty of money by the generosity of some unknown person, possibly a lover of the young girl."[127] And he says later that the Comparini forced Paolo to provide maintenance for Francesca Pompilia in the convent by threatening "that if he refused there would appear a third and unknown person who would assume the burden of it to their [the Franceschini's] dishonour."[128] The pro-Comparini pamphleteer, arguing that even if Guido did intend to avenge his honour he should have killed only his wife and not her parents, continues: "And why should he lay such plots through many days to procure the death of that kind benefactor, because the latter had been moved to pity and had ministered to their aid in the said lawsuits? Upon him there has never fallen a suspicion prejudicial to Guido's honour. For while the wife was in Arezzo he was staying at Rome."[129] No other references to this unidentified benefactor appear in any of the MS. sources, and the suggestion of his over-kindly interest in Francesca Pompilia is probably baseless. On the other hand it may explain what Guido meant when he said that the Comparini had acted as *ruffiani* to their daughter,[130] a word which means not "ruffians," as Mr. Hodell translated it, but panders. One conjecture might be that this benefactor was the Domenico Tighetti whom Francesca Pompilia made her residuary legatee,[131] and probably the guardian of her son.

Though they failed to find this mysterious object of their search, the murderers were successful in their principal object. Despite the fears of the women, who seem to have anticipated Guido's vengeance, Pietro Comparini opened the door at Caponsacchi's name, and death was swift to enter. Violante was struck down at once. Francesca Pompilia tried to extinguish the light and summon help, but the murderers were provided with lanterns, forbidden though they were in Rome, and she tried in vain to hide from them under the bed. The wretched Pietro was slain in his own room, shrieking that he wished to confess. Guido's wife, desperately making vows to the miracle-working effigy of the Virgin at Santa Maria delle Fornaci,[132] was dragged out and wounded twenty-two times, then flung down at her father's feet and left apparently lifeless but still sufficiently conscious to hear her husband urge his confederates to hurry and return to the vineyard.

The screams of the victims had roused the neighbourhood, but when Francesca Pompilia had recovered enough strength to call for help there was no answer, for the neighbours feared that the murderers had not yet departed. Finally, however, the corporal of the constables, urged on by Marchese Nicolò Gregorio,[133] ventured into the house and found the two old people riddled with wounds, their heads attached to their bodies only by a strip of skin,[134] and their daughter dying, but still capable of giving the information which led to her husband's arrest.

Again Guido's avarice and stupidity betrayed him. He had contracted for his accomplices at a bargain rate,[135] had paid them only part of the stipulated sum, and refused to pay the rest until they were all safe in Tuscany.[136] Moreover he had not secured a permit to hire horses for the return journey, and had made no other provision for a quick escape from the States of the Church, though almost certainly if he had reached Tuscany his influence there would have saved him from punishment, since the defence of honour was a valid justification for uxoricide at that period. Serious too was his mistake in not making sure that his wife was dead, for if, as he had intended, the whole Comparini household had been killed, he would not have been pursued, even if he had been suspected of the murder, until he was safe at home. Ill judged indeed had been his mention in her hearing of his destination.

Little need be said here of the trial which followed, except that the volume of evidence had swelled by that time to over 699 pages,[137] some taken from testimony gathered for the previous lawsuits but much of it fresh.[138] The case was intensely interesting to the lawyers because, though the cause of honour was a valid defence if vengeance was taken at once, in this instance there had been a delay of seven months, during three of which Francesca Pompilia had been as accessible to her husband's avenging dagger as on the day when he actually killed her. But, even so, Guido would probably have been granted his life if there had not been so many aggravating circumstances attending the murder. Dionisio Pignatelli, who drew up the final plea for his defence, missing in the OYB and published here,[139] evidently is aware that his client's case is hopeless but is making an attempt to save him from the scaffold by suggesting, as Caponsacchi's lawyer had done a few months before, alternative and lighter punishments. But Innocent XII, a man of austere principles, feared that if this crime went unpunished it might encourage other foreigners to break the laws against carrying arms in the Papal States, and might even cause more murders to be committed in Rome.[140] He may, too, have been swayed by his own knowledge of the persons concerned in the case. Pietro Comparini had secured several favours as well as a small pension from the Pope,[141] whose accessibility to poor petitioners was well known.[142] And both Paolo and Guido Franceschini were familiar to him from the previous lawsuits as quarrelsome and vindictive, not content to let justice take its course but using all their influence in noisy appeals to half the dignitaries in Rome, including himself.[143]

An appeal had been made by Arcangeli, the Procurator of the Poor, for delay in order that proofs of Guido's clerical status might be brought from Arezzo, but the Pope with his own hand signed an order for the execution. The final arrangements were carried out with great expedition (the sentence was given on the 18th of February, the Pope's decree on the 20th, and the execution took place on the 22nd) so that, according to an anonymous writer, no plea might be made for mercy which the Pope would find it embarrassing to refuse.[144]

Guido was prepared for death in his last hours by one of the members of the Confraternita della Misericordia. This Company,[145] whose function it was to prepare condemned criminals for execution, had been founded in 1488 by some pious Florentines, and had received official recognition from Pope Innocent VIII in 1490. It had numbered many distinguished Florentines living in Rome, including Michelangelo, among its members. The secretary of the order was formally notified by the authorities when an execution was to take place, and four or more of its members then spent the night in the condemned cell, persuading the doomed man to confess and receive absolution, aiding him to make his last testament, and encouraging him to bear himself bravely during those last dreadful moments whose publicity, to those of noble birth at least, was an added torment. Then the whole Company proceeded with him to the scaffold, chanting litanies, while his special comforters constantly whispered words of encouragement to him and reminded him of the eternal joys which lay beyond the fast-approaching brief agony.[146] Later they bore the body to their chapel, and there buried it. San Giovanni Decollato, the church of this Society, is still to be seen in Rome, and in its historical museum is the bronze crucifix, dark as ebony, which was carried in the procession that escorted Guido to his execution. The cloister still contains the bodies of the buried men, but no inscriptions mark those graves whose tenants left only a shameful memory behind them.

As I have said, the account of Guido's death which is given in the Cortona codex[147] was probably written by a member of the Confraternita della Misericordia. Though the records of the society for 1698 are missing, Guido's name occurs in the index, and we know that an account of Beatrice Cenci's death was written and her will drawn up by a comforter,[148] so that it is reasonable to suppose this to have been the case in our story as well.

This document is most interesting as a reflection of the devotional fervour which in the seventeenth century often existed side by side with so much eagerness for the things of this world. It was a point of honour with the Confraternity to bring its clients to a state of edification, and it is evident that this was not at all difficult with Guido. He spent his last hours in a frenzy of religious emotion, and even brought himself to order masses for the Comparini family whom he had murdered. It is impossible not to feel some sympathy for him in his evident anxiety to die as befitted his rank. The details of his courtesy to the members of the Company (many of whom of course were known to him),[149] of his solicitude for the one man who had been kind to him in prison, spy though he was,[150] of his grief over the destitution in which he was leaving his family, of his particular thought of the self-exiled Paolo, all have something touching about them. And it is plain that his comforters, though they had to acknowledge officially the justice of his punishment, sympathized with him and felt that he had been the victim of an unscrupulous plot against his honour. If there had not been the element of self-interest, the determination which had become an obsession to obtain the dowry out of which he had been cozened, the sympathies of his fellow nobles would have been entirely his.[151] Certainly he protested to the end that his one concern had been his honour, and his final reference to his wife indicates that he considered her too, at least in part, a victim of those about her.[152] His life had been one of sordid failure, during his last year on earth he had been the butt of public ridicule, but before his death he achieved a momentary dignity.

It was one of the ironies of Guido's tragedy that the last act was played out very near where the first had begun. The scene of his execution was the Piazza del Popolo, where Pietro Comparini had taken his daughter for walks when she was a child. The Porta del Popolo, through which Guido had fled after the murder, opens out of the Piazza. Into it run both the Corso and the Strada Paolina. The sombre procession to the scaffold led him down the Corso, past the shop of Antonia Scarduelli, in which five years before he had bought a wig and planned a marriage. The church of S. Maria di Monte Santo[153] in which the brothers of the Company waited to receive his mutilated body is at the corner of the Strada Paolina where Francesca Pompilia had spent her brief unmarried years, and where she and her parents had met a violent death at his hands. And by a final coincidence, the witnesses who had testified that she had no right to the name of Comparini had all sworn that they remembered her birthday because it was also the feast of the Madonna di Monte Santo.

The aftermath of the story is still obscure. Beatrice Franceschini died in 1701,[154] and the next year Caponsacchi resigned his charge as Canon of Santa Maria della Pieve in Arezzo,[155] after which no more of him is known. Paolo also dropped out of sight for a few years, though Mr. Griffin says that he published a poem in Prague in 1699.[156] In 1708 he was in Milan, and from there went to Barcelona in the train of the Duca de Moles, hoping to secure a pension from the King of Spain which would prove to Rome that though it had ruined his family and neglected him he still could find a powerful patron.[157] His letters of that date show a bitterness which was natural in an age when even the slightest degree of influence sufficed to save a murderer from the consequences of his crime.[158]

Whether Francesca Pompilia's child lived or died, the Franceschini family no longer existed in Arezzo by 1775, though the Caponsacchi and Guillichini familes still survived.[159] But these words of one of the anonymous writers on the case have proved prophetic: "Indeed Guido's name was not buried with his body, for if it is not immortal it will at least be renowned, both for the kind of vengeance which he took, and for the remarkable defence put forward in his trial."[160]

III

The new material in the documents of the Cortona codex and the Florentine archives is as we have said valuable only as it adds to our knowledge of the characters and scenes of Browning's poem. It must be pointed out that the majority of these documents, and particularly the testimony of the witnesses, set forth the Comparini rather than the Franceschini side of the case, and that three items alone of the new material (the argument for the prosecution in Caponsacchi's trial, the sentence of the court in the suit against Guillichini and Francesca Pompilia, and Pignatelli's plea in defence of Guido) support the latter side. We still have none of the testimony given at the murder trial itself, except in a few quotations from it by the lawyers. It is very much to be hoped that some day Guido's own deposition will come to light, as well as that of the thirty witnesses secured by Beatrice in her suit for theft and adultery.

A few of the minor details borrowed by Browning from the Old Yellow Book now appear to be incorrect: for instance, the wig-maker was not herself acquainted with the Comparini, though the marriage was arranged indirectly through her; Violante's confession was made before and not after her return to Rome from Arezzo; there was a fourth Franceschini brother, the youngest, Antonio Maria. These details, however, are unimportant, and it is unfortunate that the two major problems in the case, the origin of Francesca Pompilia and her innocence or guilt of adultery, must remain problems still.

The episode of the birth of Francesca Pompilia is covered very fully by the new documents. Violante's negotiations with the midwife, the latter's dealings with the mother and aunt of the child, the cunningly laid plot to ensure against detection and to carry conviction to the bystanders, are most graphically described. Many of the details are very convincing, such as the reluctance of the aunt to surrender the child without knowing where it was to be taken, and the vivid image conjured up of Corona's older daughter, exiled to the attic during the actual birth, stealing down the stairs drawn by her curiosity about the mysterious event taking place below, and summoned triumphantly to see the baby sister whose lot was to be so different from her own. Corona's solicitude for the child which poverty had forced her to part with is human and touching, and there is still no documentary evidence for the repeated references in the legal documents to Francesca Pompilia's mother as a woman of evil life. The only suggestion that the child was not legitimate is a remark of Corona's sister.[161]

It must be admitted, of course, that the story of the substitution at birth seems a little too well-timed to be convincing, and the witnesses to it are not above suspicion. Yet the wealth of detail, much of it unsavoury but very circumstantial, poured forth by Violante and her former maids, as well as by the child's "aunt" and "sister," bears the stamp of truth. It may be noticed that while the six witnesses agree in all the main points, their memories are never improbably accurate. Giovanna Bobba and Petronilla Feure are uncertain about the godmothers and the people present at the baptism; Petronilla cannot remember about dates, and is not sure in what year the child was born. And no witness seems to have been produced to contradict any part of their stories, though surely Paolo must have made a painstaking search for someone who could swear that, for instance, the child borne by Corona had really been taken to the orphanage. True, the judges did not find the story completely convincing, and decided in favour of Francesca Pompilia and her husband, but they may have been only reluctant to alter a state of affairs which had lasted so long.[162]

Less new light is thrown on the even more vexed problem of Francesca Pompilia's innocence or guilt. We already have a wealth of information and evidence, much of it conflicting, on this subject in the Old Yellow Book, which it may be well to review before the fresh material is considered. It is difficult to disregard the decisions given against her by two courts. The Tuscan judges passed on her a sentence (suspended because she was already confined in a convent) of lifetime imprisonment for theft and adultery, naming both Caponsacchi and Guillichini as her partners in guilt.[163] The court of Rome found Caponsacchi guilty of adultery with her, though the separate sentence against her was still pending when she was murdered. The charge of adultery with Guillichini may be dismissed as spite on the part of the Franceschini family, but it seems more than probable that the charges against Caponsacchi were justified. There is some question, however, as to whether he had been her lover before the night they spent together at the inn during their flight. It was maintained by the defence that this would have been impossible because Francesca Pompilia was so closely watched.[164] But she mentions in her letters absences of her husband from Arezzo,[165] and in her deposition she refers to two private interviews with Caponsacchi during one of these absences.[166] Moreover, a witness was produced at the hearing in Arezzo who said that she had seen Francesca Pompilia letting Caponsacchi out of the Franceschini house.[167] This witness, Maria Margherita Contenti, was discredited during the murder trial as being a prostitute[168] (it may be pointed out that no defence was made at the trial in Arezzo), but one of the lawyers who made the objection weakened it at once by half-admitting the truth of her testimony.[169] And in one of her letters Francesca Pompilia warns Caponsacchi that the street-door is now kept closed, and suggests that he may find another door open.[170] The Franceschini maid, Maria, was her ally, and is mentioned as a go-between both by her and by Caponsacchi.[171]

There is every indication that Guido was not the father of her child. She had concealed her pregnancy from him before she fled from Arezzo, though according to her own story her barrenness was one of his principal reproaches against her.[172] He suspected her condition before her elopement, and used his suspicion, still unconfirmed, in his suit against her and Caponsacchi.[173] The Comparini tried to keep her state from his knowledge, and had her released from the convent on the plea of illness, though the truth became known when she was examined by a physician.[174] There was even an attempt to keep the birth of her son a secret, and it was sent out of the house as soon as it was born.[175] There was, apparently, no mention of it in her will.

The suddenness of her flight from Arezzo is an added suspicious circumstance. Giovanni Battista Bottini, Advocate of the Fisc in the trial for murder, maintained that she had written to Caponsacchi only to urge him to assist her to flee from her husband's cruelty.[176] But there is no mention of flight except in the final letters, and in one at least Francesca Pompilia speaks of her husband as being well disposed towards her.[177] Indeed her only complaint against him is his jealousy, for which she was giving him just cause, and in one letter she says that all the affection she once felt for him is now directed towards Caponsacchi.[178] This seems to indicate that her relations with Guido had been amiable before he was enraged by her flirtation.

The strongest arguments in favour of her innocence have, of course, always been her death-bed declaration that she had not committed the sin for which she had been slain, and the affidavits of the friar and others who attended her during her last hours. But Bottini points out[179] that the attestations of her innocence brought forward by the defence[180] were not the spontaneous testimony of persons moved by her saintliness, but had been procured by her heir to protect her estate from the Convertites,[181] and that some of the signatories were beneficiaries of her will who would lose their legacy if her guilt was presumed. It is evident that the Comparini had some very powerful protector in Rome who had used his influence to delay both the sentence against Francesca Pompilia after her elopement and the enforcement of the court order to Pietro to complete the payment of the dowry. If, as I have suggested, this protector was Domenico Tighetti, the heir (whose station or profession is nowhere described), it is reasonable to suppose that he brought his influence to bear on the court which supported his claim to the inheritance against that of the Convertites. This supposition would weaken the argument favourable to Francesca Pompilia of the decision of the court in September, 1698, declaring that, as proof of adultery had not been established, her reputation was restored to its pristine good fame.

Professor Beichner, dealing with this aspect of the case,[182] says: "One should remember that affidavits signed by more than one person indicate by that very fact that someone is soliciting testimony and that some kind of pressure is being exerted; that no confessor ever offers testimony concerning a penitent for use in court unless some sort of pressure is brought to bear on him, and since he cannot reveal what he knows from confession, he must give a favourable impression of the penitent when a refusal to speak at all would be an admission of guilt. In an ecclesiastical court such testimony of a confessor would be worthless, and volunteered testimony of anyone else would be suspect." And he goes on to point out the ambiguity in wording of Fra Celestino's testimonial.

As for Francesca Pompilia's dying protestations of innocence, the writer of one of the anonymous pamphlets makes an observation which, cynical though it may be, is still worthy of consideration because it represents a contemporary viewpoint: he says that anyone who has confessed and received absolution is then technically innocent, and that thus Francesca Pompilia would have been justified in declaring herself guiltless.[183] Professor Beichner observes (as did more than one of Guido's lawyers), that a person is under no obligation to incriminate himself. He says: "If all are bound to respect the right of another to his secret and his good name, that person has all the more right to keep the damaging knowledge to himself. Pompilia would have had that right."[184] To the persistent questioning of those around her[185] she was, then, almost obliged to give answers which would protect not only her reputation but also Caponsacchi's. This point is made most forcibly by Arcangeli when he says: "Since she stands convicted by the aforesaid proofs of having broken her matrimonial faith, it would be absurd that an exculpation made that she might seem to die an honest woman, should be of such efficiency as to destroy the proofs of her baseness."[186] He might have added that she was also protecting her son's right to an honourable name.

In a modern court of law a dying statement is accepted as having as much validity as a statement under oath, but it must not be forgotten that in her sworn testimony after her arrest Francesca Pompilia had made many statements whose falseness was palpable. It is not impossible that on both occasions she was still translating into the terms of her real life the romantic standards of constancy to a lover which she had learned from her favourite reading.

The new light cast on this phase of the story comes from the documents concerning the trial for abduction, which, as we have seen,[187] support the supposition of the eloping couple's guilt. The argument on behalf of Guido gives an excellent summary of the case against the wife,[188] pointing out the contradictions between her story and Caponsacchi's, showing that there is no word of cruelty on the part of her husband in her letters, and refuting the suggestion that the correspondence was forged by offering to prove the handwriting of both parties.[189] In Caponsacchi's defence Lamparelli, the Procurator of Charity, relates the full story of the marriage and its financial background, and quotes several hitherto unprinted fragments from the correspondence between Paolo and the Comparini while the latter were in Arezzo.[190]

The Florentine document also belongs to this development in the tale, and gives a clearer picture than has before been available of the atmosphere of intrigue surrounding the flight, and of the part played in it by Guillichini.

It is now evident that material from both suits was employed at Guido's trial for murder, but that the Roman lawyers made less use than they might have done of the new evidence presented by Beatrice's witnesses.

One detail in the story of Francesca Pompilia's childhood is also relevant here. It is now known that she had attended school for four years, though at an early age, and thus the legend of her illiteracy and consequent inability to write the love letters is destroyed.

Though supplementary circumstances rather than startling new facts in the drama have been discovered, some addition has been made to our knowledge of the actors, and in its light Browning's interpretation of his characters may be examined. His estimate of the minor personages remains for the most part unchallenged. Judge Gest has succeeded in rehabilitating the lawyers on both sides in the murder trial,[191] and it is now evident how scrupulously they perused all the evidence and the arguments brought forward in the earlier cases. Some proof of Browning's charge of frivolous quibbling, however, is certainly apparent in the pleas for the prosecution and defence of Caponsacchi. The quotations from Ovid, the references to Scipio's superhuman chastity, the insistence on Caponsacchi's chivalry in refusing to leave Francesca Pompilia unguarded during the night, all, despite the sober Latin of the law courts in which they are couched, suggest that the legal experts may have shared the general amusement at Guido's appearance in the traditional comedy role of the deceived husband.

Among the other minor figures, Violante appears more odious than ever, as we read her unashamed account of her plot to obtain a child and financial security at the same time. Pietro's lack of judgment is even more evident now that his at least partial knowledge of the Franceschini financial situation is revealed. Heedless of warnings then as he was later, when with fatal obstinacy he opened the door to his murderers, he was willing to sacrifice his daughter's future to relieve his own immediate necessity. At once weak and quarrelsome, penniless and a spendthrift, he is a fitting match for the Franceschini brothers in his litigious lack of good faith. It is quite credible that Violante may have concealed from him her plan for the pretended birth, though it was to his advantage as much as to hers, because she feared that his lack of discretion and his intemperate habits might lead to discovery.

A little more is now known about two of Guido's accomplices. Alessandro Baldeschi, according to the Cortona codex version of S, had already committed several murders before he was hired by Guido, and on one occasion had killed four travellers after robbing them.[192] And we learn from the Angelica version of C, that Biagio Agostinelli (who in his last hours gave his comforters first so much trouble, then such edification)[193] was the servant of Paolo, and was added by Guido to his little band without any explanation of the purpose of the expedition. It was this youth who was told to guard the door of the Comparini house and to let no one enter. His ignorance of Guido's intention, and his innocence of any share in the actual murder, are given as the causes of his reluctance to acknowledge the justice of his sentence. This probably explains why one of the guards ran away from his post when he heard the noise within.[194] Biagio, if it were he and if his story were true, would have been unprepared for the terrifying sounds.

Though nothing in the new material conflicts with Browning's portrayal of these characters, an interpretation very different from his is given of the motives of the Pope in refusing a stay of execution for Guido and his younger confederate. Critics have claimed that the poet's picture of the Pope was not historically accurate. This is only partially true: Innocent XII was indeed a man of great piety and learning, of austere life, and of a charitable and generous nature. But Browning portrays him in only one of his aspects, that of the Pontiff, "standing on his integrity," rock-firm against the storm of public opinion, making a supreme demonstration before his death of his refusal to compromise with the easy standards of the corrupt world in which he lived. A seventeenth-century pope, however, had another aspect: he was also the temporal ruler of the States of the Church, and it was in this, rather than in his spiritual, capacity that Innocent made his final decision. It is noticeable that the author of the account of Guido's death refers to him as "the Prince." Rome had always been notorious for its many crimes, the perpetrators of which often went unpunished because there were so many embassies and national churches in the city where they could seek sanctuary. There were 180 murders during the Conclave of 1691,[195] and Diego Angeli claims that during the one-year pontificate of Clement XIII (1758–9, a comparatively peaceful era) there were 10,000 murders:[196] a figure which might seem incredible even in face of Corrado Ricci's statement that in Bologna, also famous for its murders, 3,600 people were assassinated between 1662 and 1665.[197] Innocent XII had from the beginning of his rule showed his interest in vigorous and impartial administration,[198] and his action in ordering Guido's immediate execution is consistent with his usual policy. Nor was he in this defying public opinion, for one of the anonymous writers describes the populace as unduly blood-thirsty in its demand for the death of the murderers, who were sacrificed, he feels, to the popular demand for vengeance.[199]

As for the three protagonists in the tragedy, Caponsacchi remains in these new documents almost as shadowy a figure as ever, despite our glimpse of him in a silver-trimmed hat, carrying a short sword.[200] Of all the characters in *The Ring and the Book* he is most completely Browning's own creation. The others were indisputably moulded and interpreted by the poet to fit his own purposes, but there is not a trace in any of the documents which have so far come to light of his St. George, his "warrior-priest," "pure in thought and deed." The real Caponsacchi is surely a much less amiable person—an idle young man of good family with a pretty but frivolous taste in literature, who thinks it amusing to seduce the charming young wife of a jealous middle-aged man, then is alarmed by the consequences of his success, and attempts to save both himself and his partner in guilt by flight. The elaborate plans for drugging the Franceschini family set forth in his correspondence with Francesca Pompilia have just as much the flavour of a seventeenth-century novel as have the floridly artificial endearments. But when the moment of real danger was at hand and the angry husband supported by the law confronted him it was not he but the lady who seized the sword which ecclesiastical law forbade him to wear. Then, when the romantic comedy turned into unpleasant reality with the prospect of banishment or even death, he hastened in his deposition to lay all the blame on Francesca Pompilia, insisting that she had pursued him with letters until he consented to the flight, and lying brazenly not in her defence but in his own.[201]

Professor Raymond has reviewed with succinct lucidity the attitudes of various writers to the character of Francesca Pompilia from the time when the poem was written until the present.[202] Professor Shaw's interpretation of the process by which Browning transfigured his heroine[203] is perhaps the only theory which the modern reader familiar with all the material now available on the subject can reasonably accept, borne out as it is by Judge Gest's re-examination of the legal aspects of the case.[204] Every poet sees reality through the lens of his personal experience of the world, and to Browning the tormented girl, used as a pawn by all around her from the moment of her birth, was doubly appealing because he was reminded by her of his wife and of the famous rescue from Wimpole Street.

Browning's portrait of her, as Professor Beichner points out,[205] is based principally on the assumption that her correspondence with Caponsacchi was forged, and on the testimony of those present during her last days. The theory of forgery can no longer be accepted, and her letters show her as a young wife, very much in love with a man who is not her husband, constantly making schemes for secret communications, quoting the advice of her confessor but reluctant to accept it.[206] Brought up by, if not born of, a scheming, unscrupulous, headstrong woman, married as a child to a man twenty years her senior who regarded her only as a means of obtaining some money and perpetuating his line, transferred from the colourful bustling life of Rome to the narrow, closely woven society of Arezzo, where she found herself the storm centre of two equally embittered families, Francesca Pompilia can only be pitied. There is no doubt that in the convention of the time, so close to the period of open *cicisbeismo*, she thought of her love for Caponsacchi as noble and exalted, and was genuinely shocked when he sent her indecent verses.[207] But her talent for intrigue is obvious, and many of the circumstances of her flight are ugly: the drugging of her husband and his brother, for instance, and the wholesale theft not only of clothes and jewels (which she might have regarded as her own dower right) but also of a suit of her husband's, an act so petty in its greed or malice that it does much to destroy the reader's sympathy.

She was undoubtedly pious—her remarkable survival for four days after her husband's attack was regarded by those around her as the miraculous result of her vows and prayers; but she lived in a time and place in which piety induced the sinner rather to seek absolution than to avoid sin; and nowhere in her brief life's history was there anything which might have taught her the lofty principles with which Browning endowed her.

In the new documents there is little to add to our knowledge of Francesca Pompilia after her marriage, but we now have probably as complete a picture as will ever be available of her birth and childhood.[208]

She was bartered for before she was born, and was handled in her earliest hours with the callous skill shown by those preparing an animal for the market. She exchanged the foul rags of her first swaddling for garments more suited to her new station, and her baptism was a triumphal affair, with carriages hired for thc brief ride from house to church, and a sumptuous banquet prepared for the godparents and guests. Then she passed from one wet-nurse to another, was sent to school, began to change from child to girl, and there the new record stops. We are left to imagine the eagerness with which Pietro and Violante waited for her to reach an age when she could be married, and so relieve their financial anxieties for the second time.

Just as Pompilia was not the saint, so Guido was not the subtle villain of Browning's conception, and the worst charge brought against him, that of manoeuvring his wife into an elopement and forging a love-correspondence, can now almost certainly be dismissed as fiction. He was, rather, a classic example of a man destined to fail in everything he undertook, and to mis-time every venture of his life, from his ill-advised marriage to the moment when, seeing himself "loathed by his relatives, abandoned by his friends, and laughed at by all,"[209] he washed out his disgrace in blood so clumsily that he brought complete ruin upon himself and his family.

The new material casts much more light on his character and situation than on Francesca Pompilia's, with regard both to the beginning and to the end of his career. From the inventory which he drew up for Pietro, padded though it may have been, it is plain that the Franceschini family had once been prosperous and still enjoyed powerful patronage. But Guido's repudiation of his inheritance shows that as early as the death of his father in 1680 the estate had been crippled with debts. Like the Comparini, the Franceschini by 1693 were clinging desperately to a social position which they had not the money to maintain; this explains why the publication of their former maid's testimony to their poverty was so peculiarly galling to them.[210] It also explains why the point of honour assumed such importance to Guido. His marriage had not only brought him no fortune: it was ruining him in lawsuits, and it was inflicting public infamy on his relatives.

His devotion to his family is evident, for it was his primary concern in the hour before his death.[211] And his genuine sense of outrage at being condemned for avenging his honour is evidenced by his passionate outburst to his comforters, an outburst for which he apologized but which he could not restrain.[212] His true vice was not cruelty but avarice, which he exercised on behalf of others, not of himself alone; and his treacherous deed of violence was the act of a weak man desperately trying to comply with the demands of an inexorable social code.

Throughout his story we see him taking action only three times: in his approach to the wig-maker, in his pursuit of the eloping couple, and in the murder; and to all three of these actions he had probably been urged by his mother and eldest brother. Paolo had his power of attorney and transacted all legal business for him in Rome; and it was Beatrice who brought suit against his wife and her confederates in the court of Arezzo. It is plain that in the Franceschini household he played a very minor part, and it is not of his behaviour that Pietro complains in his letters to Paolo. Guido was unable to check his wife's indiscreet conduct despite his blustering. His comforters obviously regarded him as a simpleton for accepting so ingenuously the friendliness of a prison spy, and for failing to rid himself of his embarrassing accomplices immediately after the murder and to press on into Tuscany before he could be arrested. It is open to question whether instead of being superhumanly cunning he may not have been slightly sub-normal mentally.

The penitential fervour of his last hours was unquestionably genuine, and the account given of his end portrays him as he appeared to his contemporaries: as the protagonist, that is, in a drama of more than ephemeral significance, a drama in which man rebels against God, persuaded that he can break divine laws with impunity, and is finally overtaken by the unfailing justice which allows no sin to go unpunished.[213]

If Professor Cundiff's ingenious and persuasive interpretation of Browning's gold and alloy metaphor is accepted,[214] there need be no real conflict between the historical facts of the Franceschini-Comparini documents and the poetical truth of *The Ring and the Book*, despite their frequent divergences. The personages shaped by Browning's creative imagination are unchanging and eternal: our knowledge of the once living men and women who were his inspiration is subject to expansion, and because they were the raw material for a great poet's masterpiece they are perennially interesting. Much may still be learned of the various stages of the ill-fated connection between the Franceschini and the Comparini, of the backgrounds of both families, perhaps even of the later lives of the survivors of the tragic drama. And whatever comes to light about them will derive its interest not only from the additional information it gives us about the most unfamiliar period in Italian history, but from the fact that their story was transmuted by Robert Browning from a sordid tale of greed and treachery into an epic of the human spirit.

DOCUMENTS FROM THE CORTONA CODEX

PREFATORY NOTE

In my translation I have not attempted to alter the style either of the legal documents or of the testimony of the witnesses, although I have changed the punctuation where it seemed desirable for greater intelligibility. I have also placed the title of each plea at the beginning of the document to which it belongs, instead of at the end, as it appears in the original.

In giving the legal citations throughout the documents, I have followed the forms used by Judge Gest and explained by him in detail (*The Old Yellow Book*, pp. 51–65).

The witnesses whose depositions appear in the Summary (section A) were apparently examined before a notary in the presence of Pietro Comparini, sometimes in Pietro's own house (p. 63), sometimes in the house or office of the notary (p. 53). The testimony was probably taken down in shorthand, and then the witness was examined more particularly on the principal points which had a bearing on the case. This explains such phrases as "With regard to the second," etc. After the various heads of the evidence had been dealt with in detail a connected narrative was prepared which the witness probably signed. Only Violante's deposition has no final summing up, at least as it appears in the codex. I am including these summaries, although they are repetitive, because they occasionally mention a point which appears nowhere else.

All the documents, including those of the Summary, are very much abridged, sometimes with little regard for consistency or lucidity. This accounts for references to records which do not appear in the Cortona codex, and for the occasional use of the word "aforesaid," applied to something which has not been mentioned earlier.

A

In the suit brought by Guido Franceschini against Pietro Comparini

A CASE TRIED AT ROME CONCERNING A CLAIM OF DAUGHTERHOOD AND A TRANSFER OF BONDS

A plea entered on behalf of Signor Pietro Comparini against Signor Guido Franceschini and Signora Francesca Pompilia his wife in the Supreme Court before the Reverend Father Passerino by Agostino Luciano

REVEREND FATHER. On the strength of the assumption that Signor Guido Franceschini, our opponent, possessed an annual income of one thousand, seven hundred scudi in cash, as appeared from a note written by his own hand (summary, n.1),[1] and from the deposition of the intermediary (summary, n. 2), Signor Pietro Comparini, our client, was induced to give in marriage to our said opponent his putative daughter, Francesca Pompilia, with the promise of a dowry of all and each of his goods, consisting of two houses, with shops beneath them, and forty bonds. And in order to avoid paying a tax on contracts in the city of Arezzo, native city of the bridegroom, the said Signor Pietro, our client, on June 24, 1693, signed two marriage contracts.[2] In the first he granted to Signor Guido Franceschini, the bridegroom, the free, perpetual, and irrevocable management of the said two houses, and of three bonds which were part of the entail established by the late Francesco Comparini, his father, and Domenico Canzi, his uncle, the conditions of which were satisfied in the person of the said Francesca Pompilia.

On his side, Signor Guido Franceschini, the bridegroom, promised and engaged himself to take the said Pietro Comparini and Violante Peruzzi, husband and wife, with him to the said city of Arezzo, and there to provide them with food, clothing, and suitable living-quarters; and in case the said husband and wife could not stay there for some reasonable cause, then even in that case he was obliged to take them back to Rome, with the same obligation of providing for them (as is shown in our summary, n. 3).

In the second place, indeed, he assigned to the said Guido twenty-four 20/100[3] of different bonds belonging to the entail established by Signor Francesco Comparini, together with ten bonds left to Signor Pietro Antonio Comparini for the term of his life, and three bonds transferred to the late Pietro Zacconi, with the power of freely cashing in five 30/100 bonds of the dowry, and of disposing freely of their price. And concerning maintenance, stipulations were clearly set forth in this second document: "That the aforesaid Signor Guido shall be allowed to conduct Signora Francesca Pompilia, his bride, to Arezzo, his native city, where her aforesaid parents, if they wish to go there also, shall be received and treated honourably, and shall be suitably fed and clothed in the paternal house or houses of Signor Guido, his mother and brothers" (summary, n. 4).

Later, on August 27, 1693, the aforesaid contracting parties drew up a public document in which, departing in one part and another from the aforesaid stipulations, power was given to the said Guido to cash in freely the said bonds at the end of a year, and to reinvest the proceeds in the said city of Arezzo; and for the rest the said contracts were once more confirmed; for the observance of which Abate Paolo Franceschini pledged himself, both in his own name and as holding power of attorney for Signori Girolamo and Antonio Franceschini, his brothers, acting as a principal generally and together with them. And lest any doubt should arise of the obligation of the said brothers because of their absence, both the said Abate Paolo and the said Guido promised together solemnly there to ratify and to have them ratify the present instrument, and everything contained therein, and later to be written in, and to produce a public instrument drawn up in legal form in my writing within two months from today (summary, n. 5).

In execution of the said contracts Signor Pietro, our client, freely handed over five 30/100 bonds, and the said Guido Franceschini received their price and withdrew the accrued interest up to the sum of seven hundred scudi, as is not disputed. Then the said Guido Franceschini left Rome with Signora Francesca Pompilia, his bride, and Signori Pietro Comparini and Violante Peruzzi, husband and wife, for Arezzo. And when they arrived there, because of the excessive poverty of the said bridegroom the aforesaid couple began to suffer unheard of hardships, as revealed by the witness (summary, n. 6).

In these misfortunes the said Violante, remembering the previous crime she had committed in substituting at birth the said Francesca Pompilia, and troubled by scruples on the occasion of the Jubilee proclaimed at that time, went to her confessor and told him that the aforesaid bride, Francesca Pompilia, was not and never had been her daughter, but had been imposed by herself on her husband, Signor Pietro, as such, so that she might free Signor Comparini, our client, in whose person the entail expired if he died without issue, from several debts, and avoid the alienation of the entail.

When her confessor had heard the daring act she had committed, and the crime had been revealed, he ordered her as a penance to disclose all to her husband, Comparini. The latter, as soon as the said substitution at birth had been revealed to him, immediately returned to Rome with his wife, and issued against the said couple a judicial notice concerning the nullity of the said marriage contract before Signor Tomati, Auditor Camerae. And in proof of the substitution of the said child at birth he formally examined six witnesses, namely Signora Violante Peruzzi, the alleged mother, Caterina Fiori, the aunt, and Cristina Paperozzi, the sister of the bride, Anna Maria Amadei, a neighbour, present at the actual birth, and Petronilla Feure and Anna Boba, present at the substitution of the child.

After the said six witnesses had been examined, the aforesaid Francesca Pompilia, on August 20, 1695, brought suit against our client for an order for her maintenance in assumed daughterhood, and, for the implementation of the said maintenance, for the transfer of the said bonds, assigned as a dowry, as described above; and she received a decision in her favour (summary, n. 7).

For the reconsideration of this decision our client, on the 31st of the same month, produced in written form certain arguments (summary, n. 9), notwithstanding which the same judge, on September 17th, with no other summons to attend to the implementation, issued an absolute decision absolving from the exceptions taken against the above-mentioned order for maintenance and transference respectively (summary, n. 10). And petition for an appeal against this decision is herein offered before this Supreme Court (summary, n. [*sic*]), the same for both sides, which from what is said below seems to be worthy to be signed with a clause directing the execution.

For in order to obtain an appeal for delay it would be sufficient to allege that the said judge, on September 17th, absolved the opposing side from exception that had been taken against the said order of transference and maintenance issued on a day of the previous August, and that, because of the production of new arguments which took place on August 31st, with a repetition of the same arguments on September 2nd, after the summons to produce confutation, with the decree of the admission of the said arguments (n. 9), there had been left out a written reference to Gregory (dec.140.n.16). In that passage the conclusion is delayed by the admission of new arguments even if the admission were made with a clause of reservation without any prejudice to the conclusion or the decision that had been given being preserved (also dec.157.n.6 cor. ead. Rot. dec.272.n.2.p.1.rec. and dec.69. n.5.par.6. Buratt. dec.720.n.2. Gratiano. discept.498.n.11. and in Caietano Bonorum 3. Decembris 1646 § prout etiam coram Caro).

Besides, even if the said order for maintenance were valid, yet the order to transfer the bonds would still be unjust if, in the ordered execution of it, it could not be saved from evident injustice; because there can be found in the argument no warrant saying that a daughter in the assumption of daughterhood in the execution of the said assumption can seek the transfer of her father's property to her own person, for actually the rule is to the contrary; for in the lifetime of the father the daughter can make no claim on his property.

If, however, the opposing side claims the said transference on the strength of the said contract, not only is the rest of the decree itself against it, in which was issued an order for transference in execution of the said order for maintenance, but the dower contract itself also, for in that the aforesaid Guido Franceschini, the bridegroom, promised within two months to produce a public legal instrument of the ratification of the said contract by his said brothers, and so, since he has not fulfilled on his part the said promise by producing the said instrument of ratification, the exception of the non-fulfilment of the ratification stands in the way of his taking action (Rot. dec.26.n.1.par.16.rec.).

Moreover, our said client, as the putative father of the said Francesca Pompilia, the bride, as regards the settlement of the said dowry is entitled to the benefit of his maintenance, and this not only from the provision made in common law (Castigan. de Benef. deducto ne egeat qu.7.n.7. et seqq. fol.157 where he opines that a father-in-law must be admitted to such a privilege even though he is under an obligation in the form set down by the Camera), but also from the agreements on the subject in the aforesaid contracts, in which our said opponent expressly obliged himself to supply food to Pietro, our client, and to his wife Violante.

Nor is our client to be deprived of the said benefit because he has denied that he is the father of the said Francesca Pompilia; for a father denying his paternity loses his legal privilege when in that same denial he is convicted of lying, but not if the denial is probable and likely, as this is, in which, so that the substitution at birth might be proved, six witnesses were formally examined; for until the case is lost the privilege remains, as is absolutely held, objecting to the contrary conclusion

(Castagn. de Benef. deducto ne egeat, quaest.1.fallent.5.limit.6.n.15. et seqq. fol.95.ibi). And this is true even if the distinction made by the opposition is retained, of the judgments of possession and of petitioning, for indeed in the decree of possession the said Francesca Pompilia obtained against our client maintenance in assumption of daughterhood and transference of the bonds in implementation of the said maintenance, rejecting the petitioner's plea of a substitution at birth; at the same time there must be granted to our said client, in the said judgment of possession, this maintenance in the assumption of fatherhood, the said exception of the negation of paternity being rejected equally for the petitioner, since the two terms of father and daughter are correlative, and one cannot hold good without the other (Rot. coram Cetro. dec.816.n.8, and coram Rich. dec.141.n.2). For if in the decree of maintenance our opponent is a daughter, then our client is a father, and as a father has a right to the privilege of an allowance to keep him from want.

The reply that the yield of the said bonds was partly destined for the redemption of the entailed bonds resigned by our client with the Pope's own signature,[4] and partly to satisfy the creditors of our client, who on that account could expect no benefit from them, recoils on its inventor; because if no profit could be derived from them by our client, neither could they benefit our opponent, and so the transfer of the said bonds sought by our opponent is useless, and therefore our appeal should be more easily admitted until the case is settled. Because with regard to the interest destined for the redemption of the said bonds that have been handed over, our client, already being the last beneficiary of the entail, obtained from the Pope the permission of this free cashing in for the purpose of feeding himself and his wife; and in regard to the other interest he will obtain it as soon as his creditors are satisfied, which will be soon.

Finally must be added the nullity of the said dower contracts, for inasmuch as our client promised to hand over to our opponent as a dowry all his property to the value of eight thousand scudi because he believed that the said Francesca Pompilia had been and was his daughter born in wedlock, when however by the deposition of six witnesses formally examined the contrary was revealed, the said promise was proved erroneous; because error deprives an act of consent, and essentially annuls a promise, as Clement VIII pronounced in precise terms in his printed decision (after Rembold. vot.1.n.446. et seqq. where he says: For error vitiates a transaction as well as contracts relating to it, because it removes consent, without which that transaction cannot exist; and Rinald. cons.102.n.22. et 23.lib.primo: no one loses his property because he is mistaken).

Error also vitiates the establishment of the dowry, which is an extremely favourable contract (Ias. cons.160.n.2.lib.4). Nothing is so contrary to consent as error, and if it is detected the obligation is annulled (Rot. coram Clar. dec.29.n.4. et seqq. and coram Rich. dec. 777.n.16 where he rules that as error deprives an act of consent it nullifies any contract, whether made by a woman or by a fully empowered adult). And error is said to be proved by the fact alone that the matter is otherwise (Rot. coram Pamphil. dec.454.n.12. Dunozzet. Iur. dec.590.n.6.). And the said conclusion is so true that it is admitted even against an obligation of the Camera (Rot. coram Rembold. dec. 246.n.8: "and this exception of a false cause or of error is admitted even against an obligation of the Camera").

The substitution at birth of the said child is proved from the deposition of the said Violante Peruzzi, the putative mother, who, having narrated the deplorable history, testifies that the cause was that she might inherit the said entail property after the death of the said Pietro, her husband (summary, n. 11). The said testimony is proved, first by the baptism certificate of the said Violante (summary, n. 12), which shows that at the time of the birth she was forty-eight years of age, and so considered incapable of bearing children (Rot. dec.386.n.2. et 6. par.8.rec.); and even more plainly because the said Violante during the fourteen years which she had passed with her husband had never borne children.[5] Secondly from the deposition of Caterina Fiori, the aunt (summary, n. 13), Cristina Paperozzi, the sister of the said Francesca Pompilia (summary, n. 14), and Anna Maria Amadei (summary, n. 19), who were all present when Corona gave birth to the said Francesca Pompilia; and the same witnesses in the month of July, 1680, with their own hands gave to the midwife called la Bracchiera[6] the said child, so that she might take it to the house of our said client, and so that the said Signora Violante, his wife, might make him believe that she had given birth to it (summary, n. 13,14,15). Thirdly, from the deposition of Anna Bobba (summary, n. 16), and Petronilla Feure (summary, n. 17), and fourthly from the deposition for permanent record of Agnese Santi Oliverizzie [*sic*], who not only heard from the lips of the said midwife about the substitution of the said child, but saw the child being carried by the midwife to the house of our said client (summary, n. 8 [*sic*]).

The aforesaid appeal should more readily be admitted when it is considered that it is a question of bonds, and that, since they are not subject to the pledge that they will be handed over at once, unjust compulsion has been exercised, since the said Guido Franceschini possesses nothing in this world, neither of his father's property, of which he repudiated the inheritance (summary, n. 19), nor of property of his own, as is testified by the Chancellor of Arezzo, who, having examined the register of taxable property, found nothing inscribed in his name (summary, n. 20), contrary to the assertions made in the inventory which he supplied before the marriage, in which he claimed to possess a yearly income of one thousand, seven hundred scudi. And already he has had at his disposal seven hundred scudi of the dower property gained from the sale of five 30/100 bonds of the dowry, and taken from the proceeds of the bonds which were due.

Wherefore

AUGUSTINUS LUCIANUS

ON BEHALF OF SIGNOR PIETRO COMPARINI—SUMMARY (AT ROME, IN THE TYPE OF THE REVERENDA CAMERA APOSTOLICA, 1696)

NUMBER 1. *Note of the assets and income of Signor Guido Franceschini, the opponent, written by his own hand*

N.N.,[7] 30 years of age,[8] a nobleman of the city of Arezzo, has three brothers who are all ecclesiastics and provided with ecclesiastical incomes, and one sister who 14 years ago married Count N.N.[9]

The said brothers have always lived in unalterable and enduring bonds of affection.

They own in their native city a very comfortable house in which they live, superior to that of many noblemen and inferior to that of none. The said house is furnished with everything necessary, and unfurnished is worth in scudi about 3,000

Another adjoining house, which rents every year for 15

Another house, which rents every year for 14

Of agricultural property: a farm in the county of N.,[10] two miles from the city, situated on a most lovely hill and producing everything necessary for a household, oil, wheat, wine, vegetables, firewood, fruit: it produces every year about 2,000

The same farm has its own elegant little house, in which one can pass the summer, very comfortable, and furnished with everything needful, with two excellent dove-cotes, a bird-netting ground,[11] and a garden suitable for the entertainment of other ladies and gentlemen in the summer time.

In the said county, an arable holding which is tenanted, which produces every year some 50

A vineyard in the county of N., 3 miles from the city, which produces about the worth of wine every year of 40

Another farm in the county of N.,[12] 5 miles from the city, with a house and dove-cote, which produces every year in wheat and wine about 150

Thickets for cutting brush-wood every year on the said farm 65

Chestnut woods in the counties of N.N. yield every year about 40

An olive grove in the county of N. yields every year some 30

There are the value, the income from and the yield of the livestock, which are uncertain, such as sheep, lambs, oxen, and hogs.

The said brothers have in certain liquid assets with Cardinal N.N. 1,500 scudi, which at 5 per cent yield every year 75

The same brothers have in certain agricultural assets 1,800
with Signor N.N., at 6 per cent every year 108 [*sic*]

Income from the ecclesiastical property of the brothers:

N.N., the eldest brother, 42 years of age,[13] serves as gentleman-in-waiting to Cardinal N.N. He has lived in Rome for 27 years, and enjoys a simple benefice in his native city under the title of St. James and St. Philip, under the patronage of the Grand Duke. It was bestowed on him through the intercession of Cardinal Cibo during the papacy of Innocent XI. The said benefice, situated in the county of N., yields annually 40

The said brother holds another simple benefice in the county of N., under the title of St. James and St. Christopher, bestowed on him by Innocent XI at the death of Abate Capponi. It yields every year 80

N.N., another brother, 35 years old,[14] is a canon in the cathedral in his native city. This charge yields an annual income of 80

He also enjoys a simple benefice in the county of N., with the title of St. Mary. This is in the gift of the Benedictine order, and yields annually 12

He enjoys another simple benefice bestowed on him by the Grand Duke,[15] with the title of the Three Wise Kings, situated in the county of N., which yields every year 40

He also holds another simple benefice with the title of St. Agatha, situated in the county of N., which he received from Innocent XI, and which yields yearly 10

N.N., another brother,[16] 28 years old, was also a canon in his said native city, but resigned his charge to the brother of the count,[17] brother-in-law of us brothers, during the present year, because he had been provided by the Grand Duke with an excellent parish 6 miles from the city: it is called the parish of St. N., and yields annually 500

The same brother enjoys in his native city a simple benefice bestowed upon him by Cardinal Chigi on the death of a gentleman of his court who was a relative of the said brothers. It is called St. Jacopo Interciso, is situated in the county of N., and yields 30

The said brothers have in their gift two curacies.

They have a lawsuit in progress with Signori N.N. over some entailed property alienated by their grandfather. They have received two favourable judgments, and this will bring in, in landed property 1,500

They have an active lawsuit with the nuns of St. N. over some money, which with a favourable judgment will yield 400

A pending active lawsuit with Signore N.N., which will be pressed after the other suit over the entailed property is over; which latter suit will set an example for finishing the first more speedily. It will yield in landed property 3,000

NUMBER 2. *Sworn testimony of the mediating agent, deposing how the marriage in question was arranged*

March 20, 1695. On behalf of Signor Pietro Comparini against all and sundry.

There was examined in Rome in the house which is the accustomed dwelling of the above-mentioned witness, situated in the Corso near the Piazza Colonna over the shop used as a wig-maker's, Signora Antonia, the wife of Signor Carlo Scarduelli of Genazzano, in the diocese of Palestrina, about sixty years of age, who, when the oath had been administered to her, &c. swore, spoke, and deposed, for the permanent record, as follows:

I tell your worship that about 3 years ago, on an occasion when Signor Guido Franceschini of Arezzo in Tuscany came to this wig-shop of mine to order a small woman's wig for a certain lady of Florence, as he said, after he had come several times to urge my daughter Ursula to make the said wig well and with every care, I asked him whether it was to be for his wife. He answered that he had no wife, but that if there were the chance of a suitable one, who had eight or ten thousand scudi for a dowry, he would marry her, and he begged me to take every pains to find one for him. I replied to him that if it were for a dowry of two or three thousand scudi I, who had friends in several of the monasteries in Rome, could find it for him, but that for as large a dowry as he demanded it would be difficult for me, but that nevertheless I would do my best. He told me that if I found him a wife with that dowry of eight or ten thousand scudi he would present my daughter with 40 doppie, and with this agreement he left my shop.

I thought that since my daughter used to go sometimes to the house of the Marchesa Panthasilea Capozzi, who lives in the Via de' Crociferi, I might send word to the said Marchesa by my said daughter, saying that if she knew of any marriageable maiden who had a dowry of eight or ten thousand scudi, here was a chance of a gentleman who would marry her, and who was well-born and rich. My daughter carried the message to the Marchesa, who sent back the answer that she had a nurse, who was employed in her house, and that she would tell her about it, and in case she heard of any opportunity she would inform me of it. When my daughter said that to the Marchesa there was also present the said nurse, who was employed in the house, and was called Cecilia, and the Marchesa told this Cecilia to consider a little whether she knew anyone suitable, and Cecilia said that she would think about it, and if anyone occurred to her she would tell her.

A few days later, urged by the said Signor Guido Franceschini, who came to the shop daily, though he had obtained his said little wig, I [in MS. he] asked my daughter to find out from the Marchesa if she had had any news about the maiden of whom he had spoken before. She replied that the said Cecilia had spoken to her about a daughter of Signor Pietro Comparini, who had a dowry of about eight or ten thousand scudi, but she did not know whether they wanted a husband for her. My daughter gave me this answer as soon as she returned from the Marchesa, and then, Signor Guido coming into the shop, I told him what was going on, and when he asked me who this Signor Pietro Comparini was, I, knowing hardly anything about it, told him that I would go to the Marchesa and try to find out who he was and where he lived. So I went, and not being able to speak with the Marchesa, who was engaged, I talked to the said Cecilia, who told me that he was a gentleman who had a house near the Via dei Greci, that is, in the street that goes to the Popolo; and she told me moreover that he had 8 or 10 thousand scudi to give his daughter as a dowry. When I had learned that I returned to my shop, and found Signor Guido Franceschini who was waiting for me, and told him what I had learned from Cecilia, and he was greatly pleased and comforted, and went away.

The next day, then, he returned to my shop, and told me that he would be very glad to have a list of this Signor Comparini's property, and I told him that he would have to give an account of his own property, and then we would secure the list of Signor Pietro's. Two or three days later the said Signor Guido returned with a folded sheet of paper in his hand, and told me that in that was described all his property and his revenue, as also that of his brothers, which consisted in a mansion, farms, woods, vineyards, investments, livestock, and other assets, which amounted to thousands of scudi. He told me, too, that Signor Comparini would not find other opportunities like that, because he would keep for his wife men-servants and maid-servants, and in the city of Arezzo she would rank among the first ladies; that she would live in his mansion in Arezzo furnished with ornaments and household goods suitable for a gentleman; and that in that said mansion of his they ate nothing but fowl, and only rarely did they eat meat that grew on four feet.[18]

When I had learned this and taken the said sheet of paper, it was carried to the Marchesa by my daughter, to whom I entrusted it for that purpose, and who left it with her; and because Signor Guido had learned from me that I had heard of this proposition in the house of the said Marchesa Capozzi, he sent the message, on the same occasion that my daughter took the paper, that Signor Guido wished to visit her in order to discuss this affair with her. My daughter received from the lady the reply that if he wished to go there he would be welcome, and reported this to the said Signor Guido, who from time to time came here to my shop; and the said Signor Guido went to the house of the said Marchesa, and there dealt directly with the said Cecilia, so that then the marriage was arranged, nor did I meddle further with the matter. And because he had no more need of me, neither he nor his brother the Abate showed themselves any more, though until they had discovered the identity of Signor Pietro Comparini, and until Signor Guido had dealings with the Marchesa, either one or the other had been coming almost daily to urge me to be active in this business.

And all the above-mentioned things I know, because they took place between the said Franceschini and myself; because I had learned about Signor Pietro from the said Cecilia; and because the said match had been found by my said daughter on the occasion of her going to the said Marchesa; and because of other reasons deposed by me above, when summoned for information.

NUMBER 3. *The first matrimonial contracts drawn up between Signor Pietro Comparini and Signor Guido Franceschini, in which the said*

Comparini cedes to Signor Guido Franceschini, the bridegroom, free administration of two houses and three bonds, with the obligation of taking Signor Pietro and his wife with him to the city of Arezzo, and of providing them with food, clothes, and a suitable dwelling-place

In the name &c. by the grace of God, &c. Since a marriage has been arranged between Signora Francesca Pompilia, and through her between the Signori Pietro Comparini and Violante Peruzzi of Rome, her parents, and Signor Guido Franceschini, son of the late Signor Tomaso of Arezzo; and since the above-mentioned Signora Francesca Pompilia is to go to the above-mentioned city of Arezzo with that same Signor Guido, her husband; therefore the same Signori Pietro and Violante, parents of the said bride, have decided for their greater quiet and comfort, and for the affection that they bear to their most beloved daughter, to go and dwell in Arezzo with that same husband and wife in the house of Signor Guido and his brothers, to remain and live with them as long as they survive. Therefore Signor Pietro, so that he may not have to think about his own maintenance and that of Signora Violante, his dearly beloved wife, but may leave all the burden of and concern for it to the said Signor Guido, gives, assigns, and cedes in free, absolute, and irrevocable administration to the above-mentioned Signor Guido Franceschini, during the lifetime of Signor Pietro, the universal usufruct of all the bonds, goods, shares, accounts, etc. of the entailed property left by the late Signor Francesco Comparini, his father, and the late Domenico Canzi, his maternal uncle; which bonds, goods, claims, and accounts are all generally to revert to the said Signora Francesca Pompilia after the death of Signor Pietro, her father, without male issue, legitimate and natural, in accordance with the terms of the wills of the said late Signori Francesco Comparini and Domenico Canzi, to which etc. which together with all his present and future property the said Signor Pietro now and for the future etc. gives, cedes, and assigns as a dowry, in contemplation of the present marriage, to Signora Francesca Pompilia, and mutually to Signor Guido, her future husband, including as well any and every account, liability, and emolument which may fall to the lot of the same Signor Pietro, reserving to himself only the power of making a will to the amount of one hundred scudi.

The assets, then, which the above-mentioned Signor Pietro is now ceding, for the period of his lifetime, to the free administration of Signor Guido Franceschini, and later gives him as a dowry, after Signor Pietro's death however, are as follows:

A house situated in Rome at the block of plastered houses in the Piazza Lombarda, with its own coach-house beneath, which he inherited from the trust constituted by the late Domenico Canzi.

Another house situated in Rome in the Strada Paolina, near and almost opposite the Greci,[19] where at present the said Signor Pietro is living, with two shops, one beneath the house on the said public street, and the other behind the house on the street called the Orti di Napoli.[20] The latter shop is fitted up with a glass-blower's furnace.

Three bonds (more or less) of the Monte S. Pietro, ninth series,[21] vested in the same Signor Pietro Comparini, which are part of the entail established by the late Signor Domenico Canzi.

And the same Signor Pietro also cedes to the said Signor Guido, with the same complete and absolute power of administration, and afterwards as a dowry, every other account, claim, etc. which may fall to him, against the claims of all other individuals. Concerning the aforesaid dowry, as defined above, the contracting parties agree expressly that the quarter of the dowry,[22] according to the statute of Rome, is not to run in favour of either party except for the income of twenty-four bonds, etc., which bonds under their true names will be assigned as dowry to Signor Guido in the legal instrument to be drawn up, etc. The usufruct from all the aforesaid real estate, bonds, assets, claims, and accounts, and from every other claim and account whatsoever, that in any manner or form belongs to him or may in future belong to him, the said Signor Pietro Comparini cedes, during his lifetime, as above, to Signor Guido Franceschini, as husband of the aforesaid Francesca Pompilia, and not otherwise, etc.

The other ten bonds of the Monte S. Pietro, sixth series, vested in Signor Pietro Antonio Comparini, proceeding from the entail established by the late Signor Francesco Comparini, which are enjoyed by Signor Pietro Antonio Comparini (all ten of which, or half of them, are to be realized and incorporated with the other property in trust mentioned above, after his death, according to the terms of the will of the said late Signor Francesco) and the other three bonds of the second nine-year loan, which were enjoyed by the late Signor Pietro Zacconi, sold to him by the said Signor Pietro, etc.,[23] and likewise the property entailed by the late Signor Domenico Canzi, are not assigned in the above-mentioned income to the aforesaid Signor Guido; but whether their reversion takes place during the lifetime or after the death of Signor Pietro Comparini, father of the bride, he desires that the income from those eight or thirteen bonds may go freely to Signora Francesca Pompilia, his daughter, for her pin-money *extra dotem*, as will be arranged in other marriage contracts, declaring in those that half the capital of these bonds is to fall or pass into the free disposal of the said Signora Francesca Pompilia.[24]

On the other hand, Signor Guido Franceschini, accepting the said cession of administration (declaring, however, that he is not to be required to give any account of it under any pretext whatsoever), as intended for the maintenance of the said husband and wife, Pietro and Violante, as is herewith set forth, in order to reciprocate with equivalent demonstrations of affection and esteem towards the aforesaid Signori Pietro and Violante, binds himself in the form prescribed by the Reverenda Camera Apostolica to take to Arezzo, his native city, at his own expense, the said Signori Pietro and Violante at the same time that he takes thither Signora Francesca Pompilia, his bride; and out of the income from the aforesaid property, ceded as above into his administration, to supply them not only with food but with clothing and with service, and to give them comfortable accommodation in the house or houses belonging to his brothers and mother, to feed them at his own table, and in event of illness to provide them with a doctor, drugs, and everything else necessary at the expense of Signor Guido, and to show every other affectionate regard for the aforesaid Signori Pietro and Violante as long as they continue to live in his paternal house, or houses, as above, in Arezzo.

Moreover, Signor Guido binds himself, as above, to pay the aforesaid Signor Pietro every year, from the income from the said property ceded to him for administration, the sum of twenty scudi in cash, to be used by him at his own discretion. Moreover, Signor Guido promises that if (which may God forbid) Signor Pietro should die and Signora Violante his wife should survive him, he will continue to maintain her during her whole lifetime in the same manner and esteem in which she was maintained by Signor Guido during the life of Signor Pietro. Indeed, he binds himself according to the form prescribed by the Reverenda Camera Apostolica to pay, as above, to Signora Violante the same twenty scudi in cash which he paid to Signor Pietro, and to do this every year during the life of Signora Violante. Moreover, Signor Guido undertakes, if both should die, that is Signor Pietro and Signora Violante (which may God forfend for many years), to pay freely, as above, the same twenty scudi in cash every year to Signora Francesca Pompilia, his wife and the daughter of the aforesaid, as pin-money, because thus, etc.

And if through some unforeseen contingency the aforesaid Signori Pietro and Violante should no longer wish to remain and dwell in Arezzo, but should desire to return to Rome, the aforesaid Signor

Guido shall be obliged to take them back there at his own expense; and it shall be at the discretion of Signor Guido either to return to Signor Pietro the income from the above-mentioned property assigned to his administration, or, without making any other restitution of it, to come and live in Rome with his wife, and to maintain in his own house and at his own table the aforesaid Signori Pietro and Violante, and to feed and clothe them in the same manner as he did in Arezzo. And the aforesaid Signori Pietro Comparini, Violante, his wife, Signor Guido Franceschini etc., and Signora Francesca Pompilia, the bride, bind themselves to observe the aforesaid obligations in the full form of the Reverenda Camera Apostolica.

In Rome, the 24th day of June, 1693:

I, Pietro Comparini, father of the bride, affirm, promise, and bind myself, as above, with my own signature.

I, Violante Peruzzi Comparini, mother of the bride, affirm, promise, and bind myself, as above, with my own signature.

I, Francesca Pompilia Comparini, promise and bind myself, as above, with my own signature.[25]

I, Guido Franceschini of Arezzo, the bridegroom, affirm, promise, and bind myself, as above, with my own signature.

I, Paolo Franceschini, brother of the said Signor Guido, affirm and am contented, promise, and bind myself, as above, with my own signature.

I, Francesco, Abate Cosetti, was witness to the above, and saw all the aforesaid signatures affixed.

I, Luca Santoli of Arezzo, was witness to the above, and saw all the aforesaid signatures affixed.

NUMBER 4. *Second marriage contracts, in which are assigned twenty-four 21/100 bonds of different loans, together with another ten bonds held in trust by Signor Pietro Comparini for his lifetime, and another three bonds resigned to the late Pietro Zacconi; and in which another obligation concerning maintenance is assumed*

In Rome, this 24th day of June, 1693.

A marriage having been arranged and finally concluded, by the grace of God, between Signora Francesca Pompilia Comparini, and through her between Dottore Pietro Comparini[26] and Violante Peruzzi, her parents, of Rome, on the one hand, and Signor Guido Franceschini, son of the late Signor Tomaso of Arezzo, on the other, so that its contents and agreements may be made more plain the parties have determined to come together to sign the contracts and agreements which appear below, which are to be drawn up formally and legally.

Therefore, in the name of the Most Blessed Trinity, Father, Son, and Holy Ghost, and of the Most Glorious Virgin Mary, Signor Guido Franceschini promises to take as his wife the aforesaid Signora Francesca Pompilia Comparini, and to enter with her into holy matrimony. And on their side, the Signori Pietro and Violante promise to give to the said Signor Guido, as his legitimate wife, the aforesaid Signora Francesca Pompilia. And as a dowry, then, and in the name of a dowry, for the said Signora Francesca Pompilia, the aforesaid Signori Pietro and Violante assign to the said Signor Guido twenty-four 21/100 bonds of different public loans, some of which are at compound interest, and some not, vested in the said Signor Pietro Comparini, which altogether, amounting to the sum and number of twenty-four 76/100 bonds, are constituted by Signore Pietro and Signora Violante as a true and actual dowry for the said Signora Francesca Pompilia, their daughter, and in his turn for Signor Guido; these bonds all coming from the inheritance and entailed property left by the late Signor Francesco Comparini, paternal grandfather of the said Signora Francesca Pompilia. And they agree upon the pact and special condition that, considering the aforesaid settlement of the dowry, Signor Guido shall be allowed at his pleasure to remove from the said bonds both the restriction of the entail established by the said Signor Francesco, paternal grandfather of the said Signora Francesca Pompilia, and the restriction of compound interest to which some of them are subject at present, and every other restriction whatsoever that may exist in the authorization and the accounts preserved in the Record Office. And the aforesaid parents consent to this cancellation of restrictions, giving every consent and assent whatsoever, in whatever manner may be necessary and opportune. And of these bonds assigned for the dowry, as above, Signor Guido may freely reassign, sell, and alienate the monthly payments of the five bonds, and realize their price, so that he may use it at his pleasure for the matrimonial expenses. And for the monthly instalments of the five bonds all Signor Guido's property is to be the security.

As for the remaining bonds established as a dowry, as above, Signor Guido may reassign them and realize their price freely, and, after he has freely realized it, it is to be reinvested in the territory of Arezzo, his native city, either in real estate, or in the funds, or in ground-rents, or other income-producing investments,[27] with the declaration however (which is to be put into the contracts of the aforesaid sure and certain investments to be made in Arezzo, as above, to the satisfaction however of both the aforesaid Dottore Pietro Comparini and Signor Guido Franceschini) that the money comes from the dowry of the said Signora Francesca Pompilia, as agreed above, and that therefore the investments must remain specially secured in favour of the said Signora Francesca Pompilia, and for the greater security of her dowry; with the declaration, however, that the aforesaid obligation of reinvestment, as above, shall not prevent Signor Guido from realizing freely the price of the said bonds assigned as a dowry, but that he is only obliged to reinvest it in the aforesaid manner with the mortgage of all his property.[28]

Moreover, the aforesaid contracting parties agree expressly that the aforesaid Signor Guido shall be allowed to conduct Signora Francesca Pompilia, his bride, to Arezzo, his native city, where her aforesaid parents, if they wish to go there also, shall be received and treated honourably, and shall be suitably fed and clothed in the paternal house or houses of Signor Guido, his mother and his brothers. And because Signor Dottore Pietro wishes to abound in tokens of affection towards his said daughter, he desires that if, during his life or after his death, there occurs the reversion of the ten or five bonds (which are part of the entail established by the late Signor Francesco Comparini, vested in the person of Signor Pietro Antonio Comparini, in conformity with the will of the late Signor Francesco Comparini, father of the aforesaid Signor Dottore Pietro) as also the recovery of the other three bonds of the second nine-year loan (sold by the said Signor Dottore Pietro to the late Signor Zacconi, and left by the late Domenico and Elizabeth Canzi, at present enjoyed by his heirs), the income from these thirteen or eight bonds, and half the capital from them shall be enjoyed by the said Signora Francesca Pompilia, his daughter, *extra dotem*, and, as is commonly said, for pin-money, and even in case of the death of the said Pietro, father of Signora Francesca, shall be at her absolute disposal.

And to the observance of all and each of the things said and expressed above they bind themselves in the form prescribed by the Reverenda Camera Apostolica, etc.

I, Guido Franceschini, son of the late Signor Tomaso of Arezzo, agree, promise, and bind myself to the above with my own signature.

I, Francesca Pompilia Comparini, agree, bind myself, and promise as above, with my own signature.

I, Pietro Comparini, father of the bride, bind myself and promise as above, with my own signature.

I, Violante Peruzzi Comparini, mother of the bride, bind myself and promise, as above, with my own signature.

I, Paolo Franceschini, bind myself and promise as above, with my own signature.

I, Francesco, Abate Cosetti, was witness to the above, etc., with my own signature, etc.

I, Luca Santoli of Arezzo, was witness to the above, with my own signature, etc.

NUMBER 5. *Dower settlement drawn up between the said parties, in which both Abate Paolo Franceschini and Signor Guido, the bridegroom, promised solemnly to have it ratified by Signori Girolamo and Antonio Franceschini, their brothers*[29]

August 27, 1693.

In the same, etc. 1693. First indiction, August 27th. A marriage having been contracted and by divine will concluded between the most illustrious Signora Francesca Pompilia Comparini of Rome, a virtuous maiden, the daughter in legitimate matrimony of the very illustrious Signori Dottore Pietro Comparini and Violante Peruzzi, husband and wife, through the contract to that end of her said parents, on one side, and the very illustrious Signor Guido Franceschini, son of the late Tomaso, a noble of Arezzo, on the other, with the promise and assignment as a dowry of twenty-four bonds and 21/100 of another bond of different loans, as set forth in the marriage contracts drawn up for that purpose, and with the agreements contained in the said marriage contracts signed by the aforesaid parties, which are being entrusted to me, a notary, so that they may be inserted into the present legal instrument, whose purport is, etc. And these parties desire to ratify in part and in details the said marriage contracts, and to alter some of the things therein contained, and better to agree and arrange, as will later be said, by drawing up a public legal instrument.

Hence it is that appearing in person before me, a notary, the aforesaid most illustrious Signori, Dottore Pietro Comparini of Rome, son of the late Francesco of Florence, and Violante of Rome, daughter of the late Giacinto, his wife, appointed legal administrators of the said Signora Francesca Comparini, their only daughter, and together with them the same most illustrious Signora Francesca Pompilia Comparini, their daughter, on the one hand: and the said most illustrious Signor Guido Franceschini, son of the late Tomaso, nobleman of Arezzo, on the other hand, etc. reciprocally ratify, verify, and approve the said present marriage contracts signed by these parties, and the things therein contained, except for the following, which are to be more clearly agreed upon and defined as will appear herewith. And for their final implementation the said Signor Pietro Comparini and together with him the said Signora Francesca Pompilia, his daughter, the future bride, withdrawing from the form of the assignment of the aforesaid twenty-four bonds and 20/100 [*sic*] of other bonds of the aforesaid loans, as settled above in the said marriage contracts by their spontaneous consent and every other manner, etc., as a dowry for the said Signora Francesca Pompilia, they assign to Signor Guido Franceschini, the future bridegroom, here present and accepting the contracts, the interest, accrued or still to fall due, until their redemption, of seven bonds and 87½/100 [*sic*] of another bond of the loans mentioned below, which stand to the credit of the said Signor Pietro Comparini, son and heir of the said late Francesco Comparini; which bonds are subject to conditions established by the entail executed by the same late Francesco Comparini in his last will, drawn up by the late Rodomonte Nobili, notary of the law court of Borgo, which was produced unopened on July 28th, and opened on August 4, 1645, or, etc. and subject to the compound interest of the said entail, whose conditions are fulfilled in the said Signora Francesca Pompilia, only daughter legitimate and natural of the said Signor Pietro. Which seven 82½/100 bonds of the aforesaid loans are to be set free of and released from the said restriction of the entail, and from the compounding of interest, and from all other restrictions to which, according to the said letters patent, they are subjected.

And after they are released, they are to be sold and reassigned freely by Signor Pietro, and he is to have their price and the accrued and future interest from them until they are sold and reassigned, as above. This is only to be done, however, in order that he may deposit the money, in the same act and context, in the Sacro Monte della Pietà,[30] or in the Banco di S. Spirito of Rome, to the credit of the said Signor Guido Franceschini, to be paid freely to the same Signor Guido on account of the dowry of the said Signora Francesca Pompilia, his future bride, so that he may freely use it for the nuptial and matrimonial expenses, which are to be made according to his judgment.[31]

And to this effect the same Signor Pietro Comparini and Signora Francesca Pompilia, his daughter, give every consent whatsoever, in whatever manner may be necessary, to the release of the said seven 82½/100 bonds of the said loans, and to their free transfer, and to the payment both of the said price and of the past and future interest of the said bonds which is to be made; the said Signor Pietro, however, being bound, *unico contextu*, as above, to deposit them to the credit and at the free disposal of the said Signor Guido. And to do this the said Signora Francesca Pompilia gives her power of attorney to Signor Pietro, her father, with all legal powers in every manner whatsoever, etc.

Item, seven bonds of the following loans, also standing to the credit of the said Signor Pietro Comparini, with the same restriction of the entail, and of remaining at compound interest, according to the terms of the said will of the said late Francesco Comparini, which as above is annulled in the said Signora Francesca Pompilia, only daughter of the said Signor Pietro; together with the interest past and future to be paid freely to the said Signor Guido, to which free payment to be made to the said Signor Guido they consent, and they give every assent whatsoever which is in any way necessary to have that transferred to the person and credit of the said Signor Guido, in the form and manner which shall be stated hereafter.

And thirteen 25/100 bonds of the loans mentioned below, similarly standing to the credit of the said Signor Pietro Comparini, part with the said restriction of the entail of the late Francesco Comparini, his father, and part with the restriction of the entail established by the late Domenico Canzi, his maternal uncle, as set forth in his last will, produced sealed the 27th of September, and opened the 7th of October, 1652, as, etc. drawn up by the late Gaspare Grisostomi, notary, A.C.,[32] the conditions of which are likewise fulfilled in the said Francesca Pompilia, only daughter of the said Signor Pietro, and with other restrictions set forth in their letters patent, on behalf of the said Signor Pietro, with the accumulated interest of the said bonds, and the interest which shall fall due in the future. And similarly, they assign and consign to the same Signor Guido each and every bond which may belong to the aforesaid two inheritances of the late Francesco Comparini, and of the late Domenico Canzi, and to the said Signor Pietro Comparini, with all their interest, both accumulated and future, etc. which bonds, all and every one, are to be transferred to the credit, favour, and person of the said Signor Guido.

And they consent, and give each and every consent and assent, in whatever manner may be necessary and opportune, to the abolition and cancellation of the aforesaid restrictions of the said entail, and of whatever other restrictions to which the money may be subject; the declaration to be made, however, in the transfer and in the letters and patents of the said bonds, that they are the dowry of the said Signora Francesca Pompilia; and that it shall be lawful for the said Signor Guido, after one year, to be reckoned from the day when the said marriage is contracted, to sell and transfer freely all the said bonds, and to exact and receive their price, for the purpose, however, in the same transaction and *unico contextu*, of depositing them to the credit of himself, Signor Guido, in the Sacro Monte della Pietà of Rome, not to be withdrawn from the said Sacro Monte, except for the purpose, with the order of the said Signor Guido, of investing them in real estate, or ground-rents, or stocks, or other interest-bearing investments, to the satisfaction of the same Signori Guido and Pietro, either in Rome or in the city or district of Arezzo,[33] or in whatsoever other place, etc.

And for the remainder, the said parties confirm each and every one of the other agreements, contracts, and arrangements contained and set forth in the marriage contracts, to the exact and inviolable observance of which the said parties reciprocally wish to be held and obliged, not only in this but in every other better manner, etc.

Which dowry, as above constituted, promised, and assigned, the said Signor Guido, the future bridegroom, adhering to the promise and obligation undertaken by him in the said marriage contracts, now and for all time promises that when he receives it he will preserve and not destroy the pledge, mortgage, security, and assurance placed in general and in particular on all his property, both movable and real, accounts, credits, and everything else of whatsoever kind, both present and future, belonging to him in whatsoever place, with the proviso and effect of the formal declaration,[34] in which part the said contracting parties withdrawing from the arrangement to the contrary made in the said marriage contracts, etc.

And to give further assurance to both the said future bride and the said Signori Pietro and Violante concerning the things promised and the agreement in their favour made by the said Signor Guido, both in the present document and in the marriage contracts, and made or still to be made in any manner whatsoever, they are personally guaranteed by the very illustrious Abate Paolo Franceschini, there present (brother of the said Signor Guido, also a nobleman of Arezzo, known to me the notary) both in his own name and as empowered to act for the most reverend Canon Girolamo and Rector Antonio Maria de' Franceschini, his brothers, having been especially entrusted by them with this authority, as is apparent from the public instrument of power of attorney drawn up in Arezzo on the 8th of the current month of August, and signed and made public by Signor Pietro Paolo Tamarito, a notary public, which he is giving me, the notary, so that I may insert it in the present document, the tenor of which instrument is to be recorded at the end; and nevertheless on their behalf both the said Abate Paolo and the said Signor Guido, their brothers, promise solemnly to have them ratify the present legal document and everything contained in it, or to be stated hereafter, and to produce the public instrument made legal within two months from today freely, *ita quod*, etc. *alias*, etc.

To the aforesaid instruments and marriage contracts, and to each and every thing contained therein, as principals principally and *in solidum*, etc. Signor Paolo agrees, gives security, and promises, binding himself and the said Canon Girolamo and Rector Antonio Maria, his brothers, *in solidum*, not only in this but in every other most stringent manner.

All which things, etc. the heirs, etc. property, etc. rights, etc. the said Guido and Abate Paolo oblige themselves and the aforesaid Canon Girolamo and Rector Antonio Maria in the form prescribed by the Reverenda Camera Apostolica, and also in the form of a guarantee and in every other accustomed form, with the usual provisos, etc. henceforward obliging themselves, etc. renouncing, etc. and consenting, etc. and took their oath.[35]

NUMBER 6. *The sworn deposition of a witness concerning the poverty of the said Signor Guido Franceschini, and the miseries endured by the said Comparino while he was living at the former's house in the city of Arezzo*

[The testimony of Angelica, which appears as item one in the summary for the Fisc (pamphlet 4) in the Old Yellow Book.]

NUMBER 7. *Order to put into effect the granted maintenance as in the position of a daughter, and the transfer of the bonds assigned as a dowry, with the decision*

August 20, 1695. On behalf of Signora Francesca Pompilia Comparini and her husband against Signor Pietro Comparini and others.

Summons to appear before the most illustrious Signor Gora for information, and for the execution of the instrument granted for maintenance in the position of a daughter and the transfer of the bonds in accordance with this instrument in the form prescribed by the dowry contract; and an order that they should be transferred in the form provided. The announcement having been made, there appeared Signor Teodoro Bambini, attorney, who petitioned as above. Thereupon His Worship ordered that for the purpose of maintenance, the bonds assigned as a dowry were to be transferred in favour of Signora Francesca Pompilia with the stipulations and other limitations not affecting the purpose, with peremptory command.

NUMBER 8. *Production and repetition of the various arguments for the reconsideration of the said decree*[36]

August 31, 1695. On behalf of Signor Pietro Comparini, against Signor Guido Franceschini and Signora Francesca Pompilia, his wife. Signor Agostino Luciano, attorney, in pursuance of his office, in order to prove, etc., produced a list of assets presented by the said Signor Guido asserting that he held property in the city of Arezzo, written with his own hand, to the effect, etc. Also he repeated the deposition of a witness who was the mediating agent in the marriage, and who was examined on March 20th; and to show that this same Signor Guido, the opponent, had repudiated his paternal inheritance he produced the public deed drawn up before a notary on August 12, 1681, to the effect, etc. Also, in order to prove that Signor Guido possessed nothing in this world, he produced the evidence of the register of property in the city of Arezzo, to the effect, etc. And to give information about the dowry[37] received by the late Tomaso, his father, on the occasion of the marriage contracted with Signora Beatrice dei Romani, his mother, he produced the public testimony of the tax-collector of the said city, to the effect, etc. Also he produced the baptism certificate of Signora Violante Peruzzi, the wife, from which it appears that at the time of the substitution at birth of the said Francesca Pompilia she was 47 years old, to the effect, etc. And to show how his client was treated while he was dwelling in the city of Arezzo he produced the deposition of a witness, to the effect, etc. And he repeated the depositions of six witnesses already formally examined. Therefore there can be no execution of the order for transfer claimed by the opponent, until requirements are fulfilled, arguments considered, and after a new summons and order.

NUMBER 9. *Repetition of the said arguments*

September 2, 1695. On behalf of Signor Pietro Comparini against Signor Guido Franceschini and Signora Francesca Pompilia, his wife, Signor Agostino Luciano, attorney, in pursuit of his office, and in order to show unjust compulsion, etc. and partly and in parts, etc. and not otherwise, etc. repeated the arguments produced and repeated in the proceedings before his worship on August 31st last, pleading, etc.

Summons to argue against the pleas with a decree of permission. On the same day on behalf of the aforesaid client against Signor Teodoro and Francesco Bambini, attorneys on the opposing side for Signor Guido Franceschini and Signora Francesca Pompilia, his wife, summoned to plead against the arguments produced and repeated, to have witnesses sworn to such of their previous testimony as needed to be admitted, and to order to be restored the collated copy that had been set aside. The announcement having been made, Signor Agostino Luciano appeared and repeated the arguments produced or repeated in the proceedings, and sought and obtained that they should be admitted, inasmuch as, etc. and that the collated copy that had been set aside should be restored.

NUMBER 10. *Sentence of the Reverend Father D. Tomati, absolving from the exceptions taken against the order for maintenance in the position of a daughter and for the transfer of the bonds*

In the name of Christ etc. On behalf of the tribunal in session, etc. in the case and cases, etc. and the petitions in the first or in later trials which were and are being carried on before us between Signora Francesca Pompilia Comparini and Signor Guido Franceschini, her husband, plaintiffs, on the one hand, and Signor Pietro Comparini, the defendant, on the other, concerning her maintenance in the position of a daughter and the transfer of the bonds assigned as a dowry by the said Pietro Comparini to Francesca Pompilia and Guido Franceschini, husband and wife, as described in the dower contract, as appears in the proceedings, we say, etc. that the exceptions made on the part of Signor Pietro Comparini, against the order to maintain in the position of a daughter, and transfer the said bonds, have not held good and do not hold good. And thus have I, Giovanni Domenico Tomati, locum tenens, decreed. Done September 17, 1695.

OLIVERI, notary

NUMBER 11. *The deposition of Signora Violante Peruzzi, asserted mother of Francesca Pompilia, concerning the substitution at birth*

There was examined, etc. Signora Violante Peruzzi dei Comparini, etc. aged 63, etc.

With regard to the second, etc. I have known Caterina Fiori[38] by sight for about 15 years, and I knew her by sight for the first time because Angela Bracchiera, a midwife, told me who she was. Exactly when I spoke for the first time to Angiola Biondi I have already said above, and she came because I sent my servant for her, so that I might talk to her about this matter which I have to disclose.

The conversation that I had this first time with the said Angiola was that I said to her that I was going to confide a great secret to her, and that first she must swear by the most blessed Virgin that she would not reveal it. She answered that she would serve me in anything that I desired, and that she would swear, as indeed she did swear, by the most blessed Virgin that she would not reveal it; and the exact words that I said to her were the following: "I should like to pretend to have a child, and I should like you to find some poor woman for me, an honest one if possible, who because of her poverty would not be able to rear the child when it was born, and would want to send it to the orphanage of S. Spirito;[39] because I would take it."

But I constantly begged her to observe secrecy, and to let me know when she had found someone and had arranged things, so that I might begin to feign to be pregnant. And this conversation took place, as I have said, in the month of November, 1679. Then the said Angiola replied to me that she was in contact with and knew a certain widow, who had come from outside the city a short time ago, though she did not tell me how long, and who thought she was pregnant; and that she would talk to her about it, and would tell me all that passed. So saying she left; and no one had been present during our conversation.

She returned the following day, but what day it was exactly when she returned I do not remember, and this second time the said Angiola and I talked on the second floor of the house where I am living at present, in a room, I mean my own bedroom beyond the drawing-room; and the said Angela was the first to speak, saying to me these exact words: "The woman of whom I spoke to you yesterday is indeed pregnant, and is very poor, and whether the child is male or female she intends to give it away. Therefore if you want to arrange this feigned birth, start to prepare yourself and to pretend that you are pregnant, because from time to time I shall come and visit you, so that we may give more colour of truth to the event."

This was all she said to me, and I replied to her, "Very well, now, remember to keep the secret," and at that time I said no more.

I talked with the husband of the said Angela only once, and that was the day of July 17, 1680, in my house in the first room, that is in the drawing-room on the second floor, and this was about four hours before sunset.[40] The aforesaid Pietro came at the aforesaid time to my house, and I talked to him there on the occasion of his bringing the baby and the afterbirth under his cloak, and the child was swaddled in an old outer swaddling cloth worked with a certain coarse thread,[41] and other blood-stained cloths.

With regard to the third, etc. During the time that I was pretending to be pregnant I was never visited by any woman or friend at all; because I went on Sunday mornings to mass, and pretended that my pregnancy was very trying and therefore I could not allow any visit. And when I went to mass it was very early in the morning, so that I need not dress with ceremony. And I continued to adjust my belly according to the progress of the pregnancy, and therefore none of my friends saw me or could see me.

I remember that during the months of my feigned pregnancy I dressed myself according to the seasons of the year, etc. and I wore my clothes loose, pretending that the same clothes were tight for me at the waist. During my said feigned pregnancy I did whatever I pleased about the house, etc. and I adjusted my clothes and the cloths about my belly so well that no one could doubt the truth of my pregnancy. Sometimes, perhaps, I erred in putting on more or fewer cloths, on account of the heat that the cloths caused, but nevertheless I took great care, and I always put on the cloths without ever leaving them off, because I had the convenience of sleeping alone in my room.

During my said feigned pregnancy, I remember that I went up and down the stairs of the house an infinite number of times to go to the rooms where Signor Pietro lived, but when Signor Pietro was there I never went there to see him, etc. During the said time, I used the little cushion which I myself had worked,[42] in proportion to the length of time that I was pretending; and every morning before I got up I placed it upon my body, and then tied it to me with two ribbons; and I was not provided by anyone with the said cushion, because in my house I had the opportunity of doing everything I pleased; and neither the male nor female servants, nor anyone else, could notice such actions of mine, because I never left my room unless beforehand I had prepared myself carefully with the said cushion or other cloths, and that is why they were unable to notice it; nor could they say a word about it to Signor Pietro, because since my belly was so well adjusted it was impossible to know about it, nor did Signor Pietro himself, my husband, know about it.

And only four or five days before the day of the feigned birth arrived, according to the account which the midwife gave me of the pregnancy of that woman who really was going to give birth, did I begin to complain, refusing to eat any longer at the table with my said husband, but only taking a couple of eggs, and then going back to bed; and at this he himself was pleased, so that I might take care of myself. I myself made the usual preparation of swaddling cloths, outer cloths, and all the other things that are necessary for the lying-in of a respectable person, etc. And to give more colour of truth to the event, and to show that the birth was real and actual, I had the birth chair brought,[43] and the servant had it carried by a porter, and I sent for it to the house of the said Angiola, the midwife, about two weeks before the day of the feigned birth; and the said chair was placed in my bedroom where I slept and was never removed from that room until the day of the said confinement arrived, etc. And it was placed by my orders in my bedroom, where no one ever came, etc.

Nor can I say more, save that I believe that he did not [*sic*] allow himself to be deceived. I know well that from that day when I began to feign pregnancy, saying that I wished to sleep alone and did not want him to touch me, he absented himself from me and forwent all conjugal comforts, etc. I have had in the past rooms that were decorated, etc. and other similar conveniences and ornaments, but only in such fashion that I might at my pleasure withdraw and remain there during the day; nor have I ever had a room to which Signor Pietro could not come, except when I was feigning pregnancy, during which time both through modesty and so as to oblige me he never came to my room. Nor have I ever had disagreements and controversies with the said Signor Pietro.

With regard to the fourth, etc. After I married Signor Pietro Comparini I have already said that several times I had symptoms of pregnancy, and at such times I almost always miscarried within the fifth month, etc. And because I suspected that it might have happened because during pregnancy I had had intercourse with Signor Pietro, therefore when I feigned pregnancy it was not difficult to make Signor Pietro stay away from me so that there might be no reason for a miscarriage; with the result that I could, at my pleasure, make Signor Pietro believe in my pregnancy and not perceive anything through sleeping with me; and that I could also adjust and pad out my belly with cushions and other cloths.

With regard to the fifth, etc. I have already said above whether I ever asked any midwife to find for me some baby newly born, and who the midwife was, and where she lived, and who called her, and the conversation between us. When the midwife came to me to talk in secret so as to arrange about the feigned birth Signor Pietro could never have appeared unexpectedly, because she came at a time when he was out of the house, as I had told her to do, etc. I cannot remember the exact words in which the midwife told me that she had persuaded the said woman to consent to give her the child who was to be born, but I do know that, according to her, she persuaded her to give it up because it was to fall into the hands of people who were prosperous, well-born, noble and genteel; and so she should not deprive the child of this good fortune, etc.

I know that the said woman was brought to bed on July 6th [*sic*, for 16th] in the evening, in the year 1680, as I have said above, which was the day of the Madonna di Monte Santo; because that same night the midwife came to tell me about it, and she told me that she had been brought to bed in the house of a certain Caterina, her sister, who, as I have said, lived in the Vicolo de' Sediari; and that immediately she had sent and had taken to her house the female child which the said woman had borne, with the afterbirth and the cloths all blood-stained. And that evening when the said midwife came to me and told me the aforesaid things it may have been about four hours after sundown, etc. and the said midwife that evening spoke to me in my own room where I was just about to go to bed. And the exact words which the midwife said to me (although I have already given their import above) were these: "That widow has just given birth to a female child; tell me, when do you want me to bring it to you? I have sent it to my house with the afterbirth and the cloths, so tell me, when you want me to bring it to you."

And I answered her as follows: "Now is not the right time, because everyone in the house would perceive it. Tomorrow I will send my servant to call you when I have an opportunity, and I will pretend to be in labour. Bring it to me then, and come right away, and do not forget to bring everything that you have sent to your house."

And the midwife replied, "So shall I do." And I bade her good evening and dismissed her, and locked the door of my room.

I know that the midwife met with some difficulty when she took the child away; because Caterina, sister of the mother, did not want to give it to her,[44] and the child's mother said nothing, because she had already come to an agreement with the midwife; but the midwife, coaxing the sister with fair words, bade her not to make the child lose its good luck. And she told her that in time she would tell her to whom she was giving it, but that then she could not tell her, because the greatest secrecy had been imposed on her. And in this way, according to what the midwife told me later, the said Caterina was persuaded and handed the child over to her, etc.

With regard to the sixth, etc. As to whether my feigned pregnancy was of 7 or of 9 months, I have already deposed above that it was of 9

G.V.in

Chiesa di S. Lorenzo in Lucina

1 Parte del Palazzo Ottoboni 2 Convento dei Chierici Minori 3 Parte del Pal[illegible] R[illegible]

PLATE I

FR. LAVRENTIVS S.R.E. PRESB. CARD. BRANCATVS
ORD. MINORVM CONVENTVALIVM S. FRANCISCI
CARD. LAVRÆA NVNCVPATVS CREATVS DIE I. SEP
TEMBRIS MDCLXXXI.
Ja. Blondeau Sculp

FRANC S·R·E· CARD·NERLIVS

PLATE II

months, and when I pretended to give birth it was in the 9th month; and according as the midwife came to inform me about the condition of that pregnant woman who was about to give birth I too pretended to have pains sometimes, and Signor Pietro too knew about that, because he heard me moaning sometimes. In the last month, near the time for the feigned birth, besides the other cloths that I wore upon my body to show the complete fulness of my body, I added besides the other little cushion which I had there, still another; nor was I in the habit of changing them, but rather increased them from time to time, nor was there ever anyone who assisted me in that.

When the time arrived, then, for me to send for the midwife, according to our plan, to feign the birth, I told the servant, at a time when Signor Pietro had gone out, to go at once to call the midwife, because I felt ill, and to tell her to come at once. Then I gave him certain other commissions, so that he might not come back at once; and when I gave him these orders it might have been about four or five hours before sundown, July 17, 1680, etc. And I began to let those around me know that I was approaching my time, by saying that I had certain little pains four or five days beforehand, according to the true account which I received from the midwife of the condition of the real parturient, etc.

And the midwife came very quickly, etc. and she came accompanied by Pietro, her husband, who came with her because he carried under his cloak the said child, and the said Pietro was dressed in his master's livery. And as soon as they both arrived, the first to speak was the said Pietro, and he said these exact words to his wife: "Take this girl, and these other things." And saying, "At your ladyship's service," he departed without any more talk, etc. And when the said Pietro left, nothing was imposed on him but secrecy, and he was told to remain quiet and not to say anything about this business. And the other things which the said Pietro was carrying were the afterbirth with certain soiled and blood-stained cloths; and it seems to me that he was also carrying a flask of calf's blood (I do not know whether it was a sucking calf or a wild calf) mingled with salt, so that it might not clot. In fact I can say that the said flask was certainly brought, but I do not remember whether the husband or the wife brought it; and it was brought to smear the cloths, because there was no other blood, and in order to give more colour to the birth.

Then as soon as the said Pietro, husband of the midwife, had left, I arranged the bed swiftly, and put on it a sheet folded several times, smeared with the blood which was in the flask, and this sheet, so folded, was placed inside the bed between the upper and lower sheets. And then I took off those cloths which I was wearing on my body and locked them inside a chest, always keeping the key on me. And as soon as the child was brought it was placed on the bed, and it was swaddled and wrapped next to its skin in an old heavy towel, of very common cloth, worked at both ends in coarse thread, and outside that there was an outer cloth of old wool, and the swaddling bands were old and ordinary. Nor did the said child have any mark on it. And the same child did not weep, and its head and both shoulders were smeared by me anew with the blood, and I rubbed on it the blood from the afterbirth, and the said blood was not fresh, because it was from the preceding day, and was beginning to smell a little.

When the child was placed on the bed as soon as it was brought, as I have said above, it remained all the time in the same place, nor was it ever picked up, because the time was short; and when it was smeared with the blood it was among the same cloths in which it had come on the aforesaid bed, and there likewise it was left, and the afterbirth was placed under the bed in a basin. The birth chair was not opened, and the reason was so that it should appear to be a sudden business which had given us no time to put the chair in order. At the exact moment of pretending that the child was being born I cried out, as women in labour do, for the sake of the neighbours, and the midwife placed the child between my legs as though it had just emerged from my body, and covered it with the little taffeta gown which I was wearing (but I do not remember its colour); and then, her arms bare, her sleeves rolled up, she ran to call a certain Giovanna, wife of a tailor, who had the shop beneath our house (nor at that time did she call any other woman, pretending that she was in a hurry) and the said woman came at once, although she was limping because she had had a fall. As soon as the said Giovanna arrived the midwife told her to get up on the bed on the side next to the wall, adding that she was to hold me tight under the arms. The said woman got up as she had been told and held me by the arms, and as soon as she had got on the bed and touched my arms, although I had already been crying out, at the moment when she touched me, as I have said, I uttered a shriek and gave a great start, and the midwife said at once, "Here is the child which has come forth."

The midwife, during the time when I was feigning to give birth and did give birth feignedly, was on her feet and held in front of her bosom some white cloths and swaddling bands. I remember that it took little time, only a few moments, to prepare me to pretend to give birth, and I have already said above that as I did so I shrieked and writhed in order to give colour to the action. During this action of pretending to give birth Giovanna Boba was present, and she was called, as I have said, by the midwife when I was on the edge of the bed, and with the child between my legs. I remained thus on the edge of the bed while the midwife went to call the said Giovanna, and while the latter came into the room. And in the said room, besides the said midwife and Giovanna Boba, there was no one else, neither man nor woman, when I pretended to give birth: because if there had been I would depose it for the truth's sake.

While I was on the edge of the bed (and, as I have said, no one else was present but the said Boba who held me) I saw and could see very well all the actions of the said midwife, and I do not know whether the said Giovanna saw them. And when she pretended that the child came forth, the midwife put the said child, with those cloths which she was holding in front of her, on the bed, and the said cloths were of white linen. And then the said Giovanna got down at once from the bed, and I think that she saw the child, because, as I have said, the midwife had placed it on the bed; and the child did not cry as soon as she pretended to deliver it, but refrained for some time, while the midwife pretended to deliver the afterbirth, which she took from under the bed. And when she did this the said Giovanna Boba was standing by the bed looking at the child, which never cried except after it was bathed and had been completely swaddled, and in short after all the other duties had been performed.

The bath was prepared by the said Giovanna Boba and by the midwife after I had feigned to give birth and had already got into bed; and the said bath was prepared in the same room in a large copper vessel which was carried there by both the said Giovanna and the midwife; and the child was washed in that same bath by the said midwife, and when that was done there were present only the said Giovanna and the midwife, as far as I remember. And during both the feigned delivery and the bath, the said Giovanna, the midwife, and myself held no conversation, except that when the bath was over and the child was swaddled I told the midwife to take as her present an ell of crimson damask which, while she was bathing the child, I had put on a cabinet on purpose to give to her.

I did not have any women around me, nor did I take any restorative then, though I took something a little later when Signora Barbara came, wife of Signor Torquato Caporossi, a neighbour who lived opposite. She was called by the said Giovanna Boba from the window. And I do not remember whether and by whom I was persuaded to take the refreshment. After I had lain down in bed and the midwife had performed her tasks, and had put on the fire a hen which the said Signora had brought alive, and which was plucked and prepared by the said midwife, she came to my bed and pretended to apply to me those remedies which are given to women in childbed, that is, tallow spread on a quantity of cotton, and similar things. She delayed in swaddling the child only long enough to pretend to bring away the afterbirth, which followed at once. The swaddling bands, cloths and outer cloths and everything that we needed were taken from a chest which I had got ready and placed on a sideboard, and they were taken by the midwife, and the child was swaddled on the bed, that is on one side, for the bed was large; and after the child was swaddled it was placed beside me in the bed.

The servant returned after all the actions which I have related above had been finished, and because the said Giovanna went back to her home, as she went away I told her to send for the wife of Ventura, another servant of mine, called Petronilla, so that she might come at once to do the other household tasks which were necessary. As soon as the servant arrived I called him and ordered him to go and find Signor Pietro, my husband, and tell him that I had given birth to a female child, etc. And the midwife left at the same time as the others, and carried away those soiled cloths in which the child had been wrapped when it came: she had put them among her own clothes to hide them, etc.

After the feigned birth I remained in bed on the second floor about a week, and when the baptism took place I went down to the first floor and remained there, also in bed, for two days. And during the time I stayed in bed on the first floor I was visited by those persons who attended the baptism, and it was the following day, etc. The friends who came to visit me on the first floor were three or four, the first of whom, who held the child at baptism, was Signora Barbara, who was called when I pretended to be brought to bed. Another was Signora Agata Sensimi, wife of Signor Pietro Pavolo Benefici; another was Signora Agata, wife of Signor Giovan Battista Barberij, who was the child's godfather; and still another was a certain Signora Angela, a Fleming, whose name I do not remember. They all came to visit me, as I have said, after lunch on the day after the baptism, and they found me sitting up in bed.

At that time the child was nursed by none other than the said Giovanna Boba, and she continued to nurse it for about three weeks, and afterwards the said Giovanna did not continue to nurse it because when her son, who was about 8 months old, fell ill, another nurse was found, etc. And the child was not nursed by me, not only because I was not of a suitable constitution but also because I had no milk, because I had not really borne a child, etc. But I gave Signor Pietro, my husband, to understand only that the midwife had brought me certain waters which Signora Silvia had given her, which had the power of causing the milk to dry up and turn back, and that I had bathed my breasts with it; and Signor Pietro believed everything, nor was there ever any talk about my having or not having milk, with anyone in the presence of any other, etc.

After the child was baptised, Giovanna Boba continued to nurse it for the time deposed above, etc., but after the child was taken from her for the aforesaid reasons it was given to be nursed to a wet-nurse named Maddalena, who lived near the Piazza of the Duke of Guadagnola, and who was suggested to me by the midwife, and she continued to nurse the child for about ten months, with the same salary of two scudi a month, etc. But because the said nurse's son died and she was grieved by his death her milk was affected by it, and when we perceived that our child was suffering we found another nurse, a widow, called Maddalena, who lived in the Strada de' Pontefici, and she continued to nurse the child for about two months, etc. But we took it away from her, too, because we noticed that she was giving milk to a son of hers, and that our own child was not receiving enough, and so we withdrew the said child, and took another nurse, who was a widow called Agnese,[45] a dressmaker, who was suggested to us by the said midwife and by the wife of a barber; and the husband of the said widow had been a coachman, etc. She continued to live in our house and nurse the child for about four months and then left us on good terms, saying that she had found a better opportunity. After this one, the above-mentioned Petronilla, our servant's wife, having been brought to bed, she put her child out to nurse, and came to our house to nurse our child, and continued to do so for about four or five months.

As to the seventh. When the said child had grown a little I sent her to school in a house near us, and the mistress came to call for her each time, and brought her home again when we did not send the servant for her at her proper time, etc. And this is the first and last school to which she was sent by us, because we did not send her to any other school, and she continued to go to the said school for four years, etc. I remember that I took the said little girl out walking myself, and that Signor Pietro, my husband, has also taken her in the street without me.

On the occasion of the Jubilee I resolved to forgive every injury that I had endured, and therefore I made my confession, and having examined my conscience carefully, because I saw myself in so much trouble, I reported to my confessor what I have deposed above, and therefore he ordered me to reveal everything to Signor Pietro, and to ask his pardon. And I have already said that this scruple had not visited me during my other confessions, because, as I have said above, I did not consider it a sin for the above-mentioned reasons. And as I examined my mind, wondering what serious sin I could ever have committed that I had to suffer so much because of the said marriage, the doubt came to me that it might have been a sin to have premeditated and carried out the feigned birth. And when I told Signor Pietro about it on my knees he remained motionless for a while, and then said these exact words: "However could you do me this great wrong, and not tell me about it before? Because if you had confessed it sooner I should not have ruined myself and you in this fashion." And he asked me whether there were others who knew about this, and I told him yes; and then, raising me to my feet, he said to me, "I forgive you." Nor did he say anything else then. It is true, however, that he did not speak to me for several days.

The said conversation took place in Arezzo, and at the time of the Jubilee, in the aforesaid room assigned to us in the house of the aforesaid Signori Franceschini. And I did not at that time plan to make any amendment at all.

NUMBER 12. *Baptism certificate of the same Signora Violante, from which it is apparent that at the time of the feigned birth she was 48 years old*

I, the undersigned, curate and parish priest of the famous basilica and church of San Lorenzo in Damaso of the city of Rome, certify that the following item is to be found in book 8, page 165, of the baptisms, to wit: On August 3, 1633, I baptized a child born on the 30th of the preceding month to Giacinto di Curio and Anna Lensi, husband and wife, of Rome, of the parish of San Nicola degli Incoronati, who was given the name of Violante. The godparents were Giovanni Battista Tilli and Alessandra Calice.

SILVERIO DE' GRAPPELLI, curate

NUMBER 13. *Testimony of Signora Caterina Fiori, aunt of Francesca Pompilia*

There was examined, etc. Signora Caterina Fiori, etc.[46] Aged 55, etc.

I do not remember the first time that I was summoned to be examined; it was last year, either in May or June, if I am not mistaken. And I was summoned to the home of the said Signor Pietro, who sent his wife to my house to summon me, and she said, "Signor Pietro would like to have a word with you, if it is not inconvenient for you." The next day I went to the said Signor Pietro's house, and found him in bed, ill. When I had greeted him, he asked me whether I had ever had a sister, and I answered yes. Moreover, he asked me whether I had ever lodged this sister of mine in my house, and I answered yes. He asked me, too, whether the child born to my sister had been male or female, and I replied that it had been female. He asked me, too, what midwife had delivered it, and I answered that it had been delivered by a midwife known to me as Angiola Bracchiera. He asked me, moreover, what had become of the little girl born to my said sister, and I answered that the midwife who had delivered it had carried away with her the child and everything pertaining to the birth, and that I had not wanted to give it to her, and held out stubbornly against it, because I wanted to send the child to S. Spirito, and that the midwife told me that she herself would take it to S. Spirito, and I said to the midwife, "No, sir, I will not have you take this child to S. Spirito, because I am going to send it there myself." And the said midwife, seeing that I was resolved not to give her the child, said to me, "Since you want me to tell you, I have promised to give it to a lady." And I answered the midwife, "Since you want me to give it to you, I want to know who this lady is." And the midwife said that in a few days she would tell me, but that then she could not, because it was an affair that must be kept secret. And she promised on her oath to tell me, and then my sister said to me, "Since there is this good fortune, it is better to let the child have it than to send her to S. Spirito," and she immediately wrapped the child in a towel of foreign style worked in coarse thread, and in swaddling cloths, and the midwife took it with everything pertaining to the birth.

Signor Pietro also asked me whether I knew where the midwife had taken the said child, and I answered that it was taken to his house, that is the house of your worship.[47] Then Signor Pietro became greatly agitated, heaved a sigh, and asked me whether I was a woman of conscience, etc.

I first knew Signor Pietro Comparini as Pietro Comparini about a year after the aforesaid affair of the child, etc. I learned who he was on an occasion when the said Signor Pietro was passing before my house, because it was in a street which led to his, and my sister said to me, "Sister, sister, come and see the father of my daughter," etc.

I first knew who Signora Violante was a long time after I first learned who Signor Pietro was, etc. I learned indeed who she was on an occasion when a certain man called Paolo Grande, who lived with his family next door to my house, fell downstairs. I heard a daughter of his weeping because her father had fallen, and being still at the window I asked her why she was weeping, and she said to me, "I am crying because my father has fallen downstairs, and I want to go and see him." I asked her where her father was, and where he had fallen, and she replied that he was in Signor Pietro Comparini's house. Then I said, "I am going to come to see him too," not so much to see this man, as to see this girl, etc.

Now I have no sister, but I did indeed in the past have as many as four, and of the said sisters only one married, and her name was Corona, etc. I think that the said Corona's husband died about 16 years ago, etc. After his death the said Corona stayed for a little while in Canapina, but exactly how long I do not know. After her husband's death it was not very long before the aforesaid Corona came to Rome, and she came and lived with me in my house. When the said Corona's husband died, I do not know for certain whether she was pregnant.[48] I do know that as soon as she had come into my house I said to her, "Sister, what is the matter with you that you are so dejected? You are not pregnant by any chance?" She answered nothing, but shrugged her shoulders. Two or three days later, when we chanced to be talking together, she said to me, "I am pregnant," etc.

I know that the said Corona was visited by a midwife, and this visit took place near the time of her confinement, but how many visits were made I do not know. When the visit of the said midwife took place I do not know, because Corona herself found the said midwife, who talked to her in secret sometimes, and sometimes talked so that I could not hear, etc. Corona told me several times that she was going to send the child to S. Spirito, and she said this from the beginning, because she was a poor woman and could not bring it up, etc.

When she was brought to bed the said Corona had no difficulty. I do not know the exact day on which she gave birth, but I do know that it was the eve or the feast-day of Monte Santo, and the birth took place in the evening. When the said Corona was brought to bed in my house there were present a gossip[49] of mine and the midwife, and my said gossip was called Anna Maria, and I sent for her, etc. As soon as the said Anna Maria reached my house she stationed herself near the bed, and she said nothing to Corona but "Courage!" as did the midwife, etc. I cannot say exactly how long it was after the midwife came that the said Corona was delivered, but I do know that she bore her child about an hour and a half or two hours after sunset. The said midwife did not bring with her cloths or other similar things, and I know this because she was in my house. When the child was born there were no other persons present except those named above, who remained there until Corona was finally delivered.

When the child was born it was not bathed, but it was, however, swaddled, and before it was swaddled it was seen by everybody present, and was recognized as a female. When the said child was swaddled it was immediately placed in the bed beside its mother, etc. After she had delivered the child, the aforesaid midwife remained in the house a short time, and she said that she wanted that child. I said that I would not give it to her, telling her to go on about her business, and that I would find a place where it should go, because it was my responsibility. The said midwife again pleaded to be allowed to take it away, and I still said that I would not give it to her. Hearing that, the midwife said to me, "Do not do this wrong either to me or to the girl, because where I shall take the girl she will be well off, as though she were their own child, because they are well-to-do people."[50] I replied, "In that case, if you want me to speak frankly, I want you to tell me whom you are going to give her to, otherwise I will not give her to you." Then the said midwife said to me, "I cannot tell you at present, because the affair must be kept secret. A feigned birth is planned to take place in the Via dei Greci,[51] and at present I cannot tell you about it, but I promise you before the Virgin that I will tell you, but not now."

Then the said Corona said to me, "Come, sister, it is better to give her to this lady than to send her to S. Spirito." And we agreed that it was a good thing that she was to have some luck. I do not remember if she said anything else. As soon as she had said these words the midwife left, and took with her the child and the afterbirth and the whole business, and she was seen by my gossip who was present, and by those who were in the house. When the midwife left, she told me that she would bring me back everything that the child was wearing, as indeed she did a few days later. To Corona she said, "Give her your blessing"; and so saying she took the child and went away.

As to the fourth. A few days later the said midwife returned to my house to bring back the outer cloths and swaddling bands, and the said midwife came there of her own accord to bring back the said cloths and bands, and she came alone, etc. When the midwife came, she talked to me and to Corona, and said to us, "Here are the cloths, for the child does not need this stuff, because it has plenty of bands, and is in a bed as though it were a princess." We said to the midwife, "God be thanked"; and then we asked her whether that lady was young and beautiful, and the midwife answered, "She is not young, but rather old." Then afterwards we told the midwife that we wanted to know where the child was, saying that she might tell us then since she had taken it where she wanted. And the midwife replied that she could not tell us yet, but that we were to have patience and she would tell us; and she begged us to say nothing and to keep quiet, etc.

After this conversation I did not speak to the midwife for the time being, but I did speak to her several times afterwards; but how much time elapsed between one occasion and another when I spoke to the said midwife I do not remember. I do remember that I would meet her sometimes on the street, sometimes in other places, and would say to her, "Well now, how is that bit of service turning out?" And she would answer, "Would that every mother's daughter were so well off!" I know however that the said midwife used to talk to Corona, because the latter would tell me so when she came home. How many times she talked to her I do not remember, but I do know very well that the said Corona used to go to see women who were suckling children, and from what the said Corona told me I know that she used to go to see her own child, etc. Nor do I know whether she went there alone or in company; I do know that the first time she went there with the midwife who showed her the house. And these things I know because Corona told me about them.

From what my sister said to me I know that the wet-nurse who suckled the said child lived near the Piazza of the Duke of Guadagnola, etc. From what my sister told me then I know that the said child was put out to nurse by that lady to whom it had been taken. I know for certain that the said Corona could not have been deceived by the said nurse's showing her one child for another,[52] and I know this from what Corona told me, who recognized it as soon as she saw it, and told me that as soon as she saw it her blood was moved, and she embraced the child tightly and put it to her breasts, and then, quite happy, returned home, etc. And I know that the nurse was paid by Signora Violante, etc.

From what Corona, who heard it from the nurse, told me, I know that the said nurse was changed, but what nurse took her place I do not know. I do know that I heard it said at some time after that the child was suckled in the house of the said Signori Comparini by the wife of a servant of theirs; and that I know because I heard it from my sister, etc.

The midwife who delivered my said sister is dead, I know, etc. Indeed it seems to me that she died in the Strada della Croce, and I know this because I believe that I saw her living there. Before the said midwife died, I had talked to her there, etc., and every time I talked to her I would speak to her about this affair. The last time I talked to her, etc., I talked to her indeed in the same street where she lived, and she used to answer me, laughing, that the said Signora Violante used to feign swoons, and increase the size of her body gradually, and we talked about my sister's confinement, etc. And the said midwife told me that because of this confinement she had received gifts, that is at the time of the bath a certain piece of scarlet or red material, etc., and when she brought the child she told me that she had received a handful of silver or coppers, and every time she went there she used to receive some token of gratitude, such as linen or other things, etc.

The first time that I saw Signora Violante I knew that she was Signora Violante because I was told so, and her house was pointed out to me; and the person who told me she was Signora Violante was the aforesaid midwife. I have seen Signor Pietro Comparini, but I do not remember exactly on what occasions. But every time I saw him I used to say to myself, "Poor man, rearing a daughter who is not his own," etc. I have seen Signor Pietro on one occasion only leading by the hand through the Piazza del Popolo this female child, and she was well dressed and well cared for, and I rejoiced when I saw her. I know that the said child was not Signor Pietro's daughter, because I know that she was born in my house and not in his, etc. And I could not be mistaken about this child's being my sister's daughter, because it resembled her. I know that the said child was reared genteelly by the said Signor Pietro, and if I were to see the girl today I should recognize her by her nose, because she had my sister's nose; and I should recognize her by her eyes, because they were large, and not small, but not out of proportion,[53] however, etc.

Then, the questions having been finished, she was examined concerning the principal points.

It is the truth that about 15 years ago there came to Rome the late Corona, my sister, who had been left a widow, from Canapina, her birthplace, to my house, where after some time she gave birth to a daughter. And seeing that she could not rear the child because of her poverty, she said that she intended to send it to S. Spirito. When the midwife heard that, she said to Corona, my sister, that instead of sending it to S. Spirito it would be better for the said child to give it to a lady who had asked her for one, and would bring it up as her own daughter, and that it would be her fortune. I, hearing this, said to the midwife that she should tell me who this lady was who wanted the child, and I would give it to her. The said midwife answered me that for the present she could not tell me, but that after some time she would tell me, and that I was to leave it all to her, and it would be a great deal better than sending the child to S. Spirito. So that both my sister and myself, persuaded by the words of the said midwife, who was called Angiola la Bracchiera, consented to give her the child. The very evening it was born the said midwife took it, with all pertaining to the birth and the afterbirth, and carried it away from my house, where I remained with the said Corona, my sister, and Anna Maria, my gossip; and there remained also Cristina, daughter of the said Corona and my niece.

After a few days the said Corona, my sister, being anxious to know where her daughter was, sent for the said midwife Angiola to learn from her where the child was, and as the midwife had promised to tell her where she had taken it, and to whom she had given it, Corona urged her to keep her word and tell her everything. At this request the said Corona could extract nothing from the midwife except that she would keep her word, but not then. So that after much urging about it, and even threats, at last the midwife said that she had taken it to Signora Violante, wife of Signor Pietro Comparini, and even led her right to the door of the house where she had taken it, and also begged her for the love of God not to talk about this business or confide it to anyone; and thus Corona was satisfied by the said midwife. But wishing even greater assurance, the said Corona asked her who was nursing her said daughter, and the said midwife replied that she herself would take her to the house of the wet-nurse, as indeed she did. And in that woman's house, which was near the palace of the Duke of Guadagnola, Corona saw her daughter, and recognized her as her daughter, and as such caressed her; and she went back there many times, according to what she told me.

I heard the said midwife say that Signora Violante, wife of the said Signor Pietro, had gone to bed the day after the said child was taken away from my house by the said midwife, with the afterbirth and all pertaining to the birth, and had pretended to have given birth to the said child, and had made not only her household servant, called Ventura, believe it, but also Signor Pietro Comparini, her husband, who when the child was to be baptized arranged for a magnificent and elegant baptism.

When the child had grown older I saw her often on the street, and heard that she was called Francesca Pompilia, and I saw her sometimes with Signora Violante and sometimes with the same Signor Pietro, who also used to lead her by the hand. And not long ago I heard that she had been married in Arezzo in Tuscany.

And I know the aforesaid things because I was present when my said sister Corona was brought to bed; because I heard everything that passed between her and the midwife in my presence; because I saw the child and afterbirth carried away from my house by the said midwife; and because I heard her say myself where the child had been taken and the rest that I mentioned above; and also because I heard from my sister that she had learned from the midwife where her daughter was, and that she had seen and recognized her as such in the house of the said wet-nurse, where she had caressed her (and she told me about it a short time after the midwife carried the said child away from my house); and for other reasons and causes which I explained above in the preliminary interrogation, etc.

NUMBER 14. *Another deposition by Signora Cristina Paperozzi, sister of the said Signora Francesca Pompilia*

There was examined, etc. Signora Cristina, daughter of the late Flaminio Paperozzi of Canapina, etc. Aged about 27, etc.

Before I went to make the said deposition I was aware where Signor Pietro Comparini lived, and I knew that because the midwife had told my mother about it, because the said midwife took a child there. And I knew it too because I used to go to school near there, and I knew that the said Signor Pietro lived there.

As to the second. My mother, who was called Corona, died about 7 or 8 years ago, etc. When she came to Rome I know that she went to live in the house of my aunt, who lived in the Vicolo de' Sediari; and I know this because I too lived with my said aunt. I do not know whether from the day she came to Rome until the day she was brought to bed the said Corona, my mother, was visited by any midwife. But the said Corona, my mother, told me that she had said to the midwife that she intended to put the child in S. Spirito, because she was a poor widow and already had two daughters; and that the midwife replied that she had a good opportunity for the child which would please her better than sending it to S. Spirito. I never saw the midwife in Corona's house except on one single occasion, which was in the evening, that is when the said Corona was brought to bed. In the house where the said Corona, my mother, was brought to bed there were present my aunt, and my aunt's gossip, called Anna Maria; and there was no other person present, etc.

I remember that when the said Corona was brought to bed it was either the eve or the feast-day of the Madonna di Monte Santo, and she gave birth about one hour and a half or two hours after sunset. She gave birth about 14 or 15 years ago, etc. When the said midwife came she came alone, and I know this because I saw her; and when the said midwife left, she left alone with the child, which was female; and she likewise bore away the afterbirth and everything pertaining to the birth, etc. And when she departed with the child, afterbirth, and so on, she was seen by all those who were in the house; and I know this because they were all present at the birth, etc.

When the child was delivered I do not know who was the first to take it up. After it was delivered I was coming to the door, and saw that it was a female child, and that they were wrapping it in cloths, and I could easily see that the said child was female; and I heard the midwife say that it would have been better if it had been male.

I know that the said child was not washed, and I know quite well that it was wrapped up and swaddled; and this I know because I saw the said child beside my mother, who was in bed; and the said child remained beside my mother the whole time that the midwife was occupied in washing her hands and making her preparations, as above.

I do not know how long it was after Corona gave birth before the afterbirth came away. I did, however, see the afterbirth, which I think was in a little basin when I saw it; and I saw it at no other times save that mentioned above, that is when it was in the basin. I know, however, that the afterbirth was carried away by the midwife, as I have said above, and when she carried it away she did so in the presence of all; and this I know because I was present, etc. I have already said above what the midwife carried away with her when she left the house, that is both the child and the afterbirth, and the said child was wrapped in a swaddling cloth worked with coarse thread, which belonged to my mother, etc.

I do not remember whether the midwife said anything as she was leaving, nor do I remember whether anything was said to her as she left. I do know that she wanted to take away the child; and she said that to my aunt, who asked her where she wanted to take it, and the said midwife replied to my said aunt that she was to leave things to her, and then she would tell her later where she had taken it. And my aunt replied to the said midwife that she was going to send the child to S. Spirito if she did not tell her where she wanted to take it. Then the midwife replied that she wanted to take the said child to the house of a lady, and therefore my aunt should not make it lose that good fortune.

My aunt replied that she wanted to know who this lady was, and the midwife answered that this was something that must be handled with great secrecy. Yet she promised her under oath that after some time she would inform her about it. And the midwife told Corona, my mother, to give the child her blessing, and afterwards carried it away, and my aunt was content that she should do so, and no more was said. And I know all about this conversation because I heard it, being in the next room, and because I have heard it related by my mother and my aunt. When this conversation took place the said Anna Maria, my aunt's gossip, was present, and no one else was present; because I saw Anna Maria together with the other whom I have mentioned above,[54] and I saw no one else, etc.

I know that before the said Corona, my mother, rose from her bed she was visited by the midwife once, but I do not know whether she came alone or accompanied; and I do not remember whether she came in the morning or the evening because I was not at home. But I know that she came on that occasion, because I heard my aunt and my mother say so, for I heard them say in the evening that she had brought back the outer cloths and the swaddling bands.

As to the third. I know that the said Corona, my mother, some time after she rose from her bed talked to the said midwife, but I do not know how often, etc. I do know that when the said Corona spoke to the midwife she bade her keep the promise she had given her; and I know too that the midwife replied to the said Corona that she would take her to that place where the child was. Also I know that the said Corona bade the midwife take her there, and I know that the midwife took Corona, my mother, to the door of the house of Signora Violante and Signor Pietro, and said, "It is here that I brought your daughter." I know that the midwife told Corona, my mother, to be quiet for the love of God and not to say anything to anybody, or she would be ruined. I know, too, that after the midwife took Corona, my mother, to the house of the nurse, which was near the Chiavica del Bufalo in the Piazza di Guadagnola, the midwife once more urged her to say nothing for the love of God, etc.

The reason I know that the aforesaid conversations took place between the midwife and Corona, my mother, is because Corona told me so in my aunt's house, where I was living. Just as I also know that the midwife took my mother to the house of Signora Violante and Signor Pietro, that is, to the door of their house, and from there to the wet-nurse's house, because my mother Corona told me so. I know that the said Corona, my mother, went to the house of a woman who was suckling the said child, etc.; and this woman lived, as I have said, at the Chiavica del Bufalo, near the Piazza di Guadagnola, etc.

I know that the child who was suckled by the said nurse was the daughter of the said Corona, my mother, because Corona recognized it and always had considered it as such; and the reason I know that the said child was recognized by my mother Corona as her daughter is because when she returned home she said, "I have been to see my daughter."

I know that the said child was put out by Signora Violante to be suckled by the said nurse, and I know this because the midwife told my mother so, etc. And the reason I know that the said child was given to be suckled to the said nurse by the said Signora Violante is that I heard my mother say so, etc. I do not know how long the same nurse continued to suckle the said child, but I heard that the nurse was changed, and this I heard from my aunt, just as I also heard the latter say that the second wet-nurse was the wife of one of Signor Pietro Comparini's servants.[55]

I know that as the said child grew older it was brought up in Signor Comparini's house, and this I know because the said child went to school with me at the house of a mistress called Margherita, who lived in a house 4 or 5 doors before you come to Signor Comparini's house. I know that the said mistress was the first to whom the said little girl went to school, and this I know because the said little girl was quite tiny, and I did not think that she could have gone to school before, etc. I used to see the said girl taken to school by a woman whose name I do not know because I was not acquainted with her. I do know that the little girl was well dressed with a gown, etc. When the said child came to the said school she might have been about 4 years old, and that I deduced by reckoning that she could not be older; and I deduced my reckoning from the time she was born, etc.

The first time I recognized the said child was because after I had seen her in school I heard someone say, "This is Signora Violante's daughter," etc.; and because sometimes I asked the little girl whose daughter she was, and she answered me, "I am Signor Pietro Comparini's daughter," etc. I know that Corona, my mother, went to the said school, but only once, and when exactly she went there I do not remember. I do know that she went to the said school to see the said child, because I had told Corona, my mother, that the said little girl, her daughter, was coming there; and this I told her because, having

S. Maria della Pieve, Arezzo

PLATE III

1. *Chiesa di S. Maria alle Fornaci, e Convento dei PP. Trinitarij Reformati, 2. Fornaci d' Mattoni.*

PLATE IV

returned home, I said to her that there was coming to the school the said little girl of Signora Violante, her daughter, etc.

Then when the questions were ended she was examined on the principal points.

It is the truth that about 15 years ago the late Corona, my mother, came to Rome from Canapina to the house of Signora Caterina, my aunt, and when she came there she was pregnant, and a few months later she was confined in the house of my aforesaid aunt where I was living, and I know that when she had borne a daughter, the midwife who delivered her, who, from what I heard in the house, was called Angiola la Bracchiera, took the child, with all pertaining to the birth and the afterbirth, and carried it out of the house in order to take it to the house of a lady. I also heard both my mother and my aunt say that they wanted to learn from the said midwife where she had taken the said child, although the same midwife before my said mother was brought to bed had asked her for the said child for a lady who would have preferred it to be a boy rather than a girl. So that after the midwife had taken it away from my aunt's house, my mother persisted with her, asking her where and with whom her daughter was. And finally the midwife made my mother promise that she would say nothing to anyone whomsoever, so that she might not incur the displeasure of the said lady who had feigned and substituted the birth; and when my mother had promised not to speak to anyone, she told her that she had given it to Signora Violante, wife of Signor Pietro Comparini.

I know that the said Signora Violante put it out to nurse, and my mother went to the house of that wet-nurse to see it several times, and recognized it for her own child, and said so at home, both to me and to others who were in the house. And when the child grew a little older she went to a school kept by a mistress called Margherita, where I also went to school. And learning that the said little girl was reputed to be the daughter of Signora Violante, and was the same child that came to the said school, when I went home I told Corona, my mother, that at the school where I went there was in attendance the daughter of the said Signora Violante, called Checca. And when my mother heard this she said that she wanted to come and see her at the said school, and indeed she did go there, and saw and caressed and kissed her. And I know that a little more than a year ago the said Francesca, reputed daughter of the said Signora Violante, my sister, got married in Arezzo, and this I heard from my aunt and from other persons.

And I know all the aforesaid things because I have seen or heard them, and because of other reasons which I have stated in the preliminary interrogation.

NUMBER 15. *Another deposition by Signora Anna Maria Amadei. (All these witnesses were present when Corona gave birth to the said Signora Francesca Pompilia; and these same witnesses in July, 1680, consigned the child with their own hands to the midwife called la Bracchiera, together with the afterbirth, so that it might be taken to the house of Signor Comparini, so that Violante, his wife, might feign it to be her own.)*

There was examined Signora Anna Maria, daughter of the late Ascentio degli Amadei, aged about 63.

I know Caterina Fiori, who is my gossip, and I first made her acquaintance about 35 years ago, when we lived next each other in the Strada dei Borgognoni, etc. It is about 35 years ago that the said Caterina came to Rome, but it is some 16 years ago that there came to Rome Corona, sister of the said Caterina, who was a widow when she came. This I know because I saw her dressed in black, and when I asked Caterina, her sister, who she was, she replied that it was her sister who was a widow, etc. I know that when the said Corona came to Rome she was pregnant, because I saw that her body was swollen, and so her sister told me too.

As to the third, etc. From the day that the said Corona came to Rome till her death I do not know whether she bore any other children except that of which I saw her delivered, which was born on the eve of the Madonna of Monte Santo, in the evening two hours after sunset. In what year exactly she was confined I do not know, because I do not understand dates, but I do remember that it was 14 years ago; and I was present because my said gossip came to fetch me and said, "Do me the kindness to come to my house, because my sister Corona is in labour and I do not want to tell anyone else." As soon as I was summoned I went there, and I had my husband take me, and he accompanied me to the door and then went away. As soon as I reached my gossip's house I saw the midwife there, and the said Corona, and my gossip; and there were no other persons there, because if there had been I should have seen them. When I arrived the said Corona was in the chair,[56] etc. They called the said midwife la Bracchiera, but I do not know if she was called Francesca or some other name, etc.[57]

However, when I reached the said house the said midwife was warming cloths, and was occupied with the said Corona. I know that they had already prepared the swaddling bands, and, it seems to me, also a towel for the swaddling (I mean that they had prepared a towel as well, in foreign style). And when the said Corona was delivered it was about two hours after sunset, etc. The child was delivered by the midwife, and as soon as it was born it was swaddled and afterwards was placed in bed beside its mother. And after the child was born the said Corona was immediately delivered of the afterbirth also by the said midwife.

When the child was born it was observed that it was female, and it was observed by all three of us who were present, and Cristina was called there too, who was upstairs in an attic; and it was observed once only that the child was female, as soon as it was born. As soon as it was born it was shown to the mother, and then swaddled and placed beside her, as I have said above, etc. I did not see the said child washed, and it could not have been washed without my having seen it, because I was present there, etc.

The said midwife talked to us all, and told Corona that she wanted to take the child away, and Corona answered, "Let my sister manage"; and she said no more and neither did the midwife. When this conversation took place between the midwife and Corona, I was present and so was my gossip, and Cristina was called, who was sitting on the stairs of a garret or little room. The said child when this conversation took place had already been swaddled, as I have said above, and the said Cristina had not been called until after Corona had been delivered, and we said to her, "Come and see the baby girl." When the midwife told Corona that she wanted to take the child away my gossip replied that she would not give it to her, but intended to send it to S. Spirito, and the midwife said that she must give it to her, otherwise she would deprive it of its good fortune. My gossip said, "I want to know where you intend to take it," and the midwife replied, "I cannot tell you now, but in a few days I will tell you"; because someone who had no children wanted to have a feigned confinement which should be kept secret from her husband and everyone; and the midwife said that if this lady's husband died without any more children she would be left rich, because there was an entail. My gossip said, "See that you tell me, or I will make trouble for you"; and I do not remember whether anything else was said. This conversation was heard by all of us who were present, etc.

After Corona was delivered, the midwife left within an hour, and when she left it was about two and a half or three hours after sunset.

When she left she was alone, and she carried with her the child wrapped in blood-stained cloths, together with the afterbirth; and the said cloths were taken there from the place where the child had been born; and when the midwife wrapped the child in them it cried a little, but then was stilled, etc. When the midwife carried off the child she carried it in her arms, as midwives do; and I know this because I saw it, and because I accompanied the said midwife downstairs to the door. When the midwife left she said that she was going home, nor can I know whether she went elsewhere.

After the questions were at an end she was examined on the principal points.

It is the truth that about 15 years ago in the house of Caterina Fiori of Canapina, my gossip, who lived in the Vicolo dei Sediari, opposite the coach-house of the Signori Bonsechi, there was living a certain Corona, sister of the said Caterina of Canapina, who was pregnant. One day, I do not remember the month but it was the eve of the Madonna di Monte Santo, as I have said in the interrogatory, there came to my house the said Caterina, sister of the said Corona, and told me that Corona, her sister, was in labour, and therefore she begged me to go to her house to be present at the said birth and to give her some aid. As soon as I heard this I went with Caterina to her house, which was not far from mine, and there I found the said Corona who was about to give birth, and the midwife was helping her. I do not remember the midwife's name, but people called her la Bracchiera. After I had been in the house about three or four hours the said Corona was delivered of a female child, which the same midwife, without bathing it or cleansing it in any other way, wrapped in certain cloths, as I have said in the interrogatory, and carried away to her own home.

It is indeed true that before she carried away the said baby the said Caterina made difficulties about giving it to her, and wanted instead to send it to S. Spirito; but after much discussion and argument (because the said Caterina wanted to know to whom she was going to give it) the said midwife finally said that she was going to give it to a lady who would pretend that she herself had been delivered of it, in order to prevent some entailed property from passing into the hands of others. As I said, she said that this lady was a lady who lived in the Strada dei Greci, and that in time she would tell them everything, but that then she could say no more, so that the affair should be carried out with the greatest secrecy, as I have also said in the interrogatory. And with this understanding, the said midwife carried off the said baby, together with the afterbirth, as I also said in the interrogatory.

A few years later, when I asked the said Caterina whether she had had any news of the said baby, both Caterina and Cristina, her niece and daughter of the said Corona, told me that they had indeed learned that the girl lived in the house of a lady in the Strada dei Greci, and went to school to the very mistress whose pupil Cristina also was, and that there the said Cristina had seen and recognized her.

And I know all the aforesaid things because I was present at the delivery of the said Corona; because I saw the baby both given away and taken by the said midwife, to carry to her house; and because I heard the things I have reported above from both the said Caterina and from Cristina, her niece, at the aforesaid places and times.

NUMBER 16. *Testimony of Signora Anna Maria Bobba, who was present at the substitution of the said child*

There was examined Signora Giovanna Bobba, aged 38.

As to the second. I know Signora Violante, wife of Signor Pietro Comparini, and I made her acquaintance before I was married, because my husband served her as a tailor, and this was after I was married, when I went to live underneath her house. And I went into her house sometimes to perform certain services according as she sent for me, etc. I do not know whether 15 years ago I went to the house of the said Signora Violante in the months of January, February, March, April, and May, because I do not remember; and I do not remember in exactly what month 15 years ago I went most frequently to Signora Violante's house, because, as I have said above, I went there when she sent for me to perform some services for her, etc.

I do not know whether, at the time when I frequented Signora Violante's house, her husband, Signor Pietro, slept apart from her, etc. I do know that there were two beds in the house, one on the first floor and the other on the second, etc. I do not know whether Signora Violante was ever pregnant, because I did not ask her such things, etc. Some time after I had gone to live in that house I heard that Signora Violante was pregnant, but I did not see that her body was large, etc. At what time I noticed that the said lady did not have a swollen body, as I have said above, I do not remember exactly, but it seems to me that it was at the beginning of the summer. I have sometimes seen the said Signora Violante, now with her body swollen, now with it flat, etc. And when I noticed that Signora Violante's body was swollen I was not suspicious of anything, but it seems to me that it was natural. I do not remember how long I continued to see the said Signora Violante's body now swollen, now flat, but I do know that I did not see that diversity in her body for long, etc.

During the time I have mentioned above I have seen Signora Violante dressed without a corset, but with a bodice without pleats and without projections, close-fitting from head to foot. I know that the other corsets which Signora Violante wore were laced at the back, and I know that she never had them let out because my husband served her as a tailor; and she could not have let them out herself because there were seams in them; and I remember always to have seen Signora Violante with her corsets laced quite tight, and long, as was the fashion then, etc.

I do not know who made the beds in Signor Pietro's house, unless the servant made them; and in the said Signor Pietro's house there were no other persons who could have made the beds. I do know, however, that sometimes the servant's wife, called Petronilla, went into Signor Pietro's house, though I do not know whether she made the beds. And the said Petronilla did not go every day to Signor Pietro's house, because, as I said, she only went there sometimes; and this I know because every time she went there she passed in front of my house and I saw her, etc.

Fifteen years ago I used to see Signora Violante going to mass with her husband at the Chiesa dei Greci,[58] and on other occasions I saw her ride out in a carriage; and besides the times I have mentioned above, I never saw her go outside the door. And I do not remember whether at the time mentioned above Signora Violante wore new clothes when she went to mass. I do know that the clothes she wore were well laced, and I always saw them laced in the one way, and 15 years ago when she went out I could not tell whether she were pregnant or not, etc. In my judgment it seemed that 15 years ago Signora Violante could not bear children because she was elderly; and she had no children, and I did not think there was any reason for it but what I have mentioned above, etc. I do not know whether any midwife ever frequented the house of the said Signora Violante, except that 15 years ago a certain midwife called la Bracchiera frequented it, whose real name I do not recall; and this I know because I saw her in the house several times.

As to the third, fourth, fifth, etc. I was never present at any confinement of Signora Violante's. I was indeed present at a feigned confinement of the said Signora Violante, which took place the day before or the day after the feast of the Madonna del Carmine, and that will be 15 years ago when the same date comes around again. And I was called by the said midwife, who said to me, etc. When I was called by the said midwife it was on a Wednesday after dinner, at about six hours before sunset, and I was in my husband's shop, underneath Signora Violante's house, and she came into my shop, and the exact words she said to me were, "Come upstairs, because Signora Violante needs you." Nor did she say anything else to me. Then while we were going upstairs together she added that the said Signora Violante was about to give birth; but on what landing she said it to me, and in what place exactly, I do not remember, etc.

When we reached the second floor, where Signora Violante lived, we went into the drawing-room, where there was no one, and in the said room, a little larger than this of your worship, where there was a harpsichord covered with yellow leather, etc. Then we went into the room where Signora Violante was, which was to the right, and the midwife entered a little before me, because I had hurt my knee and could not walk as fast as she, etc. And I had been in Signora Violante's house on other occasions besides this, but I do not remember how often, and I had gone only into the drawing-room and the kitchen, and had never before been in the room where she was that day. In the middle of the said room there was a gilded four-poster bed, but I do not remember whether there was a canopy: and this was 15 years ago from the eve of or the day after the coming feast of the Madonna del Carmine, etc.

When I entered the said room there was no one there but Signora Violante, who was sitting on the edge of the bed, which was on the right as you came into the room, and the side of it was towards the courtyard. As soon as I was in the room, the midwife told me to go between the bed and the wall and hold Signora Violante from behind; and Signora Violante said so too; and neither of them said anything else to me, etc. Then I climbed on the bed on my knees and took Signora Violante from behind under the arms. And during this time there was no one else either in the house or in the said room; and I know this because both the midwife and Signora Violante told me that everyone was out of the house, etc. Nor is it possible that the said servant and Signor Pietro Comparini were in the house, because when we had put her to bed I went to call my husband so that he might call Ventura's wife to come upstairs. And I have no other reasons for knowing it, but I do know it for certain, because they delayed somewhat in coming.

The time during which I held Signora Violante from behind was less than about half a quarter of an hour, and after the said half quarter of an hour the said Signora Violante was delivered, and the midwife said it was a female child, etc. While I was holding the said Signora Violante by the arms from behind I could not see in any way when the child was born; because, as I was on my knees behind her and she was taller than I, it was impossible for me to do so. When I held, as I have said above, the said Signora Violante, she was wearing no corset of any kind, but was in her shift, and had on a simple garment of silk, but I do not remember what colour it was. And as soon as she was delivered I took off her garment and put her to bed, and we covered her with the bedclothes; and we did not perform any other service for her then, only I and the midwife went and bathed the child, and when we had washed it we swaddled it. And the said child was born as all other children are born, except that it seemed to me that on one arm and on the back and hair the blood was rather dry.

After we had done all that I have deposed above, I called from the window to Signora Barbara, wife of the steward of Cardinal Maidalchini, who asked what I wanted, and I told her that Signora Violante had been brought to bed of a daughter, and to come upstairs. She came up at once with her waiting-woman, and I went and opened the door for her, and saw that the waiting-woman had a hen in her hand. And when I had told them to go and see Signora Violante I went off to my own house and told my husband to go and call the servant's wife. And that evening before nightfall I went back to see Signora Violante, who did not rise from her bed for several days, etc.

After the birth, the first time that she got up I saw her go to the first floor on the day of the baptism, etc. I must say, however, that before she went down to the first floor the first time, on occasions when I went to see her I saw her out of bed several times.

When the midwife and I went into the room where Signora Violante was confined, as I have said above, the midwife remained always with me and never left, except when she went to throw the afterbirth into the latrine, and I noticed its smell, etc.

Whether I have ever heard it said that Signora Violante was not really brought to bed at the aforesaid time, I reply to your worship that I have heard it said, by both men and women, that the confinement was feigned, etc. And the said men and women said these exact words: that the child could not possibly be hers because she was not of an age to bear children; and they did not say anything else. Though I may mention that it was also said that they had obtained the said child from some place in order to acquire their property, etc.

I know that when the said girl grew up she did not resemble her father or her mother, because I saw her sometimes. Where the aforesaid Checca Pompilia may be at present I do not know.

Then when the questions were ended she was examined on the principal points.

I declare to your worship as the truth that in the year 1680, which was about 14½ years ago, while I was living with my husband, Giovanni Boier, in the shop under the house of Signor Pietro Comparini in the Strada dei Greci, one day after dinner there came downstairs from the house of the said Signor Pietro a midwife whose name was Angela, called la Bracchiera, and she told me to go up to Signor Pietro's house, where Signora Violante, his wife, was in labour. So that hearing this I ran off at once, and went up to the second floor of the said house, where the said midwife had returned shortly before. Coming into the room where Signora Violante was, I found her seated on the side of her bed, without a dress and with only a little bodice, and as soon as I arrived the said midwife told me to hold the said Signora Violante from behind, and I had only been in this position for a moment when I heard the midwife say, "Here is a female child." At once Signora Violante lay down in the bed, and after that the bath was prepared in which the said child was washed, and when it was washed it was swaddled and put to bed beside Signora Violante.

When that was over, I called from the window a certain Signora Barbara, who was wife to the steward of Cardinal Maidalchino, and who came at once to Signora Violante's house, and brought with her a hen. After she had come I went downstairs to my own dwelling and told my husband what I had seen, and told him too to go and summon Petronilla, wife of Ventura, servant of the said Signor Pietro. And so my husband went there, and the said Petronilla came. And I too returned there to give milk to the said child, and I stayed there for many days and nights, and slept in the same bed as Signora Violante, and in all the time I slept with her I observed that never did milk come to the said Signora Violante's breasts. And that was for the duration of six or eight consecutive days, because from the day when I saw the said child born I always slept at night with the said Signora Violante.

Before I was called by the said midwife I had been acquainted with Signora Violante, and many times had seen her with her body swollen, and many times again I saw her with her body flat, that is, smaller than as I had seen it on the preceding day. Some days after I had seen the said child born, the said Signora Violante rose from her bed, which was in a room on the second floor of her house, and she went down by herself to the first floor, where formerly Signor Pietro, her husband, had always slept from the first moment she said she was pregnant, according to what I have heard the said Signora Violante say. And in the afternoon of the said day the said child was taken to be baptized in the church of S. Lorenzo in Lucina, and because of this three carriages went there; in the first there were the midwife with the child, Signora Barbara, wife of the aforesaid steward of Cardinal Maidalchini, and a widow, friend of the said Signora Barbara, and there was Signora Agata Massimi, wife of Signor Giovan Battista Barberij, Pietro Comparini, etc.; in the third carriage then, which was an open carriage, there were myself and the aforesaid Petronilla. And with these three carriages the child was taken to S. Lorenzo in Lucina, where it was baptized and given several names, and among others Francesca Pompilia, by which it has always been called, etc.

And I say that in all the time that I slept in the house of this Violante she never had milk in her breasts, as pregnant women do when they bear children; from which I argued that Signora Violante had not really been confined, and that she had feigned the said birth, as I have deposed more fully in the interrogatory, to which I refer.

NUMBER 17. *Another deposition by Signora Petronilla Feure*

Petronilla, daughter of the late Pietro Feure, about 32 years of age, was examined, etc.

As to the first. My said husband when he married me lived in the house of Signor Pietro Comparini and his wife Signora Violante, and as far as I know always remained in his house, although he served and had served other masters, because he had been brought up from a boy in Signor Pietro's house, etc. I have borne children to my husband, that is a daughter, and I miscarried of a male child, etc. The said daughter is alive, and I brought her up, etc. I do not know Caterina Fiori, but I do know well by sight Giovanna Boba, and I have talked to the said Giovanna because we were neighbours, but some time ago, and it is probably about 15 years ago that I talked to her; and at the time when I talked to her I was living in the Orto di Napoli, and the said Boba lived at the top of Strada Vittoria in the tailor's shop, etc.

As to the second, etc. I know Signor Pietro Comparini, and it is about 15 or 16 years ago that I began to know him on the occasion of my going sometimes to Signora Violante, his wife, together with my mother, and the said Signora Violante gave me work to do, etc. I lent a hand with the household tasks in the said Signor Pietro's house at the time when I got married, which was at Easter, and the tasks which I did in the said Signor Pietro's house consisted of sweeping, making the beds, and other household tasks, etc.

I saw Signora Violante once when she seemed to me pregnant, and this was about 15 years ago; if not quite that long ago, not much less. I do not know however whether she ever had a miscarriage. She seemed to me pregnant because she had swooning fits, and because she told me so. I do not know, however, whether Signor Pietro knew that Signora Violante was pregnant. This appearance of pregnancy lasted 9 months, and of this pregnancy the said Signora Violante feigned to be brought to bed. I was not, however, in Signor Pietro's house, but was summoned by the husband of the said Giovanna Boba, who said that I was to go at once to the house of the said Signora Violante because she was in labour, so that going there I found that they had swaddled the child, etc.

I did not see the said Signora Violante pregnant at other times than the time mentioned above when she seemed so to me; and if she had been pregnant at other times during the period that I frequented her house I should have known it, and should have been able to know it either from the signs or from Signora Violante, etc. Nor do I know whether the said Signor Pietro ever kept maid-servants. I do know that he had men-servants, and as far as I have seen he had for servants my husband and another, who was called Domenico, etc.

I do not understand dates, and therefore I cannot say how many beds Signor Pietro had made up in his house in the years 1680, 1681, and 1682. About 15 or 16 years ago, however, I remember that the said Signor Pietro had 3 beds in his house, one of which was kept in a room on the first floor, another on the second floor, and the other at the top of the house where the servant slept. I do not remember, however, for exactly how long the said Signor Pietro continued to keep the 3 beds of which I have spoken above. And I know this because I frequented the house of the said Signor Pietro, because my husband was in his service, and I often made them. I know that the said Signor Pietro slept apart from his wife; I do not remember, however, at exactly what time he began to sleep apart from his wife, but I do know that it was warm weather, etc. From what I could see, the said Signor Pietro slept downstairs, in a little room on the first floor, and Signora Violante slept in a room on the floor above. And this I know because I frequented the house; and I imagine that they slept in separate rooms, because they had me make the beds, as I have already said above, etc.

I know that the said Signora Violante was friendly with a midwife who was called Angeluccia la Bracchiera, and I know that the said midwife has been in Signor Pietro's house, and as far as I can remember I saw her there two or three times, etc. And I know that the said midwife was called Angiola Bracchiera because I heard it said afterwards by people and by them [*sic*], etc. And as far as I can remember the said midwife came to the house of the said Signora Violante because the latter pretended to be pregnant, and I know this because when I went there I saw that sometimes Signora Violante's body was swollen, and sometimes flat, etc. And I could also understand that Signora Violante was trying to feign pregnancy because I did not see the pit of her throat throbbing frequently, as ordinarily happens with pregnant women, etc. The said Signor Pietro was not much concerned in how the household affairs were carried out, because what Signora Violante did was well done, and what she said he believed.

As to the third. This aforesaid first time that Signora Violante said she was pregnant, I did not perceive in her any sign of pregnancy, etc. And when I had occasion to go to the said Signora Violante's house, as I have already said, sometimes I saw her body swollen, sometimes flatter, and sometimes I paid no attention to it. When I saw her said body swollen I imagined that it was feigned, because sometimes I saw her body swollen, sometimes flat, and because, as I have said above, I did not see the pulse in her throat beat; and I was not persuaded of this by any other causes than those mentioned above, etc. And when I went to Signora Violante's house I have never seen her with the natural fulness of her body, because I saw her with her body now flatter, now more swollen, as I have said above, and I did not consider whether its size were natural or not, etc.

When the said Signora Violante dressed I do not remember how the clothes were made which she wore at the time when she claimed to be pregnant, and I do not remember whether the clothes she wore were loose or tight. I do remember that at the time of her confinement she walked slowly, etc. And the final months when the said Signora Violante claimed to be pregnant were in the summer, and the last month when Signora Violante pretended to be confined, as I have said above, was that of the Madonna di Monte Santo, but I cannot remember the exact day, but it was either the same day as the feast of the Madonna di Monte Santo or the day following, etc.

Nor do I remember whether I ever noticed the body of the said Signora Violante in the last month of her pregnancy, as above; I did notice it, however, in the last month but one, and it seemed to be now swollen, now flat; but exactly how swollen it was and how flat I cannot remember, etc. I remember that, from what I could see, the said Signora Violante during the last days of her pregnancy, as above, remained continually on the upper floor, and did not go about the whole house, etc. I discussed the said pregnancy, as above, with my husband, and when I talked of it no one was present, because if there had been anyone present I should remember it. I do not know, however, whether my said husband ever discussed the aforesaid pregnancy with anyone else.

As to the fourth. As far as I can remember it seems to me that it was after dinner when the said Signora Violante claimed to have given birth. I do not remember the exact hour, however, but it might have been 3 or 4 hours before sunset, and as far as I remember it seems to me that the day before I had not been in Signora Violante's house. The husband of the said Giovanna Boba came to look for me in my house, and said to me, "Go to Signora Violante, who is in labour"; and this he said to me in my house. And after I had lingered at home for a few minutes I went to Signora Violante's house, and I do not remember whether Signor Pietro was there when I was in his house; nor do I know whether Signor Pietro might have been at home without my having seen him. After the aforesaid husband of the said Giovanna had told me that Signora Violante was in labour, as I have said above, I went, as I have already said above, to her house, and there I found the aforesaid Giovanna, Signora Barbara, and the midwife, and besides these there was no one else there, etc. I remember that Signor Pietro Comparini came home that evening, but I do not remember at what hour exactly he came, etc.

I know that the preceding [*sic*] day the child was given the breast by the said Giovanna Boba, who continued to give it the breast until the baptism, which took place about 10 or 11 days later. And after the baptism it seems to me that the child was at once given to a wet-nurse, and I know this because sometimes I saw her give it the breast, and sometimes either Signora Violante or my husband told me about it. The said Signora Violante remained in bed about 7 or 8 days, and I know this because I saw it, etc. I do not know whether Signora Violante ever tried to give the child the breast, but I believe that she did not nurse it, because I have never seen her have milk, etc. I do not remember whether her colour ever changed during those days when she remained in bed, but I do remember that she looked well and rosy, etc. After the baptism the said Signora Violante got up and went freely about the house, and this I know because I saw it, etc.

After the baptism, the said midwife found the wet-nurse for the said child, who lived behind S. Maria in Via, about opposite the Piazza of the Duke of Guadagnola, which wet-nurse was called Maddalena, and was the wife of a chairman of Cardinal Facchinetti; and this I know because sometimes I went with the lady to see the child at the said nurse's. I know that after the child was returned to Signora Violante it was given to another wet-nurse called Maddalena, a widow, who lived in the Strada de' Pontefici, etc. And this nurse gave it milk for about two months, and this I know because Signora Violante and my husband told me so. I know that the said child was brought home ill, and for this reason a nurse was taken into the house, called Agnese, who suckled it for 5 or 6 months, and afterwards the said Agnese was sent away, and I gave it the breast for about 4 months, etc. And I think that it was sent to school, and the first time they sent it to school near there, two doors away from the said Signor Pietro's house, etc.

Then when the questions were ended, she was examined on the principal points.

It is the truth that about 15½ years ago Ventura, my husband, was in service with Signor Pietro Comparini, and I, as his wife, went often to the said Signor Pietro's house, and there used to see Signora Violante, his wife, and used to stop and talk and gossip with her, as women do. And I saw, too, that the same Signora Violante, who said she was pregnant, appeared with her body sometimes swollen, sometimes flat, from which I argued that her pregnancy was a mere fiction, and that actually she was not pregnant. And I observed this for the space of about six or seven months, during which time I used to go to Signora Violante's house, and particularly after I was married to Ventura, my husband, after which time I went there almost every day, and often stayed for the whole day. This gave me occasion to observe that the said pregnancy was a fiction, so that each evening when I returned to the house where I was living with the said Ventura opposite the Orto di Napoli I used to talk to the same Ventura about Signora Violante's pregnancy, and we used to say to each other that this lady was pretending to be pregnant while she gave no evidence of it in any way. And both my husband and myself had often seen her with her body swollen, and at other times without any swelling; nor during the whole time was I ever able to discern in her any evidence of pregnancy.

Finally in the month of July, about 15 or 16 years ago, one day after dinner there came someone who lived in the shop under Signor Pietro's house, and told me to go to Signor Pietro Comparini's house, because the said Signora Violante, as far as I can remember either was about to bear or had borne a female child. When I heard that I came in a little while to Signor Pietro's house, and found that Signora Violante was cheerful, nor could it be recognized in any way that she had given birth: in fact when I asked her how she had felt the pains, and how much she had suffered in being delivered, she told me that she had suffered little, and that it had happened very quickly, and that the midwife had scarcely arrived in time.

Afterwards I continued to come every day to the said Signor Pietro's house, and helped to look after the said Signora Violante and also the said Signor Pietro, whose bed I made in his customary room on the first floor for about 8 or 10 days. However before the baptism, and in all the time that I was coming to the house every day, never did I see that Signora Violante, who remained in bed in a room on the second floor of the same house, had any milk in her breasts, as women are accustomed to have when they have given birth, and this circumstance gave me even greater reason to believe that she had not really borne a child, but that the birth was a feigned one. And I discussed that, too, with the said Ventura, my husband, who held it for certain that the birth was fictitious and not true. Nevertheless, however, the said Ventura, my husband, dissimulating what he knew on this subject, in order not to seem to make his mistress' business public, admonished me not to utter a word about it to anyone. And so although other people said to me that the confinement was fictitious and not true, in order to further the wishes of the said Signora Violante I used to say to those who talked about it that they were mistaken and that the confinement was true and not feigned.

When the said child was baptized I went and attended the baptism in S. Lorenzo in Lucina, for which occasion three carriages were procured by the said Signor Pietro. In the first of them rode the midwife with the child, and the godmother who was to hold it at baptism (a certain Signora Agata, whose surname I do not remember) and there was also another lady, but I do not remember who she was. In the second carriage there was the godfather, who was to hold the child at baptism, whose name I have given in the interrogatory,[59] and there was Signor Pietro Comparini, and there were others whom I do not remember. In the third carriage, then, there were myself and the aforesaid Giovanna, who lived in the shop under Signor Pietro's house, and who at the beginning when I saw the said child in bed with the said Signora Violante had suckled the said child, and also after the baptism suckled it for some days. And so when we were gathered in the church of S. Lorenzo in Lucina the said child was baptized, and it was given the names Francesca Vittoria Angela Pompilia, and after the baptism we returned to the carriages and all went back to Signor Pietro's house, where we were all given a sumptuous repast.

Some days later the said child was put out to nurse with a certain Maddalena (wife of a chairman of Cardinal Facchinetti of blessed memory) who lived behind S. Maria in Via, near the palace which today belongs to the Duke of Guadagnola. She kept it for the space of about 10 months and then restored it to the said Signora Violante, who put it out to nurse to a widow called Maddalena, who lived in the Strada de' Pontefici, who kept it for about two months. But because the child grew ill she restored it to the said Signora Violante, who took a nurse into the house, the wife of a coachman, whose name I do not know, and she suckled it for about six months. She was dismissed because I had been confined about three or four months before, and the said Signora Violante gave it to me to nurse. I was living then in the Strada Vittoria opposite the house which at that time belonged to Signor Francesco Valentini, the lawyer. It is indeed true that I entered Signora Violante's house, and lived there day and night, together with Ventura, my husband, so that I might suckle the said child, and I continued to do so for some little time, about four months, after which I left the house of the said Signora Violante, and went back to live in the said Strada Vittoria in another house, not far from the one in which I had formerly lived. Afterwards, then, I continued to frequent the house of the said Signora Violante, where I used to see the said little girl, who in order not to call her by as many names as she had been given in baptism, was called by Signora Violante and Signor Pietro, and by all those who frequented the house, only by the names of Francesca Pompilia.

And all the aforesaid things I know because I frequented Signora Violante's house both before and after I was married, in the way which I have described above in the interrogation; and because I saw the said Signora Violante both during the time when she pretended to be pregnant and after she feigned to have given birth; because I was present at the baptism; and because I had made those aforesaid reflections on the feigned birth; and because I had talked about it with my husband; and also because I had heard other people laughing at the said confinement; and because I suckled the said child; and because I knew that the other women spoken of by me above [*sic*]; and because of other causes given by me in my said deposition in the interrogation.

NUMBER 18. *Another deposition for the permanent record, by Signora Agnese Santa Olivieri, who not only heard from the mouth of the midwife about the feigning of the said confinement, but saw the child itself being taken by the midwife to the house of Signor Comparini*

August 2, 1695. On behalf of Signor Pietro Comparini against anyone whatsoever, there was examined by me, etc. for the permanent record, Signora Agnese Santa Olivieri, daughter of Signor Giovanni Olivieri, aged about 35, and on oath, etc. she said and deposed as follows, to wit.

I depose as the truth to your worship that in the month of July, 1680, as I was passing along the Strada de' Greci which leads to the Piazza di Spagna,[60] one day after dinner, I met Angiola the midwife, called la Bracchiera, who was going with her husband along the street which leads from the Piazza di Spagna to the Greci (I do not remember its name), and I went up to the said Angiola and asked her to remember to try and find me a place as wet-nurse with some lady, as on other occasions I had begged her to do. She answered that at that very moment she was going to take a child to a lady, who, because she had no children, wanted to feign that she had given birth; and that she would manage it so that I should go and serve her as a wet-nurse. Then I turned to the husband of the said midwife and raised his cloak, and saw a beautiful child wrapped in certain dirty cloths. I asked the midwife whether it was a boy or a girl, and she replied that it was a girl. Then the said midwife told me to keep it a secret, and not to confide this business to anyone; and with these words they went on their way. I, being curious, followed them at a little distance to see where they were taking the said child, and I saw that they brought it here to the house of Signor Pietro Comparini in the Greci, where at present I am being examined.

Later I heard it said that Signora Violante, wife of the aforesaid Signor Pietro, had given birth to a child which had been baptized then as the daughter of the said Signor Pietro Comparini and Violante his wife, with several names, among the others Francesca Pompilia. I went to suckle that child in the house of the said Signor Pietro and Violante about a year later, and I suckled it for about four months, for the place as nurse was obtained for me by a certain Margherita, the wife of a barber, and by the said Angiola, the midwife.

And while I was serving as a nurse in the said house there came sometimes the said midwife to see the said child again, and she used to remind me to reveal to no one what I knew, because it might cause trouble if Signor Pietro came to know of it.

All these things I know because I saw them or heard them, or because they were said to me on the occasions which I have described above in my previous examination, etc.

NUMBER 19. *Repudiation of his paternal inheritance made by Signor Guido Franceschini*

March 2, 1693, etc. I certify as a notary, etc. that in the files of public documents, etc. from March 1, 1680, through the whole month of August, 1681, etc. there is found the following repudiation of the paternal heritage, etc. to wit: 1681, August 12th, there appeared in person before the court, etc. Signori Guido and Antonio Maria, brothers, and sons of the late Tomaso Girolamo dei Franceschini, etc. saying that they intend to execute in court and to assert certain of their rights, particularly to repudiate their paternal inheritance as follows; and, lest the judgment be invalidated, they request, as minors,[61] the appointment for them as guardian of some man of integrity, with regard to, etc.

The said minors having been given into the guardianship of Signor Tomaso, the son of the late Signor Guido dei Romani, etc. present, etc. and accepting, etc., over signatures, the aforesaid Signori Guido and Antonio Maria, sons of Tomaso Girolamo Franceschini, etc. who above, etc. inasmuch as, etc. and all, etc. with the consent of Signor Tomaso, their guardian, declare and set forth that in the month of July last there passed into the other life the said Signor Tomaso Franceschini, whose estate, since he died intestate, passed to the said gentlemen appearing before the court, since they are his sons and nearest relations, both by right and by the statute, as well as two other sons of the said Signor Tomaso, also present. And that since the said gentlemen believe that the same inheritance would be and is rather to their prejudice than to their benefit, therefore they have abstained and do abstain from it, and have repudiated and do repudiate it, declaring expressly that they do not desire either its advantages or disadvantages, in order that they may not be held responsible in any way by the creditors of the said estate, if there are any, and for every other equitable purpose and effect. And concerning the aforesaid matters they petition that all suitable and necessary decrees be made and interposed for the validity of the aforesaid act, according to legal forms and statutes, not only for the aforesaid act, but in all matters, etc.

Who, etc. the judge in session, etc. having seen, etc. admitted the repudiation of the aforesaid inheritance if and assuming that, etc. and concerning the aforesaid matters interposed his decision and authority, etc.

BERNARDO DEGLI IPPOLITI, archivist

The legal document follows.[62]

NUMBER 20. *Testimony of the Chancellor of the city of Arezzo, who having searched in the register of taxable properties found nothing written on account of Signor Guido Franceschini*

November 16, 1693.

I, the undersigned, notary and chancellor of the City of Arezzo, testify that in the official books of tax dues of the said city, existing in the public chancery of the same city, it is apparent that among the eight ranks of which the gentility of Arezzo is composed, beginning with the Gonfaloniere, the Franceschini family enjoys the second rank, and that in the said books to which, etc.

BERNARDINO BALSAMINI
V. Chancellor

Item, I testify that in the official tax-books of the said city there are described as owning several properties, some worth more than 170 florins and some less than 3 and 4 soldi, Canon Girolamo and Messer Paolo, brothers, the sons and heirs of Tomaso Franceschini; which properties, excluding the taxes for a certain levy, are worth 1,600 scudi.

BERNARDINO BALSAMINI
V. Chancellor

B

In the lawsuit brought by Guido Franceschini against Giuseppe Caponsacchi

A CASE OF ABDUCTION AND THEFT AT AREZZO[63]

Argument on behalf of Signor Guido Franceschini by Giovanni Maria Serbuceri, acting on behalf of the Fisc, A.C.

MOST ILLUSTRIOUS AND REVEREND LORDSHIP: Canon Giuseppe Maria Caponsacchi of Arezzo, our opponent, because of lust abducted from her home and the company of her husband Signora Francesca Pompilia Comparini, the lawful wife of Signor Guido Franceschini, a nobleman of Arezzo, it having been previously planned between them to give a soporific to the husband and others of the household. Having accomplished this villainy, they broke the locks of a casket and stole from the husband about 150 scudi in cash of different currencies, several jewels, clothes, and other things of no little value. Then, having accomplished their evil deed, they climbed over the walls of the city of Arezzo, because the gates of the city had been closed, and then, as the saying is, they flew to Rome in a carriage which had been stationed for that very purpose outside the gate.

The husband recovered from the drug after sunrise, and, looking for his wife and not finding her, pursued them with all diligence, and after much toil and expense he came upon them resting in a room of the posting-inn at Castelnuovo. He invoked the aid of the court, and having found them together in the said room he had them transferred to prison with the stolen money and property. The aforesaid canon, while languishing in the prison of Castelnuovo, in order to hide his crime and stung by his conscience, threw not only the woman's letters but his own as well into the latrine. The latter was searched in the interests of justice by the order of the Vicar-General,[64] and 21 letters were found, 18 of which seem to be written by the woman, but the others, numbers 12 and 14 [*sic*] by the said canon.

Now Signor Guido Franceschini is seeking to have this canon severely punished, both for abduction and for theft of the said goods and money, and to recover the money and stolen goods, reserving against his wife his right to seek the administration of the dowry: and I should suppose that he will succeed.

I am not ignorant that, for what may be properly called abduction, it is necessary to have violence offered either to the woman or to the relatives under whose authority the woman is living. In truth, the said rule is limited when the abduction takes place with the consent of the abducted woman, obtained, as in this case, by persuasions or cajoleries. In what case it is to be called true abduction, and in what case the capital punishment is modified, is shown to us in the Lex unica (§ poenas autem raptu Virginis) as follows: "this (whether it concerns boy or woman) is deduced from the treachery of the most wicked man who meditates the abduction; because unless during his solicitations he deceived him with his aforesaid artfulness he could not make him willing to surrender himself to such dishonour." And Text. in the aforesaid Lex (§ qui puero ff. de extrand. Crimin.). These authorities are followed by Farinacci (quaest.145.n.110), and by several other classical authorities, and are not contradicted by Rainaldus (ad Banimen.Bonon. Cap.22 § usque ad 10 in Urb. With only the violence of persuasion. n.37).

And although several authorities temper the said rigour, as Rainaldus states in the same place as above (n.138 and several following), nevertheless they conclude that the said tempering of the rigour of the law does not apply when the wife is under the authority of her husband or of other relatives, as even Sanfelicius says clearly. Raynaldus says the same, above (n.148), as well as Farinacci (dicta quaest.n.118).

And even if for the sake of argument it were granted that it was abduction with the full consent of the abducted woman, the abductor should be severely punished, as appears from Rossi, Decian, Menocchi, and others, as reported in the decision of Farinacci mentioned above (n.120).

However we believe that we are in the presence of a true abduction with the equivalent of violence offered to the husband, because it is the same thing, and even more so, to use force against the husband with weapons and to proffer him a drug. And violence appears even more strongly from the aforesaid drug, because if violence had been offered, the husband might have opposed them with arms, or at least have called on the neighbours for help, which he could not do on account of the drug; which your most illustrious lordship and the most wise judges are begged to observe.

That the drug was proffered to the husband with the aid of the canon is shown not only by the observed event, when the wife rose in the night from her husband's side and opened the door to the canon, and they filled their bags with things, bore away money, broke locks and coffers, and did other things safely and securely in the said house, but it may also be deduced from the letter written (p. 15[65]): "I forgot to tell you that the Signora Madre no longer has a fever. She is drinking wine, but only by herself, and it is red like ours, so tell me what I must do, and I will do it."

And also letter 12 (p. 22): "What a lot has happened to you! I don't mind your saying that my mother cannot be made to sleep as long as she is ill and is not drinking wine, and so she cannot be put to sleep. She may recover in the next few days; anyhow I will let you know."

And in letter 13 (p. 36): "As for what you want to know about the wine, I tell you that it is red now, but later I do not know how it may be. But I will let you know."

And it may be assumed more clearly from the letter written by the said canon, on page 31: "And as soon as you see that they are sound asleep, open the door for me so that I may help you to pack the bundles and collect the money. Above all, try to put some in all the flasks, and do not drink any yourself. If by some sad misfortune they should discover it and threaten you with death, still open the door, for I will either die with you or free you from their hands. And let us pray God to make this plan of ours turn out well. I ratify myself, etc. Mirtillo."

Our adversary attempts to exclude this as a true abduction because he bore off the wife in order to free her from death. This is a frivolous and ridiculous excuse, since nothing appears in the trial to verify what he alleges. In fact quite the contrary, for we learn from the letters which are given in the summary (n. 1) that there was love and a long correspondence between them. Moreover, an unavoidable contradiction of reasons appears in the examination of them both, for Francesca gives as the cause of her flight that her husband wished to kill her on account of her sterility (p. 58, verso); and also that her husband wanted to slay her because of his jealousy of his wife's love for the canon (p. 60). The canon, however (p. 60, verso, and following pages), says the cause for the flight of the said wife was the threats of her husband who wanted to kill her because of the lawsuit which he was carrying on with her father. It shall be left to the most learned judges to decide what weight there is in that far-fetched cause when we have a proved charge in the trial.

And the said excuse is reduced to nothing and our position is supported by the above-mentioned letter written by the canon (p. 31, *id.*): "And praying God to cause this design of ours to succeed, etc." Therefore the cause of flight was common to both of them, and cannot be ascribed to the woman alone.

It remains to be seen whether another requisite for abduction is present, that is, whether adultery actually took place; and I should think that it cannot be doubted, for, as Ovid says in his *Art of Love,* no one can believe that a maiden will return virgin from a young and passionate lover: for we have in the first place a great love evident between them from the aforesaid love letters, written by both parties before the abduction (summary, n. 1).

We have proof that the canon was accustomed to go by night to Francesca's home, and that he visited her: not only from the said letters (aforesaid summary, n. 1), but from the record of the trial (p. 101, verso, 108, verso, and following pages) the friendship between them is evident from common rumour and notoriety (105 and 107, etc.).

This assumption gains weight because the abduction took place at night by climbing over the walls, which, even if it did not appear in the trial, may yet be inferred from the well-known fact that the gates of the city of Arezzo are closed from the setting to the rising of the sun, and, as the proverb has it, what is obvious need not be proved. Nevertheless, it is attested by three witnesses (summary, n. 2), and is deposed by Baroncello of Arezzo (p. 90).

A further presumption of guilt arises from the fact that the canon was wearing secular dress (pp. 4 and 100).

For their kissing each other silently on the journey we even have an eye-witness (p. 100). And from that we may deduce, like the poet of Sulmo,[66] "after kisses, deeds."

The crowning proof arises from their sleeping in the same room and bed, and although there were two beds in the room, the canon ordered one alone to be prepared, which I would admit might be for a good purpose if the canon were an old man, or if we were in the cold of winter.

There follow the lies and contradictions between the woman and the canon: for the former obstinately testifies that she arrived at Castelnuovo at dawn, and denies sleeping there (63, verso, and following pages, 267, verso), while the canon on the contrary frankly confesses sleeping there, as described above, and reaching the inn in the evening, not in the morning (pp. 70 and 80).

Moreover, the woman says that she spoke several times with the canon in her home (p. 59, verso, 61, 62). The canon, however, obstinately denies such conversation, but maintains that he was urged to the flight through Maria, the maid, by means of letters written by Francesca (66, verso, and 67 and 83), which Francesca expressly denies (p. 87).

Francesca deposes that at the time of the flight the canon was stationed near her home, and went to the coach with her (63, verso). The canon, however, maintains on the contrary that Francesca alone came to the coach outside the walls, where he was awaiting her (p. 69).

Another lie of the canon is evident, when he denies that he wrote any letters to Francesca except two (p. 68, verso, and 69, including 71, verso), and yet he is convicted by the letters which were found, which are in answer to others written to him (aforesaid summary, n. 1).

And from so many and such great lies and planned tricks, no one can doubt that guilt arises (Clar. quaest.21.verb.mendac.; Farinac. Cons. 125.n.21).

And that secret adultery may be argued from all the aforesaid circumstances, all arguments to the contrary being rejected, is the opinion given by Farinacci (quaest.142.n.131, with the three following). With a great number of other learned doctors there recorded.

Nor is our adversary's argument valid that the letters are not written in Francesca's own writing because she does not know how to write; because this is proved false by the marriage contracts signed by her in her own hand, recognized by a public and legal notary, given into the hands of my most excellent judge, Venturini.

Also it is of little help to the canon to deny the letter which he himself wrote, and which was found in the latrine, because, besides the fact that it can be inspected, by a conscientious court, to see whether it is the same writing as that existing in the trial (p. 83, verso) written by order of the court, we beg the judges to consider seriously that when the letters were found in the latrine in the prison where the canon was confined there was also found the licence printed by the illustrious Apostolic Press of Arezzo for his entrance into the monastery.[67]

And although the most excellent judge may disdain to affirm that the aforesaid writing is that of the canon, we beg for the appointment of experts, so that the writing of both parties may be established, since we have undoubted specimens of both their hands.[68]

Nor can it be objected that the letter written by the canon cannot be in his possession, but should be in the possession of the receiver of the letter, because the objection is removed by that same letter, because it shows that the letter was to be returned to his hands as a sign that it had secured its effect, when it says: "Therefore if you could leave, as soon as you have read this letter of mine return to the window and throw it down to be as a sign, so that I may engage a carriage" (p. 30).

In order further to show that the cause of the aforesaid abduction had nothing to do with severities and threatened death, we beg the judge to observe, besides what we have already said, that in all the many letters which were found as described above there is contained nothing except loving emotions, warm expressions, hints, and the exchange of kisses, words of jealousy, and the like, and there is not to be read the least syllable of the wife's being bowed down with threats, or vexations, or poverty, or other miseries, no doubt resulting from it; no bad treatment, or beatings or the like, but only that our principal feared the love of the adulterer towards his wife. Wherefore it can be said in every way that the abduction took place because of lust, for nothing else appears in the trial.

Therefore we are assured that no doubt can arise concerning the punishment to be inflicted on the canon, even to the capital degree, because it is only too plain from the aforesaid proofs that the wife eloped with the evil counsel and aid of the canon; for although the judges refuse to take action against the wife for theft because of the things stolen from the husband, the doubt does not concern the associate in the theft, by whose advice it was committed, and as he is an adulterer he should receive capital punishment (Farinacci, quaest.174. n.107; Iodoc. si prax. Cap.110.n.44 and 45; Menoch. de Arbiter Lib. 2.cap.580.n.30, quoted there).

That the canon participated in the theft is apparent from the same letter, where he says: "Open the door for me so that I may help you to pack the bundles and collect the money" (p. 30, verso). That the money and goods were bargained for by the canon is evident from their being found in their possession during the official search (pp. 5 ff.).

That money and goods were stolen from our principal, and what they were is confessed by Francesca (p. 60) and the canon (p. 72, verso).

Nor can the deposition of the woman, who says: "There was some of my own money among it," stand in the way of the restitution of the money. Because that would be stupid, and it is a widely held opinion that all the goods and money are presumed to be the shameful profit offered to the man, especially as the woman was also instigated for the sake of her dowry.

The bargaining is all the more clear because she was held responsible for about 150 scudi, as appears from the restoration of the stolen money, and only 104 were found (p. 5), an evident sign that the canon had spent it.

They keep talking—uselessly, we hold—of the hunger, the neediness, and the poverty of the husband, and of the sufferings of Francesca, and we will show the letters given into the hands of the most excellent referendary, and from two letters of this Francesca, which have also been presented, we will prove just the reverse, and although it would be admitted that a wife because of these things cannot leave her husband on account of lust, as is the present case; so that this amounts to nothing, as appears in Tex. in L. Palam § non est ignoscen. ff. de lib. n. pt. Pars. Cons.23.n.45. et 60.n.42., Baiard. ad Cler. Adult. n.75. et seqq.

Wherefore, etc.

A CASE OF ALLEGED ABDUCTION AT AREZZO[69]

Plea in defence of Giuseppe Caponsacchi by Antonio Lamparelli, Procurator of Charity

YOUR MOST ILLUSTRIOUS AND REVEREND LORDSHIP: the pen of my learned opponent should have recoiled in horror in imputing the crime of abduction, adultery, and theft to the reverend canon, Giuseppe Maria Caponsacchio, my principal, who has already been imprisoned for five months, considering his upright character and inborn nobility, as well as the virtue of that most modest young woman, Signora Francesca Comparini, wife of Signor Guido Franceschini, the Fisc's client, who is claimed to have been abducted, so that it is altogether malicious to cast even the least aspersion on their good name.

I do not deny that at first sight among ill-informed men there may appear some suspicion in the flight of a wife from her husband, especially as it took place in the company of a man of susceptible age; but when one considers the circumstances accompanying that flight, the quality of the persons and the place to which the lady was taken, it is completely necessary to confess that the canon, our principal, did nothing in this but for the purpose of liberating from extreme difficulties and of restoring to her parents a daughter married outside her native city, badly treated by her husband, mother-in-law, and brother-in-law, far from her own relatives, and reduced to an almost desperate state, who on other occasions had fled alone to the Bishop and Governor of Arezzo, so that they might assist her in her troubles by means of justice. But they turned a deaf ear to her complaints and did not try to help her, as is unanimously stated by the accused in their testimony, and is proved by the sworn statements given to the most excellent Signor Venturini; so that the canon was overcome by the shame of one thought, to wit that the difficulty of performing such a good deed could deserve to be repaid by a criminal accusation.

My mind would shudder indeed, if I believed that the noble husband, not ignorant of those things which took place before the whole populace of Arezzo, and even in the privacy of the home, as I shall show later, was willing, only on account of his eager and uncertain hope of gaining her dowry, to drag his wife before the judges as an adultress and a violator of the nuptial couch, careless of what Paulo de Castro urges against similar husbands denouncing their wives in his Consil. 277 (sub n.3, near the end, vers. Sed nec Judices, lib.2; Menoch. de arbitrar., etc.).

And yet that is what we have a right to believe since, in his complaint, he asks for only this one thing, and claims only this one thing in the action against his wife.

But I hope by the following arguments to dispel all his hope, and that he will not get his desire, and indeed that the canon will be restored to his former freedom, and be given great thanks because he, as befitted an honest man, preserved the young woman untouched and unharmed for her parents.

Therefore, in order to investigate the true facts of the case, those things which are said to be the base and foundation of the whole crime (as is set forth by Bertazzol. cons.192.n.16, Giurb. cons.97.n.6, Cravetta cons.6.n.22, Vermigliol. cons.20.n.20, Casson. tract. crimin. tit. de Indic. praedit. ante delict. cap.1. & seqq., Calvin. de aquitat. lib.2.cap. 132.n.20, Menoch. de praesumpt. lib.1.quaest.17. per tot., Farinacc. quaest.50.n.31. & quaest.52.n.145, Guazzin. defens.28.cap.1.n.6), those things may first be set down here which were brought out in the civil court, and which we have confirmed by producing our Summary printed and distributed with the consent of the court.

Know then, oh most learned judges, that Signor Guido Franceschini, with an incorrect statement that he possessed in the city of Arezzo a yearly income of 1,700 scudi, induced Signor Pietro Comparini to give him in marriage his only daughter, Signora Francesca Pompilia, assigning as a dowry all his property, consisting of two houses with shops here in the city of Rome, and 40 bonds. Signor Guido in return was obliged to provide with food, clothing, and a dwelling-place, both Signor Pietro Comparini and Violante Peruzzi, husband and wife, as long as they wished to live in Arezzo: and whenever, with a reasonable cause, they should wish to return home, the said Guido was pledged to take them back there at his own expense, with the same obligation of supplying them with food.

Afterwards, the marriage having taken place, and both Signor Pietro and Signora Violante having come to the city of Arezzo with the bride and groom, the event belied the expectation: for the reputed annual income of 1,700 scudi vanished. The food, too, shrank to the amount described by the witness examined in the civil suit report (summary, printed and produced, n. 6).[70]

The said Pietro Comparini, seeing therefore that he had been deceived, began to complain at home, and because of this many quarrels arose one after another; nor did he fail to send sharp complaints by letter to Abate Paolo Franceschini, who had arranged the aforesaid marriage. So that on February 6, 1694, the latter could not reply otherwise than by urging the said Pietro to be patient: "From both parties there reach me unheard-of complaints, and incredible news, etc., and unless you and Signora Violante show a little tolerance on your side I do not know what action to take, etc." And farther down: "If your prudence and that of Signora Violante cannot make you less harsh to my family, etc."

The bitterness and hatred reached extreme lengths, as is apparent from the successive letters written in answer by Abate Franceschini, produced by the defence, as follows:

Dated February 13, 1694: "Today, however, as I hear that the enemy of God has set bitterness amongst you, I must fulfil towards you the duty of answering. You and I,[71] who have been the principal authors of this marriage, have an obligation: you, with prudence and your accustomed grace, to continue to put up with things and not to pay so much attention to trifles, and I to persuade both sides with my letters to peace and love: otherwise we shall be the talk of Arezzo and Rome, with as much prejudice to you as to us, etc."

And farther down: "But since I hear from both sides that bitterness, not to say hatred, is increasing among you, I cannot refrain from feeling great scandal that neither you nor those of my own family can treat each other with charity. This makes me reluctant to engage myself to live in one household with you and Signor Pietro, since I should not want to lose that tranquillity and peace that I desire for others, and that by God's grace I have enjoyed until now. Because I am convinced that from morning until evening and at every moment you would deafen me with chatter and complaints."

Dated March 4, 1694: "I have been so overwhelmed with grief and amazement because of the events which are taking place at home between you and my family that I was not able on Saturday to answer your letter, and I am not really able to do so now that four days have passed since that time when I received news of it. Nor do I wish to pause to consider which side is in the right, because I blame both parties for not having been able to love each other as prudence and justice would have dictated, nor even to tolerate each other as a matter of policy and to avoid scandal. And what increases my surprise is that though you write to me at great length you do not make any mention in your letter of the two headlong flights made by Signora Francesca, the news of which as they have given me both great grief and greater mortification, so an event of such importance and so completely contrary to what is becoming to our birth and your quality, etc."

And farther down: "I then, as I have always based my hopes on your prudence which has here been tested at length, trust, therefore, that you will appease in future any disagreement which might arise (may God forbid); and you, Signora Violante, must reflect that as you and I have peacefully arranged this marriage, consequently we must agree to keep it peaceful, as is demanded by God, justice, and our reputation: otherwise both you and we will be unhappy."

And farther down: "I speak to you with heart in hand and with tears in my eyes. I weep for this misfortune of yours and of ours, and for the sinister events which have been brought about rather by bad management than by nature. And I shudder to think of the mockery that must be going on in that native city of mine, and perhaps in Rome among those who have news of it, for I do not know, since I shun every occasion of meeting my fellow-townsmen or other people who may know of it, so that I may not give them an opportunity for such talk."

And finally, with the date March 6th, of the same year: "I am writing to you again to say that I will not imitate you in your manner of writing, since it is not suitable for anyone like you to scatter through your letters certain words which should be answered with deeds not words. They are so offensive that I am keeping them as a reproof and mortification for you. If in my household, contrary to my expectation, disagreements have taken place between you so great that both you and we must blush for them, I weep for it, and sigh bitterly for pity of my mother and brothers, as well as of yourself, Signora Violante, and the bride. But what remedy can I offer, when I hear that so many gentlemen friendly to both parties have intervened to compose your quarrels, and have had no success, etc."

And farther down: "Signor Pietro, you who have always figured as a wise man, learned and prudent, put yourself in my shoes and tell me what you want me to do in such evil emergencies, far away and exhausted as I am. Reflect with humanity, both of you, for the love of God, on the motives that I suggest in the long letter that I am writing to Signora Violante, and do not allow yourselves to be carried away by passion. Signor Pietro, there is no remedy for what has been done, and this threatening of yours, that the papers shall be turned into waste-paper,[72] is unlike your prudence: because if you give us trouble, which I shall never believe, you will not escape from your own share of it."

Thus the said Pietro and Violante were forced to return home, and, combating artfulness with artfulness, to seek a judgment on the nullity of the dower contract before the most illustrious Signor Tomati, Auditor Camerae, by producing and examining six witnesses on the substitution at birth of the said Francesca Pompilia, claiming that she was not their own daughter, but had been imposed as such by Signora Violante on Pietro, her husband, so that she might set free the said Pietro, in whose person the entail expired should he die without issue, from several debts and alienations of the property left in trust, all of which are in evidence, printed by court order, and submitted.

To what a point the hatred and enmity of Signor Guido, his brothers, and the mother-in-law against their respective wife, sister-in-law, and daughter-in-law increased on account of the bringing of this civil suit the most perspicacious judges may infer from the fact that it was a question of losing every penny of the dowry, from which cause those learned in the law claim that mortal hatred may arise, as does Vermiglioli particularly (cons.321, n.5) and several others quoted by Farinacci (quaest.49.n.2), where he says that a great civil cause is equal to a criminal one (citing Text. in l. propter litem, cum ibi notatis, ff. de excusat. Tutor).

They infer it from the several flights from her husband's home, as deposed to by six witnesses, all publicly sworn to and recognized and produced in the suit, one of which flights was to the palace of the Bishop, who bothered neither to receive nor hear her, as is frankly reported in those letters of theirs, also produced in the suit, by Signor Bartolomeo Albergotti and Signor Tomaso de' Romani,[73] under the dates of April 4th and 5th respectively.

As the most unfortunate young woman was living in this pitiful state, sixteen years of age, in a foreign city, far from her own family, without friends or anyone in whom she could confide, torment stimulated her mind, and she planned to return to her father, in whom she hoped to find that pity which she could not find in Arezzo even from the justice of the head of the Church. And in order to put her desire into action she begged the accused, who she had heard beforehand was going to Rome, to accompany her and be her trusted comrade; and although he refused several times yet at length, to save her from the danger of imminent death, he consented, and having prepared a carriage outside the city they set out together with such speed that they would not have stopped even in Castelnuovo, where the husband overtook them, if Francesca herself had not fainted, overcome by her sufferings, and had not insisted on resting for a little while, as our accused states in his testimony (pp. 65–70), from which Signora Francesca herself does not dissent: "Therefore I begged him to take me to my father and mother, but he replied that he would not meddle with this business on any account, because it would have been regarded badly by the whole city, so much the more so as he was a friend of my husband's family. But I urged him so much, telling him that it was a Christian duty to save from death a poor woman from another city, that I induced him to promise me that he would take me, and he told me that he would engage the carriage, etc." (pp. 61, 62).

Considering these events, accurately and faithfully reported, who will deny that Francesca had a just cause for fleeing from her husband, not indeed to satisfy her lust with the canon, as is asserted by our adversary writing with great impropriety, but so that she might regain her former freedom and quiet by returning to her native city; and that the canon consented to the aforesaid flight in order to free her from the danger of death? For when we have two reasons, one of which is lawful and permissible, and the other wicked and abominable, the one which excludes crime is to be accepted (Capitulo in poenis, de regul. Iur. in 6. & lege interpretatione 42.ff.de poen., Bald. in l.prima n.10, C. de Seru. Fugit. Censa. in l.unica § primo, n.36.vers. quod si plures existerint Causae C. si quis Imper. maledixerit). Particularly because if anyone might be moved to crime by two motives, one evil and one not, it is to be presumed that he has been activated by the motive that is not evil, as appears in the decision of Honded. (cons.105.n.60.lib.primo, & Rot. Ianuem Vot.11.n.5. & 6.post Censal. in d.l.Unica).

That it was in order to free her from the danger of imminent death that the accused consented to the flight of the said Francesca and accompanied her, was frankly protested on his arrest to the husband himself, who was denouncing him for that flight: "I am an honourable man, and I did what I have done to remove your wife from the danger of death," as is testified by Jacopo, son of the late Simone, a witness for the Fisc (trial, p. 50).

As an example we have Scipio Africanus, who, when a most beautiful maiden, the wife of Allucius, Prince of the Celts, was captured by his soldiers, said as he restored her to her husband: "Your betrothed has dwelt in my camp with the same respect for her modesty as in the house of your parents-in-law, her own parents. She has been preserved for you so that she could be given you as a gift, unharmed and worthy of you and of me," as Livy reports (*History*, book 26, p. 493 in my edition). This difference should be noted, however, that Allucius as a reward for his wife's having been returned inviolate offered to the unwilling Scipio the dowry which he was to receive from his father-in-law, as the same author goes on to say; whereas in our case the husband would be glad to have his wife have lost her modesty so that he may enjoy the dowry.

Let our adversary say what he will, quoting from Ovid's *Art of Love* that no one need believe that a maid returns virgin from a young and passionate man; for even Trasonides, as Diogenes Laertes reports (book 7, p. 434 in my edition) though he had his loved one in his power spared her lest he should be hated. And, quite apt to our circumstances, we have the example of Achilles, who left untouched his beloved Briseis when she returned to him because she had come to save his life, as Plutarch reports (*de Audien. Poetis*, p. 47 in my edition, n. 25): "The continence of Achilles must be admired, who abstained from his beloved Briseis when she returned to him, although he knew that the end of his life was at hand."

For indeed if the aforesaid flight had been undertaken for the purpose of satisfying lust, they would not have taken the direct route to Rome, where they might be seized at once by Francesca's brother-in-law and her parents, but would have fled to more distant and secure parts. Nor is it probable that they would willingly have exposed themselves to the manifest danger of detection; for just as an indication of guilt rises from a probable supposition, so from an improbable supposition rises a presumption of innocence (Farinacci, cons.22.n.34; Vermiglioli, cons.3.n.6).

Since, then, for the aforesaid reasons the motive of lust has been excluded, and since it is proved that Francesca fled of her own free will, the crime of abduction and adultery immediately disappears (Salyc. in L.1.n.6.vers. Quando patitur rapinam extra hanc Causam C. de raptu Virg. Joannes. de Anan. in cap. cum Causa n.4.vers. Nota quod Raptus propriè dicitur—extra de Rapitoribus. Vermigliol. Cons.396.n.12., Mascard. de probat. Conclus.1254.n.33). Decian (Tract. Crimin. lib. 8.cap.6.n.36) gives two examples of abductors who were freed because their abduction was carried out with good intentions and to the true benefit of the abducted maidens, as in our case (Baiard. ad Clarum § Raptus n.14. & 32, Sanchez de Matrimon. lib.7.disput.12.n.17, Farinac. quaest.145.n.75, Peguer. decis.42.n.7).

And although I am not ignorant that Farinacci (in the said quaest. 145.n.120) asserts that even though he has the consent of the abducted woman the abductor can be punished with a special penalty according

G. Vasi dis. e inc.

1. Cupola della Chiesa di S. Maria del Popolo. Porta del Popolo olim Flaminia. 2. Magazzini, e Granari. 1.

PLATE V

Altarpiece from the chapel in the Carceri Nuove, Rome

PLATE VI

to the will of the judge if the woman was under the authority of her husband or relatives, still that condition does not apply in our case, because the woman escaped to her parents, and her bad relations with her husband were the cause of the flight, as appears from the circumstances reported above, so that on that account he might be held forewarned.

And what is more, since the motive disappears, the accusations themselves collected by our adversary disappear (Bart. inter Consilia Crimin. divers. Cons.8.n.8.lib.1, Bertazzol. Cons.446.n.2. & seq.lib.2, Vermigliol. Cons.25.n.2. & sequen., Giurb. Cons.51.n.16. & cons.91. n.39, Cyriac. Controv.485.n.2, Guazzin. defens.28.cap.1.n.60); particularly as either they do not bear up, or they are of no weight or relevance.

For as to the feigned love letters found in the prisons of Castelnuovo, in the first place they are not addressed to our client, let alone signed by Signora Francesca; secondly they were denied by both in their depositions, nor were they authenticated, as they should have been before the publication of the trial in order to have any weight (Eugen. cons.76. n.114, Vermigliol. cons.55.n.18, Guazzin. defens.4.cap.14.n.5, Rota decis.772.n.9.part.2.rec.). For they might have been forged and planted by the husband himself, who was present all the time at the capture and search. In the third place, finally, even if they were authentic they only convince one more strongly of the continence of our client, to whom it is claimed that they are addressed under the name of "Chaste Joseph"; nor are they immodest, but rather calculated to persuade our client to assent to the flight.

The other allegation, that our client used to visit Signora Francesca's house at night, comes only from the deposition of Maria Margherita Contenti, a public prostitute, as I am informed, who was examined in the episcopal court of Arezzo, and who, since she is only one witness, proves nothing (Capitulo veniens, & cap. licet ex quadam de Testibus). Especially as she is proved a liar by the other deposition of Canon Conti, examined by the same court concerning his conversation with Signora Francesca in the presence of our client (p. 114, and verso).

And even supposing her testimony were to be believed, we hear besides from her that such a visit was for a good purpose, according to what she had heard Signor Gregorio Guillichini say: "And Signor Guillichini then added, 'The canon goes there for a good purpose, and because she would like to go to Rome,' and he told me too, that no evil could arise from it, because there was nothing at all wrong between them" (p. 109, verso). So against the inferences of the Fisc in this matter it is sufficient to consult Farinacci (cons.120, n.10), and Vermiglioli (cons.500.n.3).

Public rumour and repute are not only not proved, but are actually excluded both by the testimony of Canon de' Conti (p. 113, verso, and 114), and by that of Canon Franceschini, brother of the said Signor Guido (p. 95); and yet for it to have any weight it would have to be unshakable and unblemished among all men, since those things which are done publicly are presumed to be known to all (Vermigliol. cons. 36.n.12. & pluribus relatis, Conciol. ver. Fama resol.2.n.2).

The deposition of Francesco Giovanni de' Rossi, alias Venerino, that he saw them kissing each other on the journey is evidently entirely false and improbable, not only because he deposes that he saw them at night, not giving as his explanation that the moon was shining, according to the gloss (in L. Si cum exceptione § in hac ff. de eo, quod met. caus., Bursat. Cons.7.n.30 & 33. Volum.1, Surd. Cons.158.n.4), but also because it was impossible for him, when he was driving the carriage at such a speed (concerning which Costanza Donati deposes that indeed they seemed rather to fly than to proceed, p. 105), to see at the same time the accused kissing each other behind him. However a witness deposing impossible or improbable things is more than untrustworthy (Farinac. Cons.192.n.60. in fine, Vermigliol. Cons.272.n.50, Bertazzol. Cons.283.n.5, Hector Felic. alleg.129.n.6).

I may point out, especially, that Signora Francesca was well known to the witness, and so if he had really seen her kissing of course he would have recognized her, and yet he asserts that he did not recognize her, but he decided it was she as soon as, returning, he met Signor Guido Franceschini, her husband, looking for her (p. 99, verso). So this deposition must be said to have emanated from his weariness of the prison in which he was detained in solitude for several days, rather than from the truth, as is pointed out by Farinacci (cons.193.n.3), and Vermiglioli (cons.33.n.6). And as he is a single witness he is not to be considered, as we have established above.

That they slept together in the inn of Castelnuovo is denied by both, and is maintained only by Jacopo, son of the late Simone, servant at the said inn, not however from certain knowledge or because he saw them, but because they asked him for a room where there was only one bed; and from this no accusation can be made, because, since they had stopped there not in order to sleep (and the accused maintain that they did not sleep) but so that the aforesaid Francesca might rest a little while because of her weakness, one bed was sufficient. Nor was it fitting that our client should leave her alone, but it was his plain duty to take care of her and protect her: nor can an equivocal action be construed as a crime (Vermigliol. cons.322.n.10. & cons.325.n.7, Farinacc. cons. 37.n.20, Cyriac. controv. for. cap.605.n.39.tom.4, Capon. discept.323. n.20). Indeed it must always be construed as excluding the crime (Eugenius cons.86.n.53.lib.1, Honded. cons.58.n.57.lib.1, Vermigliol. cons.3.n.25. & cons.13.n.12, Farinac. quaest.85.n.5, Menoch. de praesumpt. lib.5.prae.2.n.1. & seq.).

Moreover we beg to point out that, as it is a question of a crime committed outside the state, even if it were convincingly proved, which we absolutely deny, our client cannot be punished except by the simple, isolated, penalty of exile, for illicit intercourse, according to the sufficiently familiar practice of this court.

As to the pretended theft, I shall not dwell on it, because the nobility and character of our client do not permit of his suffering even a shadow of a doubt on the subject, as the judge himself acknowledged, who refused to have that character called in question; particularly as the corpus delicti was missing, which is not proved by the simple assertion of the parties claiming to be robbed, as is claimed by the other side, but by the formal examination of witnesses who depose concerning the pre-existence of the property and its loss, as well as the complaints and reputation of the robbed persons (Bartol. & alii in l. si quando in fin. C. Unde vi bene, Roland. cons.51.n.18, Brunor. a fol. quaest.51. sub n.53, Andreol. controv.36.n.22, Capon. discept.87.sub.n.7 & 8. in fine tom.2, Crazz. ad defens. discept.25.n.76, Bonifac. de furtis § est.n.5.9. & 10, Rot. coram Pamphil. dec.644.n.10.ubi, Adden.n.13).

Nevertheless we can certify, though it is not necessary, that the money found in the possession of the canon, our client, at the time of his capture was his own, except for a few Genoese and gold coins, by means of the two witnesses examined before the court of Castelnuovo (letter A), and also by the testimony of three witnesses who state that our client before he left Arezzo managed to change 80 Florentine scudi into an equal amount of Roman currency (letter B).

Wherefore, etc.

C

In the trial of Guido Franceschini and his confederates for murder

AT ROME: A CASE OF MURDERS[74]

Plea of Signor Pignatelli on behalf of Signor Guido Franceschini and his Companions against the Fisc before the Most Illustrious and Most Reverend Governor in Criminal Cases of the Glorious City of Rome

Seek out justice, oh you who judge the earth (Wisdom, ch. 1, at the beginning).

We beg for a decision in favour of the prisoners, inasmuch as God Himself, although His honour is in no way subject to stain, has said for our instruction, "I shall entrust my honour to no one."[75]

And afterwards when he walked among us, having assumed human flesh, in His most bitter passion He complained of the blow which was given Him with such ignominy (St. John, ch. 18, v. 23).

And St. Paul, His apostle and the teacher of nations, protested, "It were better for me to die, than that any man should make my glorying void" (1 Cor., ch. 9, v. 15).

That it is better to lose life than honour we learn from Ecclesiastes and from Aristotle, cited below by Polic., where he reports, too, the words of Cicero, who said, "We are born to honour and freedom; either let us preserve these or die with dignity."

For nothing is more to be shunned than life without honour, without which he who lives is considered dead (Calder. de eis.42, n.4, vol.1, where he quotes, too, Virgil: "There you behold those who are sad because they lack honour in their death").[76]

Therefore in almost all the tribunals of Europe a husband is spared who has killed his adulterous wife even after an interval, as can be seen fully and to the most complete satisfaction in Sanz. (*De Re Crim.* controv.12; and Calder. in the place cited above; and in addition to the said decision vol.2, pp.5 ff., and especially at n.26, 34, and following. These authorities are overwhelmingly supported by Polic.*De Prehemin.*, vol.2, p.34, n.24 and 70).

These authorities and those cited by them set forth not only laws and quite clear legal opinions of many authoritative learned men, but also the decisions of Supreme Courts, particularly that of Naples, even in cases not so seriously injuring the honour of the husband as the adultery of his wife, which pierces a husband's heart more deeply than the death of his children (Ross. *De coit. damn. et punibili*, n.46), or even murdered children (as Ricc. states and De Angel. confirms, *De delict.*, lib.1, p.9, n.7).

For indeed the adultery of the wife defiles the husband with so deep a stain that it can only be washed out with blood (Sanz. as above, n.25 and following).

And so it is even in minor cases, as is daily decided in the highest court of the Consilia Sacra, whose authority is the very highest, and whose duty it is to interpret the mind of the Pope (Hirolo.cons.50, n.26; Ovil. *Ad. Compar.* resol.2, n.26).

For the cause of honour, and especially in this case, is not momentary but continuous, even wounding the heart, as the aforesaid authorities teach; as does Ecclesiasticus (ch. 25, v. 31): "A humble heart, a sad face, a wound in the heart, is a worthless woman. Cut her off from your flesh lest she may always harm you."

And as it is always permissible to appeal against continued injuries, even after the time established for an appeal to the law, as is well known, so much more is it always permissible for a husband to vindicate his honour at any time, because as he is always and continually tortured by the aforesaid most grievous wound, so he can be said to avenge himself always immediately, as is confirmed unanimously by the already cited authorities (DD. Bellon., *De potest. eor. quae. sunt incont.*, tom.2, ch.50, n.6, where he also states that this was the judgment of the Senate; and elsewhere, as in the same chapter at the end).

This is proved by the unmistakably clear text of the Holy Scripture (Proverbs, ch. 6, at the end): "Men do not despise a thief, if he steal to satisfy his soul [lit., appetite] when he is hungry; but if he be found, he shall restore sevenfold; he shall give all the substance of his house. But whoso committeth adultery with a woman lacketh understanding; he that doeth it destroyeth his own soul. A wound and dishonour shall he get; and his reproach shall not be wiped away. For jealousy is the rage of a man: therefore he will not spare in the day of vengeance. He will not regard any ransom; neither will he rest content, though thou givest many gifts."

And if that was true at a time when accusing husbands were not derided, when repudiation was allowed, when the punishment for adultery was stoning, what should it be in our days, when accusing husbands are jeered at even by the judges themselves, when repudiation is not permitted, and when the penalty for adultery is very slight: indeed in some places there is no penalty at all for this most serious crime. And on that account adulterers glory, because husbands do not dare to bring forward accusations lest they incur lasting dishonour directed against them by this corrupt world, as Clarius says (*Adulterium*, n.7, vers. "Quinimo in Gallia"). And he concludes by deploring this evil abuse (at the end of the said passage, n. "Quod in hoc Respublica Christiana aegeret reformatione").

If that same Clarius knew our times he would cry out, and would agree with Sanz. (*De Regem Regni Valent.*, ch.8, § 8, n.190, at the end) that the penalty for the husband should be lessened (or rather remitted in consideration of the quality of the act and the persons involved) or a greater penalty should be established not only for adulterers but indeed for those even attempting such a crime, in order to curb the unbridled lust of women and the greedy guilt of adulterers, lest this most serious offence, by which sacred and divine laws are obviously injured, be without remedy. Concerning its atrocity and many irreparable evils which arise from it Carptou. speaks at length (*Pract.* qu.51, n.11 and following, part 2), as do Farinacci (qu.141, n.3, and following), and all who treat seriously of this crime, which is extremely grave even though everywhere neglected.

That the wife of the prisoner committed adultery is evident, not only from the notoriety of the fact (because it was perfectly well known even to the bleary-eyed and the barbers[77]) but also from its notoriety in law, both from the trial and the sentence, or decree, on September 24, 1697, whose tenor is as follows: "Giuseppe Maria Caponsacchi of Arezzo, because of his complicity in the flight and abduction of Francesca Comparini, and for his carnal knowledge of her, is banished for three years to Civita Vecchia" (Farinacc.qu.21, n.11, 14, and several following, and especially n.18, 35 and 36).

Because of this it would be impossible rather than difficult to find a similar case in which horns were placed upon an honourable husband on a high hill in the eyes of all; so that even if there were a law expressly forbidding vengeance to a husband it would not include our case, which is most worthy of all commiseration, and particularly because of the notoriety of the deed and of the legal decision (Cresp. *Observ.*2, n.50, part 1).

To this most urgent cause of lost honour was added another, less indeed than the first but vehemently provocative to continuous anger, and even sufficient in itself; and that was that the adulterous wife who had been confined in an institution was allowed to enter the home of Pietro Comparini, though both he and his wife in their testimony had not only affirmed that she was not their daughter, but had tried with all their might to prove that she was the daughter of a most base mother, born of an illicit union; without the foreknowledge let alone the consent of the prisoner, as is stated in the account of the event in the vulgar tongue.[78] My master Rainaldus observes (book 1, p.533, n.170, at the end) and is supported by Text (ch.28, § absumpto argumento a contrario sensu ex illis verbis) "and that it may be a consolation to the kindred and kin by marriage, etc.," and in the same place, "the punishments rendered, etc." (ff. de poen.).

Nor does the objection on the part of the Fisc hold good, that the prisoner could not proceed to exact vengeance for the event because he had had recourse to law, for it was very shrewdly answered (as usual) by my colleagues, pleading the case of the prisoners, and especially pointing out that the prisoner had recourse to the judge on account of the flight, as appears in the aforesaid narrative, but it was when the prisoner was assured also that adultery had taken place by the sentence of that same judge that he proceeded to take vengeance for the deed. Crespi observes (60, n.59, part 2) that because of a new cause one may return to take vengeance for a deed. And this motive was heightened by the other cause, that the adultress was placed in the home of the prisoner's enemies by legal permission.

This with regard to the slaying of the adulterous wife, which may be considered to have been accomplished immediately, although the cause was not continuous but momentary, because the sentence was given on September 24, 1697, and the homicide was committed late on January 2, 1698, and the adultress was consigned into the hands of his enemies after she had been imprisoned for five months in a safe place, as it is supposed. But though the prisoner, living far from Rome, might be moved at once by a most just rage to avenge the aforesaid things when he was informed of them, yet he could not at once think how and in what manner vengeance might be taken in Rome and in the house of his enemies, or find assistants and all else necessary for such a long journey. Therefore even if he did delay his vengeance for six months it should nevertheless be considered, for the aforesaid reasons, that he acted immediately, although the cause was momentary, as is shown by the elegant teaching of Ugozzoni, which Baldo praised highly, and as is confirmed by Angeli (*De Malefic.*, passage beginning "Che hai adulterato la mia donna, n.21, about the middle of the verse): and even more strongly does Sanfelic. confirm it in his *Dec.* (337, n.82 ff.).

As for the slaying of Comparini and his wife, indeed, on which the Fisc lays most stress, it is answered by the learned lawyers arguing on behalf of the prisoners that not only were they conscious of and participatators in but indeed the authors, the instigators, and the inciters of the flight and adultery; to which we may add that at the time of the marriage of that daughter of theirs they handed her over to the prisoner as completely innocent,[79] and afterwards said in court too that she was not a wanton, and unblushingly did their best to prove whatever opprobrious and perverse crimes new under the sun can be imagined. By which they offered the most bitter offence not only to the prisoner but to his whole noble family, involving even the infamy of their descendants, as is proved seriously, with his ever-elegant pen, by Merlin (Pignatell. controv.38, n.7,8,11, and 12).

Because of this most weighty cause of honour he had a right to kill them even after an interval, as well as his wife for her adultery, just as, because of many atrocious insults uttered by a certain doctor against a surgeon (for he said that he was a cuckold, and that his wife was a harlot, and that he himself (the doctor) had cuckolded him, and because he had painted a bull's horns on the doors of the said surgeon's house), the surgeon was excused from the usual penalty and condemned to the galleys for life, which penalty was commuted in his favour to perpetual banishment, although he had killed the said doctor with a forbidden weapon, after an interval, and although the aforesaid insults were imperfectly proved in his defence (Calder. cit.decis.42, n.37; and following, where other similar decisions are reported).

This most atrocious injury, which of itself constantly and ever would provoke and compel to vengeance, and particularly in the case of noble souls, was renewed with good reason by the parents' persuasion and instigation of their daughter's flight, and their co-operation in her adultery at least as a cause; by their reception, apparently contrived by themselves, of the adultress into their own home, although previously they had repudiated her with ignominy, and deprived her scandalously of her claim to being their daughter; and by the continuance of the closest friendship with the adulterer; and by other serious causes, which are brought forward in the trial. Because if churchmen plunging into the depths of evil are handed over by the Church, as though impatient of so many villainies, to the secular courts to be punished (Cap. cum non ab homine de Judic. in fine), and if even light offences often repeated become capital crimes, and particularly theft, what shall be said in this case, where the wretched couple stole from the prisoner not merely goods but his honour, and plotted still other mischief? Because even in slight matters reiteration of the offence leads the injured party to greater vengeance, as my master Signor Raynaldus observes (vol.1, p.593, n.47).

And if the brothers of the ravished Dinah slew not only the ravisher but his father and others (despite the peace and the kinship by a subsequent marriage which had been established) and when they were reproved for it by Jacob, their father, they replied, "Should he deal with our sister as with an harlot?" (Gen. ch. 34), what would they answer in our case if they had killed the aforesaid Comparini and his wife because of the reasons stated above?

Therefore my most learned and upright judges are begged that before they cast their votes in this very serious case each and every one of them will consider well, imagining himself in this peculiar case, which is worthy of special note, particularly on account of the irreparable notoriety which cannot be concealed by adulation itself (involving the destruction of the honour not only of the prisoner but of his whole noble family, and so most worthy of all pity); and let him consider in his heart whether any other ablution than that of the blood of the ravishers of his honour could wash away this most vile and most glaring stain. Then let him cast that vote which sincerely and dispassionately he would desire for himself, as Polic. admonishes the judges they are to do in considering whether the evidence is above all doubt or not (*De praehimini*, vol.11, p.105, n.44).

But the circumstances aggravating the crime, such as the place, the weapons, the forbidden assembly, and the lawsuits, trumpeted by the Fisc to the stars against the prisoner, particularly in the cases handed down by Sanz. (con.12, n.29) hold good in little or nothing, even with the omission of what had been most skilfully explained, in this as in all matters, in favour of the prisoners; because in the said controversy cited by our opponent the question was that of an adulterous wife, who in her husband's absence stripped his house of goods and furniture, and fled with her lover, and was handed over by the ecclesiastical court for safekeeping to a friend, as it was said, of the adulterer himself. The husband entered the house and killed her with a forbidden weapon, then took flight with several friends whom he had gathered together for this purpose. After a few days he was captured, and condemned to the galleys for 10 years, as may be seen in that place, at the beginning, and numbers 29 and 101; where, as in another similar case, the said penalty was imposed because of the aggravating circumstance of insidious weapons, with a reference to another case in which the husband was condemned to exile. And in the 11th controversy another case is dealt with, aggravated by several circumstances, and especially because the husband behaved with too much craft, feigning an absence, taking his brother with him, and killing with insidious weapons; because of which he was condemned to exile for four years, and to a fine of 2,000 ducats, as appears at the beginning and end of the said controversy.[80]

This latter case, narrated in the said controversy, exactly corresponds to ours, because it deals with the killing of an adulterous wife, and is only different because in the aforesaid case the husband was not noble. There the adultress had fled in her husband's absence, here from the conjugal couch, and from the very side of her sleeping husband, having previously cast him into a deeper sleep so that she might take from him not another rib but his heart, his honour. There the adultress was placed in the custody of a friend, as they said, of the adulterer; here she was handed over to the most open enemies of the prisoner, so that they might honestly safeguard her whom they had claimed in court to be most base, and born of an uncertain union.

For it is according to rule that in all offences the cause should be considered, since that is the queen of all human actions (Addentes ad Sanfelic. decis.337, p.58 in my edition, in the first versicle, just before the end. Novari. decis.225, n.6). And particularly should it be sought in criminal cases, and all other circumstances serve it as queen, for the facts of the case are not considered alone, except by the ignorant crowd. (Text. in L. aut facta 16, beginning "But these four kinds must be considered in seven ways," etc. de poen. where the cause is given the first place; and in L.4 at the end where we read, "however the cause of overstaying the furlough must always be examined," etc. de rer. militar.; despite the fact that in military crimes the proceedings are always very rigorous. And Text.L.verum est 40, at the beginning where we read, "For not the deed is to be sought but the cause for the deed, etc. de furt. ch. sciendum p.o, the gloss at the beginning where we read, "Because many do not consider this they fall into a labyrinth and a snare of error, and do not judge rightly because they do not understand fully": dist.29, cap.grave 7, qu. 10, ubi Glos. Verbo quia Veritas, where we read, "For it is impossible to reach the truth unless the cause is considered," juncto cap.ibidem citato).

And another thing would seem clear, for who would be excused for a slaying, which of its very nature is a more serious offence than the circumstances accompanying it, and would not also be excused for the said circumstances, especially when they proceeded from the most weighty and excusable cause of avenging his honour, as in our case, which he could not have managed in any other way, as everyone can see? That is why the circumstances received little consideration in the 11th controversy cited (Sanz.) and the collection of accomplices none at all (see Calder. dec.65, n.99, where he says that every time is permissible, so is the use of arms). In favour of our position—among the more open-minded as regards the crime and stricter as regards the cause—is Pragn., against is Crisp. (in pratic.Crim.Tract.12, de Scrib. Scop. n.1; et seqq. n.19), according to whom all arms used by a murderer are forbidden arms even in defence. Who nevertheless goes on to say that in the case in question the penalty was commuted from death to the galleys for nineteen years.

And so, if the prisoner had been captured with his associates before the crime, would he have been condemned to the usual penalty because of the aforesaid circumstance, arranged by him not in light anger, which would have been sufficient, but in grief and fury beyond belief? Most certainly not, because any cause at all, even a bestial and a most bestial one, is an excuse even in the crime of homicide, and much more it would have excused him for the said circumstances, prepared in anger and in wrath, as has been said. For a stain to honour, and especially among nobles, cannot be washed away except with blood, as has been proved at the beginning, and as is further proved by adden.ad Sanfelic. (d.d.e 337, p.57, first column at the end).

What has been said on behalf of the prisoner must also hold good for his four associates, as weightily and with a full pen has been shown to be evident by my fellow-advocates and the Procurator of the Poor; and although the contrary has sometimes been practised, we beg to point out that it was in cases of men who had received orders, and with the aggravating circumstances of their being assassins. But as to the deed being performed with assistants, I have neither read nor heard hitherto of any limitation of the rule, which has become proverbial, that principals and assistants receive the same punishment. And I have only read of the rule being altered when the principals are excused for some reason special to their persons, such as that they were minors, but not when common fellows are excused on account of the cause through which they have committed the crime, or when the quality of their crime is considered partly with regard to their persons and partly with regard to the cause of the crime.

As for what I have read of a limitation concerning the assistants of a man who was captured by the police as he was escaping, in a case in which the accused might have been unjustly captured, and appeared innocent, my master Rainaldo comments (I, p.292, n.39, beginning ex Cavalcan. subdit.) that this may indicate a weakness in the legal rule on accessories. Which conclusion it seems must be understood with a grain of salt and the greatest circumspection.

And so if the Fisc claims in this case another exception to the undoubted rule, he must prove it, otherwise, etc.

Therefore, my most reverend judges, I beg you to permit me to ask you whether you would condemn the said assistants for the circumstances of an assassination, a parricide, or a breach of the peace, if the prisoner had committed these crimes and the aforesaid aggravating circumstances were known beforehand to the accomplices? I hear you answer unanimously, "Very willingly," because we have the teaching of the same learned Deciano (*Summi Theorici*, in Tract.crim., tom.2, lib.9, cap.35, n.8 and ff.) giving the opinion that he who gives the orders is the first motor and the first cause to which the result must be attributed, nor can any secondary cause operate except in so far as it is influenced by a first cause.

Why should that doctrine which is so willingly accepted by the Fisc be rejected as regards the extenuating circumstances, when in this case it is more easy to accept in favour of the guilty, as Deciano points out (*ibid.* n.13)?

Even if the extenuating circumstances were not known to the accomplices but they believed in another reason, since the conclusion is most obvious that sometimes opinion, sometimes truth, should be heeded, according to which is more favourable to the guilty, but this circumstance extenuating the crime should be admitted even more in the case of the accomplices, if it was known to them, and if because of it they gave their assistance, otherwise they would not have bargained with the Fisc, as can be plainly seen from their answers when they were examined.

And therefore I believe that too hasty progress has been made until now in this most serious case, as was set forth by the Advocate for the Poor, of whom it might be said that in criminal battles he was a leader rather than a mere soldier, as it is found written of the Marchese Spinola[81] in martial strife.

And therefore we beg you earnestly to deign to read and re-read each and every one of these arguments, and to examine them with great diligence, because it is a question of the life of the prisoner and of the honour of a noble family. And you must not shrink from changing your judgment, if until now it was against the prisoners (which is not credible); but in such a case do not be loath to consult Luca de Penna in the prologue of his book, the dedicatory letter to the eminent cardinal,[82] towards the end, and St. Augustine in the prologue of his book of Retractions.

And pray from your hearts to Our Lord Jesus Christ to grant you wisdom, as it was granted to Solomon, who asked for that alone, and to deliver you from your difficulties in this most serious case, as St. Augustine warns should be done in one's own concern (*De Civitate*

Dei, book 19, chap. 6, throughout and especially at the end); not forgetting Text. 1. Non puto ff.de Jur.fisc., pondering on the adverb *easy* which is to be read there, and that the voice of pity is to be listened to rather than that of severity (Glos.chap.Ponderet, verbo misericordia, dist.50).

And finally remember that if crimes are punished not because of the crimes themselves that have been committed (which no matter what penalty is inflicted on the guilty cannot be undone) but in order that others may be deterred from crimes by fear of that punishment (Carpzou. in pract. qu.142, n.3), therefore it is more profitable to the state that infamous adulterers and abominable adultresses should be deterred, rather than most honourable husbands, especially in our times, according to the most prudent and opportune observations of Sanz. cited above.

Wherefore, etc.

DIONJSIUS PIGNATELLUS,
Advocate.

DESCRIPTION OF THE DEATH OF GUIDO FRANCESCHINI AND HIS FOUR COMPANIONS, WHICH TOOK PLACE ON FEBRUARY 22, 1698

He who risks doing evil to obtain thereby some advantage has too bold a confidence in himself, and for the most part sees himself overcome by the very villainies from which he hoped relief. Evil has this special quality, that it brings its punishment with it; because the greatest penalty of sin is the sin itself, and if indeed it seems sometimes that Divine Justice winks, so to speak, at human crimes, nevertheless it is then that one must be the most apprehensive, bearing in mind that it refrains from undertaking the punishment readily, only in order to strike a blow which shall be all the heavier the later it falls.

This infallible truth was proved in the persons of Pietro and Violante Comparini, husband and wife, and of their daughter Francesca Pompilia, on the one hand, and of Guido Franceschini, a noble of the first rank of the city of Arezzo, with four confederates, on the other, as the reader will sufficiently have remarked fully in the preceding writings here added.[83] Wherefore, in order not to multiply accounts needlessly, as the saying is, I shall not dilate on the faults which caused the said Comparini and their daughter to experience the vengeance of Heaven in their slaughter, nor on the causes which moved the wrath of Divine Justice against Franceschini and his companions; for the only task I have set for myself is that of adding here at the end the execution which took place of these five guilty men, mentioning a part of that infinity which should be said about their great resignation in the will of God and the Prince, and with what emotions of true faith they embraced that cross which was to be the ladder for them to ascend by to the heavenly Jerusalem.

And because the Advocate of the Poor had alleged on behalf of Guido Franceschini his clerical status (seeing that neither the arguments brought forward in the many writings for the defence, nor the pleas to the Criminal Court added separately, were of any avail) the Criminal Congregation was assembled as already will have been seen, before reading this account, in the current printed documents; and he also alleged their status as minors on behalf of Domenico Gambasini and Francesco Pasquini, hoping by that if not to save them, at least to prolong their lives and lessen their punishment.

Our Lord, Pope Innocent XII, who wished this case to be brought speedily to a close, would not admit the delay requested so that these two points might be proved, but under the date of February 20th, with three special documents signed by his hand, he rejected the pleas of the aforesaid advocate, and ordered that the sentence should be carried out on the 22nd of the said month, on a Saturday, as was done in the following manner. He was moved to this by the fear lest, during such a delay, letters might come from royal monarchs to save the life of Guido Franceschini, and that with such an example not only Romans but foreigners might attempt to commit acts similar to that of Franceschini, who had come into Rome from a foreign state, with armed men, in order to commit such a deed.

When Saturday, the day appointed, arrived, there was to be seen in the Piazza del Popolo, in front of the fountain, the scaffold, higher than a man, and in the middle the axe to cut off Guido's head; and on each side of the said scaffold two gallows erected, on each of which two of his associates were to be hanged; and this is all that need be said of the preparations.

And now I shall proceed to relate the event from the beginning at the chapel, or rather from the moment when they were informed that they were to die, until they were buried; and I shall mention only those things which are most essential and worthy of memory, because if I tried to report everything in detail it would make a volume, not a brief and simple account.

The day beforehand the Justices notified the Compagnia della Misericordia, whose executive officer, Signor Ciccaprovi, a Florentine gentleman, summoned the commissioners and gave them orders to go at once to the secretary of that same Company in order to send a notice to its members, and then to inform the sacristans so that they might set in order the chapel inside the prison;[84] and finally, after having prepared the little chapel inside the same prison, they were to go at 7 hours after sunset to call for the comforters, as is the custom. Consequently, all having assembled at the Oratory of St. Orsola al Consolato[85] and having made there the usual preparations, they proceeded to the prison, where they arrived less than 8 hours after sunset. Having offered more prayers there, and asked for the aid of the Holy Ghost, they proceeded to receive the sufferers who were all sleeping soundly, if one may call sleep what such persons, reduced to such a state, can capture.

Guido was the first to be awakened, and when he heard the door of the prison open he asked the gaoler whether he was going to be sent to the galleys. The gaoler bade him get dressed, because he was to be moved to another prison; but, as the time of night seemed unsuitable to him, he admitted later that he had guessed at what was happening, and yet was not unduly agitated when the death warrant was presented to him.

When he reached the passage outside the chapel he was received by two brothers of the Misericordia, who were Abate Panciatichi and Cavaliere Acciaioli, and at such an encounter one would have needed to be of bronze not to be dismayed.[86] But Guido's heart was incapable of such cowardice, for besides the noble birth which had fallen to his lot he was endowed also with corresponding valour and courage. Wherefore he said only, "Then because I defended and repaired my honour must I die in this manner?" And entering the chapel between his comforters he knelt down before the altar, where in less than an hour he became fortified and self-possessed, and was made so fit for death that he was able to give to all and each such an edifying example that since time immemorial no one can remember similar and comparable things. Because, prostrating himself at the feet of Christ, he poured forth upon those most precious wounds floods of kisses, with such vehemence that he made the beholders fear lest he should break some vein in his bosom: and perhaps that did not occur only because of the sweetness which his heart extracted from that life-giving balsam.

From this first testimony the comforters perceived the perfect holy devotion of the sufferer, and, if their hearts had been capable of vainglory, they would have been perceptibly afflicted by the reflection that they could claim no merit in that deed. But if they were amazed at that commencement one might say that they were stunned when, ever persisting in the same fervour, like a thirsting Tantalus he approached the wound in the side, and seemed to desire to suck from it all that precious body, with continuous cries for mercy for his sins: and for about a quarter of an hour he never removed his lips from it. Then turning to the sacred head, it is incredible what prayers he addressed to it, what protestations he made to it, the mercies for which he besought it, the vows which he made to it, the entreaties with which he prayed to it.

Because he wished his heart to receive still more comfort from the sweetness which he would feel in kissing that divine face, before he approached his lips to it he declared that if on other occasions he had been a Judas, now he desired to be so no longer; and that he regretted not having several lives, so that he might consecrate them all to His divine will; but what was denied to him as impossible was granted to him by his ardent resolution, and therefore, as he wished that he might shed the blood of those lives in His divine service, so he desired for himself, in that single penalty which was prepared for him, the stones of St. Stephen, his advocate, the glowing irons of St. Lawrence, and, in short, all the agonies already and still to be devised by human barbarity for the martyrdom of the saints.

Having poured out his soul at length in these testimonials, he went on to entreat that same divine mercy graciously to obliterate from his conscience all those stains which might keep his soul apart from eternal bliss, to infuse within him true repentance for his sins, and perfect constancy during his sufferings, to keep him from vain and ambitious thoughts, and, in short, to grant him special and divine assistance so that he might triumph over all the assaults which the world, the flesh, and the devil might prepare against him. Thus it seemed to the comforters that they were dealing not with a man newly converted, but with a long-established penitent, so that, their hearts dissolved in a sea of tears, they began to render thanks to the Eternal God, called the God of miracles, for the grace that they were receiving, that is, of learning the holy teachings from one whom they were supposed to comfort.

With such an example it was not difficult for his associates to resign themselves also completely to the will of God, except for Biagio Agostinelli, of Città della Pieve, as shall be related in its proper place. One thing alone somewhat tormented Signor Guido and seemed to make him recalcitrant to the fatal decrees of Heaven, and that was the necessity of dying in public. Therefore with great fervour he urged those comforters to try to obtain for him the grace of being allowed to die in private; but he was told that that was not possible, because since such a crime had been committed by him in the sight of the whole world it

LA PIAZZA DEL POPOLO ABBELLITA CON LI NVOVI EDIFICI ET VEDVTA DELLA CITTA DI ROMA COME SI TROVA AL PRESENTE
Data in Luce da Domenico de Rossi Erede di Gio Giac.o de Rossi dalle sue Stampe in Roma alla Pace con licenza de Sup.ri e Priuil. del S.P. l'Anno 1692.
7. Strada di Ripetta
8. Palazzo et Giardino del Sig.r Gianchino su l M.te Pincio
9. Chiesa et Convento della Trinita de Monti
10. Palazzo Pontificio sul Quirinale
11. Campanile di Santo Andrea delle fratte
13. Chiesa di Giesu Maria su la Via del Corso
14. Cupola della Chiesa del Giesu
15. Loggia del Palazzo del Sig.r Prencipe Borghese
16. Chiesa della Rotonda
17. Palazzo del Sig. Marchese Capponi
18. Cupola di San Carlo a Catinaro
19. Campanile dello Studio della Sapienza
20. Cupola di Santo Andrea della Valle
21. Campanile di Santo Agostino
22. Collegio Clementino

PLATE VII

Cloisters of S. Giovanni Decollato, Rome

PLATE VIII

was indeed fitting that the whole world should know and see that that penalty was inflicted on him which was his just punishment for such a misdeed. Convinced on this point, the great resignation of this gentleman to the will of God and the Prince was, as has been said, as worthy of amazement and universal admiration as it was deserving of perpetual memory, for there was no need for the comforters to employ any more efforts to dispose him to a good death.

They continued to admire his moral virtues and his remarkable resignation, accompanied by such an inexpressible intrepidity of soul; and, filled with holy awe, to pray the Almighty that by His infinite goodness He might deign to continue in him and his companions the effects of His most holy grace, which was in a few hours to produce such copious fruit for the Empyrean.

In such a happy conjuncture of compunction the heart of Biagio Agostinelli alone, who was being prepared by Abate Marascelli and Honorato Mattei, remained obstinate and overshadowed by the chimeras of Satan, who is too envious of the justification of the unrighteous. His pertinacity was based on his claim that he was innocent of these crimes, and therefore did not deserve death. Hence he refused to make his confession, and at last, finding himself constrained by the reasons set forth to him by his comforters, he protested that he would not yield unless they promised to grant him a favour. This was agreed to by those gentlemen, and upon hearing their promise he revealed his request, which was that he wished them to set free for him from the galleys a man who had been with him in prison, on which occasion a friendship had sprung up between them; and to alter the penalty of five years in the galleys, to which the man had been condemned, to simple banishment from all the States of the Church. The pious prudence of these gentlemen, which in similar cases neglects no means by which souls may be gained for, or rather restored to, the hands of that God Who created them, considered that in order to persuade this soul, which seemed recalcitrant, to reconcile itself to death, it was well to tell him, after a certain time had elapsed, that our lord had at his prayers granted him the required favour: and, because he had said that he wished a token of that, there was shown to him the prisoner's rosary, which was well known to him. But the devil, doing everything in his power to profit by such an occasion, suggested to him to demand, as in fact he did demand, to see the reprieved prisoner in person and at liberty. This satisfaction too was given him, by obtaining that the captain of the prison, who was also anxious to share in securing the eternal salvation of this soul, should consent to have him taken from the prison and brought before Biagio, in order to express to him the enduring gratitude which he bore him for such a favour obtained by his means from our lord.[87]

But because the poison of the infernal dragon had corrupted the faculties of this wretch, not content with the satisfaction he had received, he remained more obstinate than ever in asserting his innocence: saying that as an innocent man he neither could nor should die. To remove him from such a diabolical impression not only all the means indicated hitherto had been insufficient, but even the persuasiveness of various good men of religion and servants of God, such as were the two Capuchin fathers and Father Machiavelli, superior of the New Church, who had been brought here for the purpose by the Brothers of the Misericordia to see whether the efficacy of their spirit, refined like gold in the fire by penitence and religious exercises, would suffice to soften in some sort that heart of adamant. Here it is easy to picture the bitter affliction which was felt by these followers of the Redeemer, when they saw that the seed of the divine word was being scattered by them on masses of living stone, and so was not bearing fruit like the other which their companions had sown in such fertile ground.

As it was now six hours before sunset, and as experience confirmed their opinion that, using these methods, their reasonable persuasions had had no effect, and that the prayers of those venerable men had availed even less to bear fruit, they resolved to use the final resort to overcome his hardness of heart. Therefore they had the executioner enter and seize Biagio by the hair with great scorn, raising his head and putting the noose about his neck.[88] Oh truly, how great are the effects of divine grace! And what can it not accomplish in the greatest needs? Such was the terror that he experienced from this action, that in an instant he became as pliable and obedient to the decrees of Heaven as formerly he had been obstinate, receiving into his heart in such fashion divine grace, and forcing the common enemy to depart. For, flinging himself beneath the sweet yoke of the holy exhortations of the two comforters who had fallen to his lot, Abate Vannini, Canon of St. Peter's, and Abate Maggi, also a canon of the Lateran Basilica, what excuses did he not make to them, what prayers for forgiveness for the scandal he had caused did he not utter, what pleas that they would not forsake him? And finally, not to be prolix, what prayers did he not offer to the Eternal Father, to His Beloved Son, to the most blessed Virgin Mary, to the saints, his advocates, and to his guardian angel, that the former might grant him and the latter entreat for him mercy for his misdeeds? And in fact the conversion of this unhappy man, if such a glorious penitent can be called so, made perfect the design formed by divine grace of adorning each of the wounds of the Redeemer with these five precious jewels, bought at the cost of all His blood.

If up to this point the salvation of this soul, almost despaired of, had caused some reasonable fear, it was also the greatest consolation to see and hear with what gaiety of countenance, with what grief for his sins, and with what confidence in divine pity, Domenico Gambasini, a Florentine, comforted by Signor Miniato Ricci and Don Giovanni Fiorini, embraced more than willingly that death which in a few short moments was to make him immortal. Here I feel that it is better not to describe at length the expressions of joy that he uttered, exclaiming continually, "Paradise, Paradise," and similar things such as would have softened stones let alone the bystanders, who through tenderness all dissolved in warm tears. Nor shall I report the actions of all the other penitent companions, so that I may not become too tedious nor depart from my purpose, which is to write fully only what happened concerning the person of Guido Franceschini, mentioning however in passing the more noteworthy particulars concerning his companions.

So when all these five heroes had been disposed to die well and had prepared to make their confession, it was a miraculous thing to see the readiness which Biagio Agostinelli showed for it, considering that at first he had been so obstinate against conversion: for he demanded it with vehement insistence, maintaining extravagantly that he feared to be swallowed up by the very earth if he delayed longer in ridding his soul of those crimes which had made it in such a degree an enemy to God. But because the chaplain of the company was occupied with Francesco da Montacuto he could not be satisfied until Domenico Gambasini, Franceschini, and Alessandro had all confessed, while the said Ciampalanti, comforter and priest of Alessandro [so in MS.].[89] And perhaps God permitted this in order to increase his fervour, because deprivation begets appetite.

When at last the confession was over, Guido, recognizing there the Duke of Zagarolo,[90] begged his pardon if he had through preoccupation failed in the reverence due to him; and after other courteous speeches he begged his comforters to allow him to spend a few moments in talking to His Excellency. This request was immediately granted, and he stayed with him about half an hour, and, as was heard later, implored the patronage of that prince for the members of his family, and obtained from him the promise that His Excellency would write to all his relatives and assure them of every possible assistance in their needs; and especially as regarded the Abate Paolo, his brother, who was in Venice.

Then the other members of the Confraternity, seeing that the conversation was no longer on secret matters, approached also, and the subjects were introduced of his imprisonment, and of his lack of circumspection in having tried to escape after he had committed the murders. He answered assuring them that he knew that it had been brought about by Almighty God in order to save his soul, considering that before he had taken the risk he had considered that having companions who were not known to each other might result in his greater security, particularly since N.N.[91] was such a trustworthy man that he would rather have doubted a brother than him: and that he did not separate himself from them after the event because they protested that they wanted to accompany him to the place where they had joined him, and so he could not help giving them the other ten scudi, the last instalment of their reward, as he had intended before leaving the Porta del Popolo. When they received this information those gentlemen told him that he was under a greater obligation to God for such grace.

Then, abandoning his conversation and sitting down at the table with the executive officer of the Company, Guido left in his hands his will, which he dictated to him; and, remembering the company of a prisoner which he had enjoyed secretly in prison, the confidence shown him by that man, the assurances of friendship which had been made to him, the kindly offices rendered him, even though it was simulation, he felt that it was fitting to make some recognition of it at this time. So he ordered that two scudi should be given to the man from that money which had been found on him when he was imprisoned, and asked that with the rest of the money masses should be celebrated for his own soul, and for those of his wife and her father and mother. If the comforters had been very much struck by his earlier heroic behaviour, they were completely stupefied when they considered his magnanimity in rewarding a man who as a spy had rather harmed him than otherwise. Nor could they believe that he had not been aware that that was a feigned prisoner, placed there by the government, as is the custom in such cases; because a person of such a degree of intelligence easily perceives the artifices of such people.

It was also a most amazing thing to observe that Guido, from the moment that he received such dismal news until the last moments of his life, displayed the greatest intrepidity of mind, so that he never shed a tear or uttered a sigh, ever thanking God who had given him such an interval for repentance, since without it he might have been killed unexpectedly by some apoplectic stroke, by poison, by a musket-shot, or some such thing, and with his life might have lost his soul also;[92] whereas dying in this fashion he had had time and opportunity to set all his affairs in order, as indeed he did, first of all with a good confession, and then with many acts of penitence and protestations of faith in that God who desireth not the death of a sinner, but rather that he may turn to Him and live.

And because on an earlier suitable occasion he had talked at length, as has been said above, about the merits of his case, beginning with the marriage with Francesca Pompilia, and touching on all the dealings which had taken place between him and the Comparini down to the time when he was induced to commit the well-known murder, so that none of the bystanders might conceive the idea that he had done so because it grieved him to die, and to die in public at the hands of justice, he declared that that recital was a first impulse, an outburst demanded by nature and the flesh, which for the most part insistently presumes to rebel against reason; whereas he was more than willing to meet that end which had been allotted to him by divine and human justice, knowing that it was an opportune means of going to enjoy forever the presence of his most beloved Creator. And that if the latter, in order to redeem his soul, had actually died upon the cross, after having shed all His most precious blood, he, Guido, might well repay this act of unbounded love with those few sufferings and that death which lay before him, hoping that from that death he might obtain true life.

During this conversation it chanced that his wife was mentioned, and after various remarks on this subject he added that if men of this world had been capable of depriving him of her dear company in this life, they would not be able to do so in the next, where in a few moments he was going to enjoy it in Heaven, and to be joined with her in the indissoluble bonds of perfect charity.

It was even more amazing and unusual to see and hear with what efficacy he disposed his companions to a good death, and to seek refuge in the wounds of Jesus, in Whose side he had already placed all his hopes. His exhortations were so lively that the bystanders could not hear them with dry eyes, and without tender compassion. So that he employed the whole time that he remained in the chapel in meritorious acts and the holiest of exercises, with which he continued to fortify his heart to constancy, and prepare his soul to receive from the hand of God greater grace and strength to resist the snares of hell: so that he never ceased to recite psalms and prayers, and to utter protestations at the feet of the Crucified, neither consenting nor being willing ever to consent to the temptations or suggestions that might be insinuated to him by the devil, who always goes about seeking whom he may devour.

Guido redoubled these protestations when he saw Abate Lelio Tempi dressed in his sacred vestments to celebrate the first mass, which both he and his associates attended still on their knees, reciting psalms and prayers. But because at the second mass both he and the others were to be enriched with the precious balm of the most holy Eucharist, he asked for a quarter of an hour to make solemn preparations to receive it. It would take quite another pen than mine to relate in detail all that happened at that time, so I shall not attempt it, only begging the reader to believe more than is credible about his acts of contrition, his pleas for mercy, his desire that his sufferings should be much greater, and the like.

Meanwhile, all five having fed during the second mass on that celestial food, it was apparent what constancy it had given their souls, while they were set amidst that sweetness of Paradise, eternal glory and bliss, so that the executive officer could scarcely make them tell him how they wished him to use the 25 scudi of alms which were given to them by the comforters themselves; to whom they all replied unanimously at the same time that they wanted the money used for masses for the benefit of their souls.

At last the appointed hour for proceeding to the scaffold arrived, and at four hours before sunset, coming to the prison with a crucifix,[93] the Compagnia della Misericordia waited for these fortunate penitents, in order to conduct them to the Piazza del Popolo, the place that was destined to be the lists where they were to test their own constancy and triumph over the common enemy. And now indeed even a stony-hearted man would have dissolved in tears on seeing that Guido, kneeling at the feet of that Christ with acts of true faith and hope in His mercy, made a fervent speech in which he recommended his own soul so that He might deign to receive it in His most holy arms, and present it to the Eternal Father, together with those of his four companions. From this one may judge the quality of his faculties, considering that as the term of his life drew near its close divine grace increased in him. And one may see, too, how divine grace can manifest itself for the comfort of those in tribulation.

When Guido had finished this adjuration to the Crucified, and had kissed with great devotion His most holy feet and side, he went forth, and mounting the cart with extraordinary firmness, he recommended himself to the people assembled there in great numbers, and begged them all to say a Pater, Ave, and a Salve Regina, so that His Divine Majesty might give him strength at that last moment: and so in turn did the others, and then set forth from the prison. The procession went in the direction of the Via del Governo, and from there to Pasquino, where, as is customary, the Compania delli Agonizzanti[94] has the Blessed Sacrament exposed; and there Guido, approaching it, made a brief but efficacious prayer to the Venerated Host, as did his companions also. Then the procession went on through the Piazza Navona, to the Pantheon and Via Capranica, to the Piazza Colonna, whence it entered the Corso, and finally reached the Piazza del Popolo.

The concourse of people of all ranks who were to be seen assembled in all the places by which the procession passed was so great that there is no memory of anything similar. The most amazing thing was that the evening before, when the news of this execution became known, people began to go to the said Piazza del Popolo in such numbers that almost all night, while the executioners were making their preparations, it was continually frequented, and much more so in the morning, as though people were going to witness the triumphal entrance of the ancient Caesars. Therefore there had been set in order a great number of stands, which were to be seen in the Piazza, which at the hour of the execution was so full of carriages and carts and people on foot as well that it is probably an understatement to say that there were more than 40,000 persons; which will not be difficult to be believed, since the windows were rented at as high as 8 scudi apiece.[95]

As for the roofs, it was a miracle that they did not break under the weight, they were so laden with people; and one may say, finally, that the shops were all closed, for the very tradesmen flocked to witness the tragedy.

When the procession arrived at the Piazza del Popolo, these sufferers descended from the cart in the usual place adopted for use as a chapel, and there, according to the order set forth in the mandate,[96] when they had been confessed by the confessor of the Misericordia and had made the customary act of contrition at the foot of the crucifix, the chief executioner began to take to the scaffold the four sufferers, each of whom was exhorted by Guido to be constant at that moment on which depended an eternity either of glory or of torments. And then he added that when they arrived before the tribunal of God they were to pray for him, so that he might be granted strength and constancy to endure that imminent death by means of which he was soon to follow them.

The courteous expressions of Guido to the above-mentioned Company during the time that his companions were dying cannot be fully related. First, particularly, they were addressed to all those who had then raised their hoods, and whom he knew: he called them by name, and bidding them draw near him he kissed them; and then he begged the whole body of the Order to consent to help his family if the opportunity ever arose, and especially Abate Paolo, his brother, "who," he said, "is an honourable man, and one who, it may be said, was born in Rome, whence he has been forced to depart because he no longer has the face to appear among men of honour." Then he begged them all, and particularly those gentlemen who had comforted him, to bear with him if he had not derived from their pious instructions as much profit as he should. And last he thanked them for the great charity which they had shown in helping him; and finally all the body of the Company. Then he whispered for a while to the Duke of Zagarolo, and, when that conversation was over, went on to say several prayers, psalms, passages of Scripture and of the Gospels, with the prayer for the Passion which begins, "Our Lord Jesus Christ, who didst deign to be born and circumcised," and afterwards the other which follows, in honour of the Virgin, and finally a Te Deum upon the most holy conception of Our Lord, with the verses corresponding to those in the breviary.

Then, renewing his protestations of rejecting the temptations of the Devil, he desired to be confessed again.[97] At this moment the news came that the others were dead, and, with the same intrepidity as at first, he went to the end of the chapel where, kneeling at the feet of the Crucified, he offered up a most beautiful prayer. Then the chief executioner, taking off his fetters, tied his hands behind him, and, blindfolding him, led him to the scaffold. As he left the chapel he intoned in a clear intrepid voice, "I was glad when they said unto me, we will go into the house of the Lord"; and continuing to recite this he came to the scaffold, and ascending it he begged the people to say a Pater, an Ave, and a Salve Regina for his soul, recommending it to God at that last instant; and calling the confessor he desired to be confessed again. Then of his own accord he placed himself upon the plank, or trestle, whichever it should be called, putting his neck beneath the axe; and as it beheaded him he restored his soul to its Creator. Then the executioner, showing the head to the people, repeated several times, "This is the head of Franceschini."[98]

So fell these five victims, sacrificed to the public wrath of the people of Rome, which showed itself almost too thirsty for their blood because of the rash slaughter of an entire household, committed in the manner that is known, under the specious pretext of honour, and with vengeance greater than is suitable for a private individual.

When the execution was over, the Company went into the neighbouring church of the Madonna di Monte Santo, and, reciting the customary prayers on behalf of those souls, awaited the hour for taking away the bodies. This was done shortly before the Avemaria by the Company, which, according to the customs, bore them to S. Giovanni Decollato, where after the usual service they were buried at about 2 hours after sunset. Guido Franceschini was interred in the church before the altar opposite that of the Crucified, to distinguish him, as his birth demanded, even in his burial, from the other four who were placed beneath the loggie. But indeed Guido's name was not buried with his body, for if it is not immortal it will at least be renowned, both for the kind of vengeance which he took and for the remarkable defence put forward in his trial.

In describing this dismal event I have not aimed at writing for publication, but only at giving a simple account of the end which Guido and his companions made, so that it might be added to the preceding documents which came out during the time of his imprisonment. Therefore I have set it down without any ornament, and just as it has come from my pen, which would have been employed only too unworthily in polishing this little offspring of mine, which is designed not to see the light but to remain as though dead in my bookshelves.

ADDITIONS TO THE DOCUMENT ENTITLED "SENTENCE OF THE CRIMINAL COURT OF FLORENCE" IN THE OLD YELLOW BOOK

Sentence of the Criminal Court of Florence in the case against Gregorio Guillichini, Francesca Pompilia Comparini, and Francesco Borsi

This is the document which appears in an incomplete form at the beginning of the Old Yellow Book, as an abridgment made in Guido's defence during the murder trial. The original is in the Archivio di Stato in Florence. The first part is identical with that given in the OYB, and my translation commences where the deviation starts, at the end of the inventory of the stolen property. The last item in the inventory is:

. . . *a coat of her husband Guido*. They took these by forcing and breaking the lock of a chest in which he [Guido] kept part of the aforementioned goods, and they converted everything to their own use against the said Guido's will, the first accused [Gregorio Guillichini] and the said Canon Caponsacchio with the second accused [Francesca Pompilia] having scaled the walls of the city, as well as the second accused having committed adultery with them, and the third accused [Francesco Borsi] having facilitated the flight of the second accused and the said Canon in the manner described above.

This is apparent from the corpus delicti of the theft, from the forcing and breaking of the lock of the coffer observed in the official visit of inspection, and from the description of the said goods resulting from the report made of them by Beatrice, mother of the said Guido Franceschini, in his absence, and deposed by her, as well as through complaints made about them testified to by witnesses n. 6, 12, 13, and 14, who attest that their existence is very probable because the Franceschini are very well off, which is borne out by witnesses n. 10, 11, and 30, who also depose that Guido is an honourable and worthy nobleman of this city.

The circumstances prejudicial to the second accused are: first, that she is accused by the said Beatrice, mother of the said Guido, her husband; second, her flight from her husband's house on the said night, after having drugged the wine which the said Canon Franceschini and Guido drank, as has been deposed by the said Beatrice and, as concerns the flight, by the driver, the third accused, who drove her out of the said city on the said night to Camoscia towards Perugia, and by the witness n. 28 who met her during the journey from this city towards

Cortona. Both the latter testify that she was accompanied in the coach by Canon Caponsacchio, and that she and the Canon were guilty of the said flight is said publicly throughout the city, as is testified by witnesses n. 1, 4, 5, 6, 7, 9, 10, 11, 12, 13, 14, 15, 16, 19, 24, and 30.

One may add to all this the said Canon's behaviour for some time before the flight showing indications of adultery, that is, his frequent walks through the Borgo de' Cenci where the Franceschini house stands, as testified by witnesses n. 1, 8, 11, and 14; the affectionate intercourse shown by exchange of greetings, testified to by witnesses n. 1 and 8; his coming out of the Franceschini house, where the second accused stood at the door with a light and locked the door again when the Canon had gone out very softly, which is testified by an eye-witness, n. 1,[99] in her second examination (and at other times standing at the window she would lower a letter down to him); the exchanged kisses which are testified to by the coachman while they were going from this city towards Camoscia; and finally the scaling of the walls, since at 3 hours after sunset the said second accused was at home, as is seen by the trial, at which time the gates of the city were locked, because the porters of the city had closed them half an hour after sunset, as they aver, nor did they open them again until the morning; and she appeared at seven hours after sunset at the Horse Inn outside Porta S. Clemente, as the third accused says, coming from the direction of that part of the walls where there is a broken or ruined tower, which makes it easy to descend from the said walls, as was observed in the official inspection; and many witnesses say that they passed that way (that is, n. 12, 14, 16, 19 and 30). And the third accused states this too, and also testifies that the second accused had a very large box which she placed in the coach.

As for the assistance and aid given in all this by the first accused, indications are his confidential relations, friendship, and intimacy with the said Canon Caponsacchio, shown by their often walking together in the said Borgo de' Cenci and visiting the Franceschini house, testified by witnesses n. 1, 8, 11, 14, 24, and 30. Secondly, the threats which he makes to the said Maria Margherita, assuming that she has spread the news about his conduct and that of Canon Caponsacchio observed by her, as the said Margherita says and the witness n. 24 confirms.

Third, the confidential relations between him and the second accused, which can be inferred from his throwing snowballs at the window where she was standing during the last Carnival, testified to by the witness n. 8.

Fourth, the fact that on the said night of August 28, 1697, at about 5 hours after sunset, he was abroad in the city, not far from the Franceschini house, armed with a short sword, as is testified by witnesses n. 15, 16, 17, and 19.

Fifth, the fact that he was in the company of the said second accused and Canon Caponsacchio on the said night when they fled, having accompanied them to the place where they got into the carriage, as the third accused testifies.

Sixth, his flight and withdrawal into a place of immunity, asserted by the complainant and confirmed by witnesses n. 16, 18, 25, 26, and 30.

As for the assistance and aid given by the third accused, they consisted only in acting as coachman in the carriage in which he drove the said second accused and Canon Caponsacchio towards Camoscia on the way to Perugia. In this he was at fault for co-operating in something which both in appearance and in substance was unlawful, that is the flight of an ecclesiastic, very well known to him, with a woman, at an incongruous time and place, the Canon being dressed in clothes unsuited to his position, that is, wearing a hat edged with silver and carrying a short sword, as he says; although he excuses himself by saying that he did not know the woman personally.

The first and second accused are contumacious to the summons to appear before the court, and so must be presumed to confess themselves guilty of the aforesaid crimes, which are extremely serious, both because of the value of the stolen goods, and because of the injury done personally to the husband, a noble gentleman of this city, who is injured both in his honour and in his property, for which reason this criminal action for theft has been brought against his wife who eloped with an adulterer.

It must however be taken into consideration concerning the first accused that although from the aforesaid indication his knowledge and awareness of the aforesaid facts are to be deduced, from which and from his connection with the flight it can be said that he lent his immediate aid and co-operation to the said crimes, nevertheless, because it is very probable that the second accused carried out her bold deed at home without assistance, or at the most with the assistance of the most interested party, that is of the Canon with whom she was eloping, since the stolen goods were convenient and easy to carry off; and since perhaps even without his assistance the aforesaid crimes would have taken place; therefore it would appear that he should be condemned to a serious arbitrary penalty, considering his absence and his circumstances, but that he should not be obliged to make restitution.

Passing on then to the third accused, it can be considered only a slight fault in him to have lent a hand to an unlawful thing; and even for this fault he may be excused, because he is only a stableboy and works as a rule under the orders of his master, and neither of them had forewarning that in the carriage with the Canon (who ordered it for himself alone) there would be a woman, as we learn from his said master. It would seem then that he was sufficiently punished with the imprisonment which he has suffered until now, and which he is still undergoing. He is then to be released freely from the said prison without further proceeding to fine him for his defence, since this has not been done in the case of the contumacious, and so, etc.

The Commissioner and his judge are of the opinion that the first accused should be condemned to 5 years banishment at Portoferraio, on pain of the galleys for the same length of time if he does not appear within the space of two weeks to justify himself. The second accused is to be condemned to the Stinche[100] for life, and is to restore the stolen property, with the same reservations. The third is not to be prosecuted further, and is to be released from the prison.

The Court has ordered an inquiry to be made whether Guido has returned, what has happened to his wife and the Canon, how old the woman was and what she looked like, and what happened to the missing property, since the trial showed that no parcels were put into the carriage, though on the other hand it is apparent that the said property was carried away.

Because of this the Rector has added:

Guido Franceschini is about to return to Florence, where he went when he came back from Rome, where he had gone because of the flight of his wife with Canon Caponsacchi, according to the mother of the said Guido, and witnesses n. 1 and 2. It is learned that the wife and the Canon arrived at Castelnuovo, in the Papal States, and were there overtaken by Guido who was pursuing them and had them arrested by the constables of that court, and they were taken as prisoners to Rome, where the Canon was put in the Carceri Nuovi, and Guido's wife in a place of safekeeping, as Guido's mother and witnesses n. 1 and 2 attest.

It is learned that the woman is seventeen years of age and beautiful in appearance, according to Guido's mother and witnesses n. 1 and 2. They also assert that when the two were captured all the stolen money, clothes, and jewels were found, and when an inventory had been made of them they were taken before the court of the Governor of Rome.

The aforesaid investigation having been carried out and the citations repeated, the Commissioner and his judge consider it advisable to refer to the vote already carried out in this case, viz. The Court has ordered that the first accused should be condemned to the galleys at the pleasure of your Serene Highness [the Grand Duke of Tuscany, Cosimo III] with the aforementioned reservation. As for the second, who is confined in Rome in a pious establishment, the execution of the sentence is to be suspended. And for the third, who has committed no wrong intentionally, the order has been given as in the investigation.

[Added in the handwriting of Francesco Panciatichi][101]

The decision of the Court is approved.

APPENDIX

The Cortona version of the Secondary Source

The most complete version of the narrative first known to us through the Secondary Source appears as the first document in the Cortona codex. As this version is only slightly longer than the Baylor MS. which was translated in 1939 by Professor E. H. Yarrill in the *Baylor Bulletin* I am translating here those portions alone which are new. The translation is italicized to distinguish it from my own comments. I am adding also an occasional comment on material which occurs only in the Pesaro MS.

Deplorable and wicked homicide committed in Rome by Guido Franceschini, son of the late Tomaso Franceschini, and four other companions on the persons of Pietro Comparini and Violante Peruzzi, husband and wife, and Francesca Pompilia, their putative daughter and wife of the aforesaid Franceschini.

The Pesaro MS. has here the following two paragraphs, which appear in no other version:

"The aforesaid event took place in the street called Paolina near the Chiesa dei Greci at about one hour after sunset on the 2nd of January, 1698, in the reign of His Holiness Pope Innocent XII.

"With the execution of the slayers, which took place on the 22nd of February of the same year."

Reader: he who has prepared to describe this barbarous massacre, as you see makes no pretence to do more than give a simple account and a brief narration of what he has seen and heard and gathered from various arguments and summaries printed by many authors, some in favour of the guilty, others against them, claiming always to leave the truth unaltered, and to deprive the subjects of his account of no tittle of their birth and station. Nor has he desired to avail himself in order to adorn his tale of any flowers of rhetoric, since it did not appear to him that the story which he has undertaken to describe deserved such ornaments. And if while your eyes peruse it your heart should prompt you to some tears of compassion, accompany them with devout prayers for the souls not only of the slain but of the slayers. Because they too have paid the penalty of their crimes through their execution, one beneath the knife, the others on the gallows. And remember that to the Lord God whatever we do for our neighbours is most pleasing.

As I have explained in the Introduction, the Cortona account is divided into chapters by headings.

The first head is: *Commencement of marriage negotiations between the Comparini and Francesca Pompilia their daughter with Franceschini; the marriage is accomplished.* There are few variations in this section, except unimportant details of spelling or word order.

The second section is headed: *Departure of the same from Rome, and reception in Arezzo, and slights received by the said Comparini from the Franceschini mother and brothers.* When angry words are addressed to Violante *they caused her so serious a stroke that it made a great to-do.* When she locked herself in her room, the writer adds: *where she remained all day Saturday weeping, without anyone being moved to compassion for her. Then in the evening Franceschini said that she was to be taken out of that room.* At the end of the section, after describing how the door had been locked against Violante and Pietro so that they had to spend the night, she at a neighbour's, he at an inn, there is a final sentence: *Wherefore early next morning this couple made no complaint at what had happened, so that their daughter might not be abused on their account.*

The third head is: *Departure of the Comparini from Arezzo, and disclosure that the birth of the said Pompilia was a pretence.* In this section there are a few additional words after the statement that the Pope had proclaimed a Jubilee: *The said Violante, thinking about herself and realizing her unhappiness, decided that she wanted to make her confession on that very occasion of Jubilee; and indeed she put her thought into effect and revealed to her confessor that the said Francesca Pompilia was not in any way her daughter.*

The fourth section is headed: *Resolve of Pompilia to flee to Rome and the results of her journey.* One addition here is minor, that Canon Conti was moved to pity *seeing with his own eyes* that what Francesca Pompilia told him about her sad state was true. Another additional passage is important though it is omitted in all other versions, except in the Pesaro MS. Conti has approached Caponsacchi, and the flight has been agreed on. *While the manner of such a departure was being planned, Signor Ruggiero Guillichini, who was also a close relation of Guido Franceschini, learned about it and he too thought the time was ripe to put into effect what he had formerly discussed when he had talked in Rome with Pietro and Violante de' Comparini, and that was to take the said girl to them in Rome. Therefore he did not fail to write both by a messenger sent from Arezzo and by the post to the said Pietro and Violante, representing to them that it would be opportune and con-*

venient to free their daughter from the abuse of her husband and from death. He asked Pietro to inform him if he still held to the same purpose as before, and said that if Pietro gave his consent he offered not only his own services for that but also those of the said Canon Caponsacchi, a man of a good presence, of the highest nobility, and very God-fearing; as appears from the original letters produced in the suit. So he obtained, not surprisingly, an answer from the said parents consenting to the said departure.

And a few sentences later the Cortona MS. says that Caponsacchi hesitated to undertake the task *although urged to do so by Guillichini,* and finally yielded to the instances of Conti *and Guillichini.* It is striking that these references to Guillichini, which appear both in the Cortona and in the Pesaro MSS., have been omitted from all other versions of S.

Towards the end of this section, which is lengthy, there is an addition after the statement that Francesca Pompilia was transferred to the house of the Comparini, a fine of 300 scudi to be imposed if she failed to appear at the summons of the court. *The said Abate* [Paolo] *however refused absolutely to agree to this unless Pietro Comparini bound himself by an agreement drawn up legally (as he did in the end) to provide food for the said Francesca for as long as she remained in his house without any possibility of reimbursement.*

So, having resigned from the service of his employer, the said Abate sold all his books, furniture and everything else, and having caused to be given to him the 47 scudi found on the said Pompilia at Castelnuovo, he departed from Rome.

Meanwhile on December 18th the said Francesca Pompilia bore a son, which was given to a wet-nurse to be brought up, and the latter had it baptized in the church of S. Lorenzo in Damaso (the Pesaro MS. says S. Lorenzo in Lucina), *and gave it the name of Gaetano Franceschini.*

The fifth and sixth sections are entitled *Resolve of Franceschini to go to Rome with four companions*, and *Homicide committed by the same and its results.* Neither section contains any additional material.

The seventh section is headed *Flight of Signor Guido Franceschini and his companions.* Here the Pesaro MS. alone gives the detail that the Genoese knife belonging to Guido was placed, apparently as an exhibit, in the Castel Sant'Angelo. Towards the end of the section there are three additions which appear in the Cortona MS. alone. After saying that it was by God's will that Francesca Pompilia survived long enough to reveal the identity of her murderers, the author adds: *And it was truly a miraculous thing, when the surgeon reflected on the deep wounds that had been inflicted on her, that she remained alive thus during that whole length of time, because grace had been granted her so that she might be able to reconcile herself with God.*

Guido when arrested was put into a carriage and, guarded by sbirri, was taken back to Rome. *The said Franceschini did not spare himself, and asked the constable who accompanied him how the deed had been discovered. "I do not know," said the constable; but later when Franceschini again urged him to tell him how such a discovery had been made the constable replied that his wife was alive. Guido was amazed and stupefied, and said with raised brows, "What, is my wife living?"; and the constable answered, "Yes, sir, your wife is indeed alive."*

Then when the accomplices are mentioned further details are given about Alessandro Baldeschi from Città di Castello. *This Alessandro among the other murders he had committed numbered one which is very notorious because he confessed it during the trial. He had attacked four persons who were travelling and after he had taken from them the money which they were carrying he had deprived all four of their lives.*

The eighth section is headed *Stupefaction of the people on seeing the dead bodies in the church*; and there another ghastly detail is added to the description of the slain Pietro and Violante. The sight of two old people so brutally murdered *caused great compassion because not only had their murderers cut their throats but they had also cut through the head just where it joins the neck, so that it remained attached to the body only by a strip of flesh and a little skin; and what caused even more marvel and stupefaction was that they were riddled with stabs.*

The ninth section is entitled *Resignation of Francesca Pompilia and her preparation to die well.* It gives the added detail that Francesca Pompilia insisted on the comforts of religion *during the whole time that was left to her* before she restored her soul to her Creator, and that *the resignation of that unfortunate girl was such that the priests themselves were amazed when they saw with what compunction of heart she replied to and joined in with the very prayers which they contrived to suggest to her.* When she had pardoned her enemies, *she desired the same night to make her will, leaving many legacies for her soul, and to her benefactors, which in part were confirmed and in part revised in the second will which she made the day before her death.*

Then the doctors decided to let her blood, *because they did not want to fail in carrying out a most distinguished treatment, although they despaired because the wounds were so inflamed and angry and were festering, so that there was more than certain danger that she would not survive. It was however decided not only by the doctors but by the surgeons too to bleed her.*

When her body was exposed in the church of S. Lorenzo in Lucina it was *clad in the habit of a nun. Her corpse was accompanied by an enormous crowd, and people of every condition assembled in the streets so that the church was so full that the bier could scarcely obtain entrance amidst a murmuring and chattering that caused both marvel and stupor.*

In the tenth section, *The trial of Franceschini continues, in which there were not lacking writings from many learned pens,* we are told that when Alessandro Baldeschi had the judge called and admitted his guilt *he said that his guardian angel had inspired him to confess* such a crime. And at the end of the section the Pope, we are told, ordered the sentence to be carried out *by issuing a decree in which every objection of age and clerical status was set aside; and so our lord ordered that they should be put to death, which was hastened on by the said Governor.*

The eleventh section is called *Death of Franceschini and his companions.* Here we are told in the description of the crowd in the Piazza del Popolo that *more than one house opposite* (the scaffold) *which was rented for that day was hired for a price equal to 3 months' rent by some Flemish noblemen; and the next day the keys of the house were given back, and permission was granted to rent it again, and a present was made of the excess money which had been paid.*

We also learn that Biagio Agostinelli welcomed his death *as a penalty for his sins,* and that Domenico Gambasini *was often seen to raise his eyes to heaven, calling on the name of God and of all the saints, with such an infinite number of like fervent acts that even the member of the Confraternity who was assisting him wept and sobbed so that he could not utter the words which are usually said before an execution.* And as Domenico died he invoked the Blessed Virgin *and the name of Jesus, and made many acts as a true Christian.* Alessandro Baldeschi, on the contrary, though most contrite *was observed not to make any act of true repentance, but only to stand there like a dead man.* Guido's voice as he asked the people to pray for him was *most intrepid.*

In the last section, *Features of the said Guido and his clothes,* there is an additional paragraph. *After some months it was learned that at the instance of the heir Francesca Pompilia was absolved of the alleged adultery charged against her by her husband by a full council meeting of the Government on August 19, 1698, and that she was by the said assembly declared innocent and restored to her pristine reputation. Otherwise she would have been held guilty of adultery, and that is plain from the sentence pronounced against her.*

There are other minor differences, such as that Beatrice's name is correctly given as de' Romani; the wig-maker's address near the Piazza Colonna is mentioned; it is explained that Pietro had to borrow money for his journey because the Franceschini would not give him enough; Francesca Pompilia's mother is called a woman from outside Rome, not a washerwoman as in the Baylor MS.; Violante confesses to her husband because the priest has made it a matter of conscience.

NOTES

Notes

NOTES TO THE INTRODUCTION

A simple page reference (e.g., p. 120) refers to a page of this translation. The abbreviation OYB refers to Charles W. Hodell's translation of the Old Yellow Book in the Everyman edition.

1. MS. 250 (333). I have already described this codex in an article "New Documents on Browning's Roman Murder Case," in *Studies in Philology*, XLIX (3), July 1952, 520–33.

2. John Marshall Gest, *The Old Yellow Book* (Philadelphia: University of Pennsylvania Press, 1927).

3. "Browning's 'Roman Murder Story' as Recorded in a Hitherto Unknown Italian Contemporary Manuscript," in the *Baylor Bulletin*, XLII (4), Dec. 1939, 23–47.

4. W. O. Raymond, *The Infinite Moment* (University of Toronto Press, 1950), pp. 95–104.

5. This is probably the missing document mentioned by Antonio Ugolinucci in his letter to Francesco Cencini (OYB, p. 338).

6. Archivio di Stato di Firenze, Ruota criminale, anno 1697, filza 86.

7. The OYB contains only documents which are concerned with or which appeared at the time of Guido Franceschini's trial for murder. The sentence of the court of Florence as it appears there is simply a transcript made for Guido's defence, giving an inventory of the objects alleged to have been stolen by Pompilia and Caponsacchi, and proving that in the opinion of the Florentine court the accused were guilty of adultery.

8. This collection contains 18 items, number 3 being the story of Beatrice Cenci, number 6 the story of Vittoria Accoramboni, and numbers 16 and 17 dealing with the heresy of Molinos.

9. This narrative was translated by W. Hall Griffin in the *Monthly Review*, Nov. 1900. It was re-translated by C. W. Hodell, and published in his edition of the Old Yellow Book. The original Italian has never been published.

10. This very typical collection, which originally belonged to Marchese Pietro Pietrucci, is entitled "Narrazioni diverse di esecuzioni giudiziarie." It contains 9 items: number 4 is the story of Vittoria Accoramboni, number 8 that of Beatrice Cenci. These details serve to show how certain favourite stories recur constantly in such repertories.

11. A microfilm, which I was allowed to transcribe, of this MS. is in the library of Bishop's College, Lennoxville, Que.

12. Two other items proved to be disappointing except as further proof of the widespread interest in the case. One, from the Biblioteca Giovardiana at Veroli, 191 (42-1-45), vol. XI, item 4, was the printed pamphlet (n. 15 in the OYB) written in support of the Comparini. The other, from the Biblioteca Universitaria of Bologna, 1784 (3901), item 4, was an incomplete copy of the anonymous pamphlet in favour of Guido (OYB, n. 10) and of the Summary on his behalf (OYB, n. 7).

13. *Novelle*, I, 4 and 26.

14. Cardinal Pallavicino was Governor of Rome at the time of Guido Franceschini's crime; it is not impossible that he wrote the original of C.

A whole collection of criminal cases during the pontificate of Urban VIII was written by Giovanni Battista Spada, Governor of Rome during that period (Biblioteca del Comune of Cortona, MS. 234 (317).

15. The wording in the versions of both S and C is nearly always identical, though occasionally the very much abridged Angelica version of C paraphrases for the sake of brevity. The copyists are neither consistent nor careful, which is why the Baylor version of S gives November as the date of Guido's wedding, and the Secondary Source December, though the month is correctly given as September in the Pesaro and Cortona versions.

16. See p. xlvi.

17. "Nomi dei giustiziati assistiti negli ultimi momenti dall'Arciconfraternita di S. Giovanni Decollato (detta della Misericordia) in Roma. Desunti dai Registri del Pio Sodalizio depositati nell'Archivio Romano di Stato il 23 Novembre 1891, che principiano coll'anno 1499 e terminano col 1870, ultimo della dominazione Pontificia."

18. See pp. 20–1, where we also learn that Francesco Comparini was a Florentine by birth.

19. Canzi died in 1652 (p. 22).

20. Throughout the text I have translated the word *fedecommesso* as entail.

21. Violante, Pietro's wife, would evidently have preferred the child to be a boy (pp. 44, 47).

22. Both Pietro and Francesca Pompilia make wills in which apparently there is no mention of any entail (OYB, pp. 121, 160–1). The dower contracts speak of the conditions of the entail being satisfied in Francesca Pompilia (p. 21).

23. Now the Via del Babuino. Sir Frederick Treves (*The Country of "The Ring and the Book*," London, 1913, p. 102) identifies Pietro's home as the one at the corner of that street and the Via Vittoria. However it is further described in the documents as having two shops beneath it fronting on the Orti di Napoli, and as being almost opposite the Chiesa dei Greci, Sant'Atanasio (p. 15), then owned by the Jesuit Order. Of the four houses shown in the 1676 plan of Rome (Treves, p. 300) which have fronts on both streets, the one best answering to this description is the third from the corner, a large house which must have been a valuable property.

24. Most of my information on this subject is taken from Antonio Coppi's *Discorso sulle finanze dello Stato pontificio dal secolo XVI al XIX* (Rome, 1855).

25. Giulio de' Medici, who naturally as a member of the great banking house brought to Rome Florentine methods of establishing a public debt.

26. I have translated this as the second nine-year loan.

27. Coppi, *Discorso*, p. 15.

28. See p. 8.

29. For this breach of the conditions of the entail Pietro had to gain the permission of the Pope himself (p. 7).

30. Pp. 26–36.

31. None of the witnesses mentions the fourth name, Camilla, which is recorded in her baptism and marriage licences.

32. OYB, p. 95.

33. See p. 47.

34. See pp. 35, 46. This is one of the most curious details in the story. I have not been able to find any record of secular day schools for girls in seventeenth-century Italy. And it must have been an unusual school, since it took children of both the middle class and that very poorest class to which Francesca Pompilia's alleged sister, Cristina Paperozzi, apparently belonged. Also the age-range of its pupils was very wide: Cristina must have been sixteen when the four-year-old Francesca Pompilia began to go to school. It seems strange that a poor girl of sixteen was not at work rather than at school. However, this part of the evidence does not appear to have been questioned.

35. OYB, p. 160.

36. See p. 41.

37. Coppi, *Discorso*, p. 17.

38. OYB, p. 145. According to Bishop Burnet (*Travels through France, Italy, Germany and Switzerland* [1685–6], London, 1750, p. 179) many investors were ruined by this refunding.

39. Pp. 64–5. The youngest Franceschini brother, Antonio Maria, is not mentioned anywhere in the OYB.

40. Archivio dei Laici, Arezzo, MS. 12, pp. 76–77. Grades of nobility were determined by the age of the family and the public offices and dignities which its members had held.

41. P. 65.

42. Pietro Faruli, *Annali . . . di Arezzo* (Foligno, 1717), p. 354. Faruli gives no date for this certificate, but says that Porzia had obtained it "ultimamente," very recently.

43. In 1546 the family had been declared eligible for the office of gonfaloniere, and a Tomaso dei Romani had been appointed to the post in the following year. In 1756 Filippo, the son of Guido's uncle Tomaso, was inscribed with his descendants in the Golden Book of Patricians of Arezzo. U. Spreti, *Enciclopedia storico-nobiliare italiana*, V, 778.

44. P. 3. Cardinal Flavio Chigi (1631–1693) received many favours from Cosimo III, among them the marquisate of San Quirico which he entailed on his sister and her son.

45. Faruli, *Annali*, p. 258.

46. Alderano Cibo (1613–1700) was created Cardinal by Innocent X in 1645, and became Secretary of State under Innocent XI. Pier Matteo Petrucci dedicated to him his *Contemplazione mistica acquistata* (1681), which is Molinistic in tone. A patron of letters and the arts, he had a chapel built in S. Maria del Popolo under the direction of Carlo Fontana, with an altarpiece by Carlo Maratta. In 1689, the year of Guido's death, he assembled a synod meeting at Velletri. *Enciclopedia cattolica*, art. "Cibo."

47. The title-page reads: "Presagio / di prosperità / all'armi cristiane / nel presente assedio / di Vienna / di / Paolo Franceschini Aretino / all'Eminentiss. e reverendiss. sig. cardinale / Lorenzo Brancati / di Lavria / in Roma, nella Stamperia di Nicolò Angelo Tinassi Stamp. Camerale / MDCLXXXIII / con licenza de' Superiori." (A copy of this poem is in the Biblioteca Vittorio Emmanuele in Rome.) Lorenzo Brancati, Cardinal di Lauria, was a distinguished member of the Conventual Franciscans. Born at Lauria in Lucania in 1612, he taught theology and philosophy at the Sapienza in Rome, was consultant to the Holy Office and Prefect of the Propaganda Fide and of the Vatican Library. He was made a cardinal by Innocent XII in 1681, and died in 1693. Pious and

learned, he wrote many theological works, some of which were reprinted as late as 1899. *Enciclopedia cattolica,* art. "Brancati."

48. Francesco Nerli (1636–1708), Archbishop of Florence and appointed nuncio in Paris in 1672, was made a cardinal in 1673.

49. This odd commission may be explained by the fact that in 1692 Cosimo III had imposed a tax on wigs in Tuscany which the lady was probably trying to evade. G. Conti, *Firenze dai Medici ai Loreni* (Florence, 1909), p. 275.

50. Pp. 11–13.

51. The writer of C gives an elaborate description of the deplorable familiarity of Violante with this intriguing Antonia—another proof that he had never seen the legal documents concerning the lawsuit.

52. P. 13.

53. E.g., p. 17.

54. P. 55. Benedetto Maidalchini, great-nephew of Pope Innocent X, was not created Cardinal until 1681, but at the time of Pompilia's birth was Grand Prior of Rome. His steward would be a person of some importance and probably much influence.

55. P. 57.

56. P. 53.

57. P. 75.

58. According to one of the anonymous pamphleteers, Paolo was surprised when the inventory was produced by Pietro during the first lawsuit. Guido, when reproached by his brother for its falsifications, said that Violante had urged him to draw it up (OYB, p. 146).

59. P. 14.

60. Pp. 12–17.

61. Pp. 17–20.

62. The references to numbers and fractions of bonds in the contract are so self-contradictory and so ambiguous (e.g., thirteen or eight bonds) that they are further proof that the documents are incomplete.

63. Pp. 20–4.

64. The certificate of Guido's repudiation of his inheritance is dated March 2, 1693 (p. 64). This date is probably too early, for the certificate seems to have been obtained after June 24, when the first contracts were drawn up, and before August 27, when the third contract shows that Pietro is aware of the repudiation.

The certificate that the Franceschini belonged to the second class of nobles is dated November 16, 1693 (p. 65).

65. This refutes the contention of one of the pamphlet writers that five bonds were freed from the entail and realized against Pietro's wishes (OYB, p. 212). The arrangement given in the settlement was apparently never carried out, and ultimately only five 30/100 bonds were cashed (p. 4). They amounted to the sum of 700 scudi.

66. P. 7.

67. Peter Beckford, *Familiar Letters from Italy to a Friend in England* [written before 1785] (London, 1805), I, 390–1.

68. Corrado Ricci, *Anime dannate* (Milan, 1919), pp. 141, 175.

69. Beckford, *loc. cit.*

70. P. 1.

71. E.g., OYB, p. 112.

72. Detail in longer versions of S.

73. OYB, p. 89. Only Girolamo is mentioned in the OYB as actually living in the Franceschini home. Antonio Maria had surrendered his position as canon of S. Maria della Pieve in Arezzo to Porzia's brother-in-law, and may have been living at his parish, six miles from the city (pp. 10–11).

74. P. 4.

75. OYB, pp. 49–53.

76. *Ibid.*, p. 113.

77. The first recorded letter is dated February 6, 1694 (p. 74).

78. P. 74.

79. OYB, p. 90. It is possible that it was these jewels that Francesca Pompilia stole before her flight, and that the Comparini regarded them as the equivalent of part of her dowry. Their value was over 400 scudi (OYB, p. 6).

80. P. 75.

81. P. 76.

82. The purpose of this Jubilee was to invoke divine aid for peace among Christian people.

83. P. 45. Here both S and C are at fault, for they say that Violante's confession was made after her return to Rome. Probably it was one of the causes of the return, for the Comparini would never have dared to make their public repudiation of Francesca Pompilia and the dower contract while still in Arezzo and exposed to the Franceschini's anger.

84. P. 36.

85. Detail in longer versions of S.

86. P. 4.

87. P. 36.

88. The testimony of Angelica (OYB, p. 49), and of Agnese Olivieri (p. 63).

89. P. 5.

90. Pp. 9–65.

91. P. 41. Petronilla Feure says that the neighbours laughed at the mock "confinement" (p. 63).

92. P. 47.

93. Pp. 36–64.

94. P. 110.

95. OYB, pp. 90–5.

96. *Ibid.*, p. 160.

97. P. 107.

98. These books have been identified by Professor J. E. Shaw in "The 'Donna Angelicata' in *The Ring and the Book*," *PMLA*, March 1926, pp. 55–81.

99. OYB, p. 160.

100. *Ibid.*, p. 93.

101. *Ibid.*, p. 245.

102. *Ibid.*, pp. 95–6.

103. *Ibid.*, p. 96.

104. *Ibid.*, p. 91 (my own re-translation). Maria Margherita Contenti was evidently on good terms with all three young men, Canon Conti, Guillichini, and Caponsacchi, and Guillichini seems to have felt obliged to reassure her about the innocence of Caponsacchi's journey to Rome (p. 79).

105. OYB, p. 135.

106. *Ibid.*, p. 189.

107. *Ibid.*, p. 122.

108. Doubt has been cast on the inventory of stolen goods which was drawn up by Beatrice (OYB, p. 6); it may be as padded as Guido's inventory of his property. Sir Frederick Treves (*The Country of "The Ring and the Book,"* pp. 62–3) is convinced that the goods, except for a few trinkets, never existed, a doubt expressed also by Caponsacchi's lawyer (p. 81). However, Francesca Pompilia does not question the inventory made by the treasurer at Castelnuovo, saying only that the list makes it obvious that the "many trifles" were her own possessions (OYB, p. 93). The coachman testified that she had with her on her flight a "very large box" (p. 108).

109. P. 79.

110. For instance, the argument that the coachman's evidence was not admissible since he had not said that he was able to see the pair kissing because the moon was shining (p. 80).

111. The title of the charge against Caponsacchi, though not the charge itself, was altered in the sentence. The change was made so that the still undecided suit against Francesca Pompilia might not be prejudiced (OYB, pp. 229–30).

112. Temporary confinement in a convent after an elopement was not uncommon at that time, as it protected a fugitive wife or daughter from summary vengeance.

113. OYB, p. 217.

114. Though the suit for divorce is mentioned in the OYB several times there is no specific information about it, and we still do not know on what grounds it was brought. As Judge Gest has pointed out (*The Old Yellow Book*, p. 12) it could only have been for legal separation, not for true divorce.

115. OYB, p. 151.

116. P. 107.

117. P. 108.

118. Guido's visit to Florence may have encouraged him to have this action taken.

119. P. 110.

120. P. 108.

121. P. 110.

122. P. 75.

123. OYB, p. 151.

124. P. 97.

125. OYB, p. 19.

126. The child was born on December 18. Sir Frederick Treves was unable to find any record of its birth in the register of San Lorenzo in Lucina, the Comparini parish church. One of the Vatican MSS. gives its place of baptism as San Lorenzo in Damaso, where Violante had been baptized.

127. OYB, pp. 150–1.

128. *Ibid.*, p. 155.

129. *Ibid.*, p. 224.

130. *Ibid.*, p. 137.

131. *Ibid.*, p. 121. This identification is supported by longer versions of S, which say that her fortune was left to "her benefactors." The term certainly applies to those who attended her at her death, but may include Tighetti as well. (P. 118.) Francesca Pompilia's choice of an heir who was no relation to her family was criticized by Arcangeli, the Procurator of the Poor, in his defence of Guido. It may be noted too that Tighetti gave his murdered benefactress such

a magnificent funeral that it was the subject of public comment (detail in longer versions of S).

132. S. Maria delle Fornaci was the result of a rural mission, begun by Giuseppe Faraldi in 1683, near the brick kilns from which it took its name. The first church, an octagonal wooden structure, designed by the architect Francesco Antonio Bufalino, was built in 1689 around the tiny original chapel containing the miraculous picture of the Virgin. This had been sketched from a revelation received in prayer by one of Faraldi's devout penitents, Anna Maria Villa, and then painted by a Flemish artist specially chosen for his piety, Gilles Hallet (who died in Rome in 1694 after spending most of his life there). It represents the Virgin wearing a crown and holding up one hand of the crowned Christ Child in the gesture of blessing, as though gently compelling Him to bestow the favour sought of Him. Miracles were performed as soon as the altarpiece was put in place, and for the next couple of decades all Rome flocked to the shrine, whose record of wealthy patrons and valuable offerings was enviable.

The church as it appears in the illustration was re-built, still preserving the original chapel, about 1713 after the plans of Francesco Multò; the façade was added in 1735. Padre Celestino de' Santi, *Storia della Chiesa di Maria Santissima Interceditrice di Grazie alle Fornaci fuori Porta Cavalleggieri* (Rome, 1903); Antonio Nibby, *Roma* (Rome, 1839), III, 374–5.

133. He is called only "a marchese" in S, but we can probably identify him from OYB, p. 60.

134. P. 118.

135. OYB, p. 276.

136. Detail in Cortona codex and Pesaro versions of S.

137. OYB, p. 136, where "page 722" is evidently a reference to a page of the testimony.

138. Now that we have documents from the earlier cases it is evident how often the lawyers in the murder trial were summarizing or quoting former arguments.

139. Pp. 82–91.

140. P. 92.

141. OYB, p. 145.

142. L. von Pastor, *The History of the Popes* (London, 1940), XXXII, 576–7.

143. OYB, p. 275.

144. P. 92. The only ruler who might have been expected to intervene on Guido's behalf was Cosimo III de' Medici, but apparently the Emperor too was interested in the case (OYB, p. 237).

145. My information on this subject is derived from V. Moschini, *S. Giovanni Decollato*, in the series *Le Chiese di Roma illustrate*, no. 26 (Rome, 1926), pp. 11 ff.

146. Such a procession is described by Dr. John Moore in his *A View of Society and Manners in Italy* (London, 1781), pp. 476–83, a book which was brought to my attention by Miss S. Pantazzi. He attended the hanging of someone who was to be executed for his fifth murder, and says: "First of all, there was a procession of priests, one of whom carried a crucifix on a pole hung with black; they were followed by a number of people in long gowns which covered them from head to foot, with holes immediately before the face, through which those in this disguise could see everything perfectly, while they could not be recognized by the spectators. . . . All of them carried lighted torches, and a few

shook tin boxes, into which the multitude put money to defray the expence of masses for the soul of the criminal. . . . Immediately after them came the malefactor himself, seated in a cart, with a Capucin Friar on each side of him. The hangman, with two assistants, dressed in scarlet jackets, walked by the cart. This procession having moved slowly round the gallows, which was erected in the Piazza del Popolo, the culprit descended from the cart, and was led to a house in the neighbourhood, attended by the two Capucins. He remained there about half an hour, was confessed, and received absolution; after which he came out, exclaiming to the populace to join in prayers for his soul, and walked with a hurried pace to the gallows. . . . During the time appointed by law for the body to hang, all the members of the procession, with the whole apparatus of torches, crucifixes, and Capucins, went into a neighbouring church, at the corner of the Strada del Babuino, and remained there till a mass was said for the soul of the deceased; and when that was concluded, they returned in procession to the gallows, with a coffin covered with black cloth. . . . Two persons in masks, and with black gowns, mounted the ladder and cut the rope, while others below, of the same society, received the body, and put it carefully into the coffin."

147. Pp. 91–103.

148. Corrado Ricci, *Beatrice Cenci* (London, 1926), II, 196 ff.

149. P. 97.

150. P. 98.

151. The sympathies of the Roman populace lay with the Comparini, the sight of whose murdered bodies, Francesca Pompilia's clad in the habit of a nun (p. 118), moved them to pity and a desire for vengeance, particularly as vengeance would take the form of one of those public spectacles of bloodshed which were at once a semi-religious rite and a theatrical entertainment.

152. P. 99.

153. One of the twin baroque churches in the Piazza del Popolo. Its architects were first Rainaldi and later Bernini, and it had been completed in 1662. The feast of the Madonna of Monte Santo, or of Mount Carmel, had become increasingly popular during the seventeenth century, and was a special favourite with the poorer classes in Rome. The following description by the Marquis de Coulanges in his *Mémoires* (Paris, 1820, p. 207) of the procession for this feast, which he saw in 1690 when he was living in the Palazzo Bigassi in the Corso, shows convincingly how the date of Pompilia's birth would have been established in the minds of the witnesses, particularly as the Comparini house too was so near the site of the festivities. "Two days ago a spectacle took place which made us marvel more than ever at the singular devotion of the Italians. We saw a procession pass by in which at least two hundred men pulled along with tremendous effort a many-wheeled machine on which an altar had been erected in the middle of which appeared an effigy of the Virgin, life-sized, dressed and bedecked in the style of the most fashionable ladies of this land, lighted up by a great number of candles, and known as the Madonna del Carmine. This spectacle had drawn crowds of the common people into the streets, and had brought the nobles and their ladies to the windows." [Translated from the French.]

154. W. Hall Griffin, "The Murder of Pompilia" (translation of the Casanatense MS.), in the *Monthly Review*, Nov. 1900, p. 118, note 3.

155. OYB, p. 286, note 34.

156. Griffin, "The Murder of Pompilia," p. 125. There is no authority given for this statement, and I have not been able to trace the poem.

157. F. E. Faverty, "The Absconded Abbot in *The Ring and the Book*," in *Studies in Philology*, XXXVI, 88–104. (It may be remarked that Paolo Franceschini was not an abbot. The title *abate* in the seventeenth century meant only "the reverend.")

158. Dr. Moore (*A View of Society*, pp. 471–2) attributes the prevalence of murder in Italy even a hundred years later to this interference with justice and to the ease of escaping to another state, as Guido had attempted to do. He says:

"The murderer is pretty certain of gaining some church or convent, where he will be protected, till he can compound the matter with the relations of the deceased, or escape to some of the other Italian States; which is no very difficult matter, as the dominions of none are very extensive.

"Besides, when any of these assassins is actually carried to prison, it is not a very difficult matter for his friends or relations to prevail, by their entreaties and tears, on some of the Cardinals or Princes, to interfere in his favour, and endeavour to obtain his pardon."

159. Arezzo, Biblioteca dei Laici, MS. 106, pp. 72–4.

160. P. 103.

161. P. 38.

162. It is curious that no suit appears to have been brought by the family which would have had a claim to the Comparini fortune if Pietro had been childless.

163. P. 107, and OYB, p. 5.

164. OYB, p. 223.

165. *Ibid.*, pp. 101, 103, 104.

166. *Ibid.*, p. 93.

167. *Ibid.*, p. 118.

168. *Ibid.*, p. 81.

169. *Ibid.*, p. 183.

170. *Ibid.*, p. 103.

171. *Ibid.*, pp. 103, 96.

172. She actually uses this defence at her examination in Rome on May 13. OYB, p. 91.

173. *Ibid.*, p. 136.

174. *Ibid.*, p. 122. The statement in C (OYB, p. 276) that the Comparini hoped that Guido would be moved to a reconciliation by the birth of the child is most unconvincing. C is always the least reliable of the narratives.

175. OYB, p. 121.

176. *Ibid.*, p. 182. This argument was not used at the earlier trial of Caponsacchi.

177. *Ibid.*, p. 103.

178. *Ibid.*, p. 105.

179. *Ibid.*, p. 137.

180. *Ibid.*, pp. 57–61.

181. The Convertites were apparently so convinced of her guilt that they laid claim to her property as soon as she was dead (OYB, p. 152), taking advantage of the law by which prostitutes were forbidden to make a will, their goods being forfeit either to hospitals of poor honest girls or "to the maintaining of those guards that are to watch over their deportment." Richards Lassels, *The Voyage of Italy* (London, 1686), II, 128–9.

The desire to protect Francesca Pompilia's estate from the Convertites may explain the revisions in her will, and it might be suggested that some of the legacies were deliberately used as bribes to elicit testimonials to her innocence (p. 118).

182. P. E. Beichner, "Fra Celestino's Affidavit and *The Ring and the Book*," in *Modern Language Notes*, May 1943, pp. 335–40.

183. OYB, p. 156.

184. Beichner, "Fra Celestino's Affidavit," p. 338.

185. OYB, p. 59.

186. *Ibid.*, p. 121.

187. Pp. xliv–xlv.

188. Pp. 66–72.

189. P. 70.

190. Pp. 74–6.

191. Gest, *The Old Yellow Book*, pp. 45–50.

192. P. 118.

193. Pp. 95–7. There is some confusion about the identification. The Angelica MS. does not name the confederate, but calls him a "giovanetto pievano": Biagio Agostinelli alone was from Città della Pieve. But it later speaks of him as the youngest of the accomplices, and, according to the longer versions of S, Domenico Gambassini, the other guard at the door, was a few months younger than Biagio. Yet it was Biagio who was obdurate in his last hours, protesting that he was ignorant of Guido's murderous intentions. This declaration of innocence is contradicted by Biagio's own confession (OYB, pp. 136–7), and if it appeared in only one document would have to be discarded as an invented detail. But it is dwelt on at such length in the narrative of Guido's death that it may be supposed that the confession was the result of torture, though it is corroborated by Guido's own story (OYB, p. 135).

194. Detail in longer versions of S.

195. Lacy Collison-Morley, *Italy after the Renaissance* (London, 1930), p. 146.

196. Diego Angeli, *Storia romana di trent'anni* (Milan, 1945), p. 10.

197. Ricci, *Anime dannate*, p. 55.

198. Von Pastor, *History of the Popes*, XXXII, 583–6.

199. P. 102.

200. P. 109.

201. Pp. 69–70. See also p. xxxii.

202. Raymond, *The Infinite Moment*, pp. 213 ff.

203. Shaw, "The 'Donna Angelicata,'" pp. 69–80.

204. Gest, *The Old Yellow Book*, Preface, and chapter XIII, in which he examines the evidence, points out the falsehoods in Francesca Pompilia's deposition, and quotes the *Decisiones Criminales* of Francesco Dino, published in 1713, where Guido Franceschini's case is cited as that of a husband whose slaying of his adulterous wife was punished because of the attendant circumstances, despite the wife's guilt.

205. Beichner, "Fra Celestino's Affidavit," pp. 335–6.

206. Shaw, "The 'Donna Angelicata,'" p. 65. I am referring to Professor Shaw's translation of the letters in preference to that of Mr. Hodell, which is not always accurate. There is, moreover, in the Everyman edition of the OYB (p. 103) a misprint of *Fate* for *Frate*.

207. Shaw, p. 67.

208. Pp. 26–64.
209. OYB, p. 130.
210. *Ibid.*, p. 181. This testimony was not admitted to the record (*ibid.*, p. 110).
211. Pp. 101–2.
212. P. 99.
213. P. 91. Many of these narratives of a condemned man's final hours have some such prelude or conclusion.
214. Paul A. Cundiff, "The Clarity of Browning's Ring Metaphor," in *PMLA*, Dec. 1948, pp. 1276–82.

NOTES TO THE DOCUMENTS

1. These numbers refer to the Summary which follows.
2. Pp. 13–20.
3. I am unable to explain these fractions of bonds, unless they refer to the state of maturity of the bonds with cumulative interest. Some bonds in these Monti were bought at, say, 87 scudi, and were redeemable after a certain number of years at 100.
4. This refers to the three bonds pledged to Pietro Zacconi (p. 15).
5. This is one of the strongest arguments in support of the feigned birth contention. It is most unlikely that a woman of Violante's age after several miscarriages (p. 29) could have borne a living child.
6. The nickname probably indicates that Angela's husband was a huntsman in the service of some wealthy family. He is described elsewhere as wearing his master's livery (p. 31).
7. Abbreviation for *Non Nominatus*, the equivalent of the English X.
8. Unless the compiler of the documents copied this figure inaccurately, Guido falsified even his age. As he was baptized in January 1657, he was 36 in 1693.
9. Conte Conti, whose brother, the Canon, helped to plan the flight from Arezzo.
10. This was probably the villa at Vitiano where later Guido planned his wife's murder (OYB, p. 136). She may have met Caponsacchi there occasionally in that garden which was so suitable for the entertainment of pleasant company (*ibid.*, p. 103).
11. A bird-netting ground is thus described by Montaigne: "Among other things I saw there [at a villa near Lucca] the form of certain little thickets which they make in rough places. Within an area of about fifty paces they plant divers trees, of those that remain green all the year round. This place they encircle with little ditches, and within it they lay out little sort of covered alleys. In the middle a place for the fowler, who with a silver whistle and a number of thrushes caught for the purpose and tied, having disposed on every side a number of bird-lime snares, at a certain season of the year, say about November, he will in a morning catch 200 thrushes." *The Diary of Montaigne's Journey to Italy in 1580–1581*, trans. E. J. Trechmann (London: Hogarth Press, 1929), p. 252.
12. Possibly at Sovara (Shaw, "The 'Donna Angelicata,'" p. 65).
13. Paolo, in the service of Cardinal Lauria, was actually 43.
14. Girolamo Franceschini was really 39.
15. Cosimo III de' Medici.

16. Antonio Maria Franceschini.

17. This "brother of the count," is of course, the Canon Conti who helped Francesca Pompilia to leave Arezzo.

18. This detail may have been elicited by the Comparini's lawyer with malicious intent: the deposition of Angelica about the niggardly housekeeping of Signora Beatrice also forms part of the Summary.

19. The Chiesa or Via dei Greci.

20. Now part of the Via Margutta. These gardens were on the site of Domitian's naumachia.

21. Nine Monti (to a total of 209,271 bonds) called San Pietro at 3 per cent were instituted by Innocent XI to refund all the other Monti except a part of the Novennale secondo (Coppi, *Discorso*, p. 17). The value of these bonds rose from par of 100 to 127 scudi.

22. There was a system by which the bridegroom made a gift to the bride proportionate to the dowry, which may explain this reference. C. Calisse, *A History of Italian Law* (Boston, 1928), p. 578.

23. Evidently he had gained the Pope's permission to alienate only the interest of these bonds. He had probably surrendered them to Pietro Zacconi as security for a sum of money which was to be repaid out of the interest, and when repayment was completed he was probably to recover the bonds. This would explain the reference on p. 7.

24. Pietro apparently tried to protect his daughter's interests more carefully than his own. It is almost impossible to believe that unless he had had some secret agreement with Guido he would have surrendered so completely his right to even a small income. This is all the more evident because there were laws forbidding a dowry to be disproportionate to the estate of the father of the bride (Calisse, *A History of Italian Law*, p. 377).

25. It is Francesca Pompilia's signature to this and the other dowry contracts which was adduced later as a proof that she knew how to write before she went to Arezzo.

26. Both here and on pp. 17, 19, Pietro Comparini is styled *Dottore*, which is certain evidence, since the title appears in a legal document, that he had graduated from a university, probably in law. This is the only indication we have of his social status.

27. The provision that the bonds could be cashed and the proceeds reinvested was probably made so that Guido might secure a higher rate of interest on the capital. Since the Monti could be sold at a high premium, this reinvestment would be a very sound way of increasing his income.

28. This, of course, was the weak part of the agreement, as Guido had no property of his own; and his brothers, as the event showed, were not willing to give him any rights in their benefices.

29. This is the promise of ratification which was not fulfilled, and which consequently gave Pietro a good excuse for refusing to complete the payment of the dowry.

30. The Monte di Pietà was the public loan society, exercising the function which in England was performed by pawnshops. It made loans on pledge, and part of its capital was derived from investors who received interest on their money. It was one of the safest investments available.

31. In the original contracts Guido was granted only the price of five bonds

(p. 18). He may have found in the meantime that his immediate financial needs were greater than he had anticipated.

32. A.C. stands for Auditor Camerae.

33. The preceding document had stipulated that the money was to be reinvested in Arezzo only (p. 18).

34. This clause indicates that, as I have suggested in the Introduction, Guido had entered into some arrangement with Pietro, the record of which no longer exists. The other contracts do not mention any property of Guido's which could be mortgaged or held as security for his fulfilment of his engagements.

35. There are no signatures given for this document, so we still do not know whether, as the writer of C states (OYB, p. 270), Cardinal Lauria was one of the witnesses.

36. This document is a list of the contents of the "Summary."

37. Nothing appears concerning this dowry in the tax-collector's certificate as we have it (p. 65), which indicates that like other documents in the Cortona codex it is only a summary of the original.

38. Caterina Fiori was, according to this story, the aunt of Francesca Pompilia, who is claimed to be the daughter of Corona Paperozzi, Caterina's sister.

39. The hospital of S. Spirito was thus described by Richard Lassels in 1661–3. "This hospital of S. Spirito is one of the fairest in Europe both for bigness and revenues. It has a thousand beds in it for the sick; a prelate to govern it; store of priests physicians and under officers to attend on them, and a revenue of 70,000 crowns a year. There is also a monastery of women in it, in a place separated from the rest, capable of 500 young girls. . . . There is also a grate towards the street, where little infants are put into a square hole of a turn, and so turned in by night by their unlawful mothers, who not daring to own them, would otherwise dare to destroy them. The person that brings the child in the night, rings a little bell, whose rope hangs at the outside of that grate, and an officer within comes presently and receiveth it, and having first asked whether it be baptized or no, carrieth it presently away, and recommends it to a nurse, of which there are always store in readiness entertained there at the cost of the hospital on the woman's side of the house. When the children are grown fit for instruction, they are set to trades, the girls are carefully brought up by religious women there, till they be fit for marriage or a nunnery, according to their vocation." Lassels, *The Voyage of Italy*, II, 47–8.

40. I have not attempted to translate the times of day into modern terms. How difficult it is to do so is explained by the following passage from Beckford's *Letters* (II, 299): "The modern Romans reckon 24 hours, which end soon after sun-set. The first hour after is called one hour of the night. It is convenient enough at night, but in the morning, when they talk of the 16th or 17th hour, it is not always intelligible. As the length of each day differs several minutes from the preceding one, to avoid a daily alteration, which would be inconvenient, they wait till the difference amounts to 15 minutes; all the clocks then make a skip of a quarter of an hour on a day appointed, of which the Almanack will inform you." Following this system, 20 hours would be four hours before sunset, no matter whether the sun set at 7 or 8 P.M.

41. The Italian baby at that time was first swaddled in bands or strips of material, and then apparently an outer cover, consisting of a wide piece of cloth or a towel was fastened over these, covering it from neck to feet. This is some-

times called in the documents a foreign fashion, and may have been imported from Spain. A glorified version of this outer swaddling cloth may be seen in the portrait of the infant prince Federigo d'Urbino by Federico Baroccio (1532–1612).

42. According to Collison-Morley, "the coronation of a Pope meant a distribution of half a giulio to each poor person applying for the dole: women with child received double, with the natural consequence that many of them padded themselves with pillows." *Italy after the Renaissance*, p. 177.

43. The birth or delivery chair, or obstetrical stool, as it is variously called, is described in Harvey Graham's *Eternal Eve* (London, 1950), pp. 143–4, in a quotation from Richard Jonas's *The Byrth of Mankynde*, a 1540 translation of a Latin work by Rosselin. It was chiefly popular in Germany and France, but began to go out of favour there in the seventeenth century, when it was used only by ignorant midwives (*ibid.*, p. 217).

44. Violante does not mention offering any bribe to the mother, but Caterina's reluctance to surrender the child was probably an attempt to extort a larger price than had originally been stipulated. A present to the midwife is mentioned in this document (p. 33), and the price she received is more fully described later (p. 41).

45. This is the witness who claimed to have seen the child being taken to Pietro Comparini's house by the midwife and her husband (pp. 63–4).

46. It is unfortunate that the status of Caterina Fiori has been omitted, so that we know nothing of her position in life.

47. "Your worship" is evidently Pietro Comparini, in whose presence the deposition was made.

48. This, as I have mentioned in the Introduction, is the only suggestion in the evidence that Francesca Pompilia was not a legitimate, though posthumous, child. Nowhere in the depositions is there any statement about the social position or employment of her relations, though it is evident that they were of the poorest class.

49. I have used this old English word for *comare* as the nearest equivalent. Literally *comare* should mean godmother of one's child, a relationship which in Italy was, and in some regions still is, an extremely close one. It often, however, means only intimate friend or neighbour.

50. Rather a less glowing description than the one attributed to her by Violante, who insists on nobility as well as prosperity (p. 30).

51. This slight inaccuracy in the address may have been intentional, though the various references to the Comparini house do not always tally. It may be noticed that in the 1692 etching of the Piazza del Popolo used as an illustration in this book the Strada Paolina alone is not given a name.

52. Obviously the notary who is taking the deposition is anticipating all the objections that might be suggested by the other side, and is excluding any idea of mistaken identity.

53. This is the only description of Francesca Pompilia that we have, apart from the scattered statements that she was beautiful.

54. I.e., the midwife.

55. This is one of the details which show that the witnesses had not been too well drilled in their stories. Giovanna Bobba was the first wet-nurse to suckle the child (p. 34), Petronilla Feure the last (p. 35).

56. I.e., the delivery chair.

57. Another indication that the witnesses had not been coached.

58. S. Atanasio, attached to a college founded by Gregory XIII in 1580, almost across the street from the Comparini house. Their parish church, of course, was S. Lorenzo in Lucina, a little farther along the Via del Babuino, or Strada Paolina, as it was then called.

59. All details about the baptism are omitted from the earlier part of her deposition as we have it here.

60. Actually the Via de' Greci does not lead to the Piazza di Spagna but runs between the Via del Babuino (which does lead to it, and which she is obviously describing in the next clause) and the Corso. Agnese is evidently confused in her topography, and speaks later of Pietro Comparini's house as being in the Via de' Greci, instead of the Strada Paolina. See also note 51.

61. In many parts of Italy the age of legal majority was then 25. In 1681 Guido was 23 and Antonio Maria was apparently 21.

62. *Sic.* This document does not exist in the Cortona codex.

63. Both this plea and the following counter-plea are frequently quoted (without quotation marks) by the lawyers during the trial for murder.

64. This account seems to dispose of the theory that Guido hid and caused to be found the letters which he had gone to the trouble of forging, though it is an accusation made by the opposing counsel (p. 79).

65. These references are evidently to pages of the evidence prepared for this trial. The reference (p. 79) to page 114 shows what a bulk this evidence must have reached. It is to be hoped that some of it has survived and will yet be found.

66. Ovid was born at Sulmo, the modern Solmona. This quotation is, as Judge Gest points out (*The Old Yellow Book*, p. 157), very popular, and is elsewhere ascribed to Cicero. It is not to be found in the works either of Cicero or of Ovid, and seems to be a synthetic quotation, a summary of a passage in Lucian's *Amores* (section 53).

67. I cannot explain this reference, but the licence was probably connected with the original cause of his journey to Rome, about which he is very mysterious even in his deposition (OYB, p. 95).

68. The offer by the prosecution to have the handwriting of both parties established is almost conclusive proof of the strength of Guido's case. It was rejected on the insubstantial ground that the authentication should have been made before the trial (p. 79).

69. Antonio Lamparello after Guido's execution presented the case for clearing Francesca Pompilia from the charge of adultery, and so enabled Tighetti to inherit her fortune. It will be evident from a comparison of this document in the codex with the later plea (OYB, pp. 241–51) that in the latter he is only reiterating his old arguments, and can find nothing new to say in her defence.

70. This is the testimony of Angelica, and the number refers to the Summary as it appears in the Cortona codex.

71. I.e., Violante, to whom this letter is evidently addressed. These extracts from Paolo's letters are more lengthy than any in the OYB, and show that the unfortunate elder brother, evidently glad to be in Rome, far from the battlefield, was doing his best with all the tact and diplomacy which he had learned in his Cardinal's service to persuade both sides to tolerance, endurance, and discretion.

72. Probably a threat, as I have suggested in the Introduction, to invalidate the dower contracts.

73. I.e., Guido's maternal uncle. These letters have not so far come to light.

74. Of all the documents, this presents the most corrupt and difficult text. It is obviously very much abbreviated, and was so carelessly copied that in many places it was almost unreadable.

75. This argument is borrowed from one of the anonymous pamphlets (OYB, p. 155).

76. *Aeneid,* VI, 333.

77. Another hackneyed quotation, this time from Horace (*Satires,* I.7.3).

78. The anonymous pamphlet supporting the Franceschini (OYB, pp. 145–56).

79. See above, p. 20.

80. In this and the following paragraphs Pignatelli, evidently sure that his client will be found guility, is ingeniously suggesting that lighter penalties than the death sentence have been imposed in similar cases.

81. Marchese Ambrogio Spinola (1569–1630) was appointed by Philip III of Spain as supreme commander in the Low Countries. He appears in Velasquez's painting, "The Surrender of Breda."

82. Luca de Penna (*ca.* 1320–*ca.* 1390), a celebrated Neapolitan jurist, dedicated his *Tres Libri Codicis* to a still unidentified Cardinal Petrus Sanctae Mariae Novae.

83. This is the most complete of the three versions of the narrative in the Cortona library.

84. The Company had its own little chapel in the Carceri Nuove (where Guido was imprisoned). The altarpiece of Christ on the cross which inspired such devotion in the condemned is still in the museum of the Confraternity. Moschini thinks that it is probably by Giovanni Bizzelli, a pupil of Alessandro Allori, and was painted in 1575 (*S. Giovanni Decollato,* p. 53).

85. The church of S. Orsolo and S. Caterina in the Piazza del Popolo. It belonged to the Ursuline Order.

86. To understand this comment one must remember that the brothers of the Order wore, when engaged in their sombre mission, an all-enveloping black cassock and a pointed hood with narrow slits for the eyes (see Dr. Moore's description above, p. 129, n. 146). The first sight of these ill-omened figures would have assured Guido of his fate.

87. I am unable to determine whether the unnamed prisoner really was released, or whether the comforters considered that a pious lie was justified, the captive himself consenting to the dismal comedy in order to save Biagio's soul. If this is true, as seems probable, the episode is an unpleasant one.

88. This curious scene has many parallels in other documents of the period. There is a particularly striking one in another case described in Vat. lat. 13685 (pp. 286–307), entitled *Decapitazione dell'Illmo. et Eccmo. Signore Protomedico Giovanni Tomassini, Lettore di Sapienza et Esaminatore.* This gentleman, who was executed on June 9, 1666, for having killed another physician with a dagger, was obdurate when visited by his comforters. To soften his heart by a show of humility they put cords around their necks and attempted to kiss his feet. He refused to permit it. Then they threatened him, and put a lighted candle near his hands to give him a foretaste of hell. Still he was obstinate. Then, one after another, all the most persuasive members of the Confraternity tried their elo-

quence on him, but in vain. Then members of the Capuchin Order were called in; then Carmelities. Still in vain; and when he was taken into a chapel he refused to kneel. A notary of the Governor's came in to inquire what progress was being made; and when a brother of the Company told the doctor that he was now to be executed he retorted with threats to reveal scandals about prelates and cardinals.

Then the executioner entered, gagged him, put a rope around his neck, and cut off with shears all his hair, which, says the anonymous writer, was very long and beautiful. More orations were made to him, which moved all but him to tears. Finally the procession accompanied him to the gallows. But what piety had not effected vanity accomplished, and as he mounted the steps he sighed, removed the gag, and offered to repent on condition that he was to be taken back to the prison to receive the sacrament, that a wig should be made from his own hair or from some like it which he could wear as he was being executed, and that he should die not by the hangman's rope but under the axe. His conditions were fulfilled, and he died "with God, like a good Christian."

There was a manual for the use of the comforters on such occasions, *Memorie a fratelli della ven. archiconfraternita di S. Giovanni Decollato detta della Misericordia, della Natione Fiorentina in Roma per la solita prattica di aiutare a ben morire i condannati a morte* (1659). This has never been printed, but many manuscript copies still survive, two in the Vatican library, one in the Casanatense library (Moschini, *S. Giovanni Decollato*, p. 18). At least one such handbook was printed, Fra Zanobi de' Medici's *Trattato in conforto de' condannati a morte per via di giustizia* followed by *Ragioni da confortar coloro che per la Giustitia publica si trovano condannati alla morte, raccolte per M. Tullio Crispoldo da Riete—Alla devota compagnia di Santo Giovanni Decollato di Roma, et a qualunque altra persona, che per sua carità si diletterà d'andare a confortare coloro, che sono dalla giustitia condannati alla morte* (Rome, 1565), printed at the expense of the Confraternita. This volume contains a woodcut of St. John's head on a charger, a common emblem for the Compagnia della Misericordia in many cities of Italy.

89. If it were not for the lacuna one might consider this document the original, for it is more complete than either of the other versions of this narrative. But it too is evidently only an abridged copy of some still unknown original.

90. Giambattista Rospigliosi (1646–1722), who had been created Prince of the Holy Roman Empire in 1658 and invested with the duchy of Zagarolo in 1668. He had married Maria Camilla Pallavicini, heiress to Cardinal Lazzaro Pallavicini (Spreti, *Enciclopedia storico-nobiliare italiana*, V, 799). Despite his undoubtedly powerful influence he does not seem to have carried out his promises, as we know that Abate Paolo probably died in exile with the bitter conviction that his family had been ruined (Faverty, "The Absconded Abbot").

91. Probably his servant, Baldeschi. It is reminiscent of Manzoni's Don Rodrigo and Il Griso that Guido should have had in his service this murderous ruffian who already had a criminal record. He may have felt, again like Don Rodrigo, that he could depend on the man just because he had sheltered him from the law.

92. Such pious reflections were apparently not unusual. Beckford (*Familiar Letters*, II, 261) says that a member of the Misericordia told him of accompany-

ing to the gallows "an old offender: an assassin by profession, and a most hardened sinner. He told the Abbé that he had often prayed to God that he might die on a gallows, rather than be killed in the street, and he thanked him for his kindness."

93. The bronze processional crucifix, which is of very fine workmanship, and dates from the middle of the sixteenth century (Moschini, *S. Giovanni Decollato*, p. 53).

94. "The Fathers of the Agonizzants, whose vocation is, to be the Seconds of those who fight against death itself; that is, whose profession is, to assist those that are in the agony of death; and to help them to make those pious acts, which Christians should most of all then rouse themselves up to." Lassels, *The Voyage of Italy*, II, 15.

95. It is evidently from this narrative that the writer of S took his account of the execution.

96. The manual of instruction used by the Misericordia.

97. It is apparent from these repeated confessions that Guido was still inwardly rebellious against his punishment, and constantly felt the need of absolution for those moments of resentment.

98. Charles Dickens describes an execution which he witnessed in Rome in 1844 beside the church of S. Giovanni Decollato which is similar to this in many details. *Pictures from Italy*, Everyman edition, pp. 384–8.

99. This witness can be identified as Maria Margherita Contenti, whose character was attacked by Caponsacchi's lawyer (p. 79). Witness number 8, who is often joined with number 1 in this evidence, may be Maria Margherita's maid or one of the other "insignificant women living opposite" the Franceschini house of whom Francesca Pompilia speaks (OYB, p. 91, my own re-translation).

100. The prison in Florence where in the seventeenth century prisoners from other parts of Tuscany were confined on criminal charges.

101. This writing can be identified, though there is no signature, because Panciatichi's signed ratification appears on many other documents in this collection.

LIST OF AUTHORS CITED

ANGELI, D. *Storia romana di trent'anni.* Milan: Garzanti, 1945.

BECKFORD, P. *Familiar Letters from Italy to a Friend in England* [1787]. London, 1805.

BEICHNER, P. E. "Fra Celestino's Affidavit and *The Ring and the Book.*" *Modern Language Notes,* May, 1943.

BURNET, Bishop GILBERT. *Travels through France, Italy, Germany and Switzerland* [1685–6]. London, 1750.

CALISSE, C. *A History of Italian Law.* Boston: Little Brown, 1928.

CELESTINO DE' SANTI, Padre. *Storia della Chiesa di Maria Santissima Interceditrice di Grazie alle Fornaci fuori porta Cavalleggieri in Roma.* Rome, 1903.

CINELLI CALVOLI, G. *Biblioteca volante,* continuata dal dottor Dionigi Andrea Sancassani. 2nd ed., Venice, 1735.

COLLISON-MORLEY, L. *Italy after the Renaissance.* London: Routledge, 1930.

CONTI, G. *Firenze dai Medici ai Loreni.* Florence: Bemporad, 1909.

COPPI, A. *Discorso sulle finanze dello Stato pontificio dal secolo XVI al XIX.* Rome, 1855.

COULANGES, PIERRE PHILIPPE EMMANUEL, Marquis de. *Mémoires de M. de Coulanges, publiés par M. de Monmerqué.* Paris, 1820.

CUNDIFF, P. A. "The Clarity of Browning's Ring Metaphor." *Publications of the Modern Language Association,* Dec., 1948.

DICKENS, C. *Pictures from Italy.* Everyman edition.

Enciclopedia Cattolica. Vatican City, 1948–54.

FARULI, Abate PIETRO. *Annali, overo notizie istoriche dell'antica, nobile, e valorosa citta di Arezzo in Toscana dal suo principio fino al presente anno 1717.* Foligno, [1717].

FAVERTY, F. E. "The Absconded Abbot in *The Ring and the Book.*" *Studies in Philology,* XXXVI.

FLACK, ISAAC HARVEY. *Eternal Eve.* London: Heinemann, 1950.

GEST, J. M. *The Old Yellow Book.* Philadelphia: University of Pennsylvania Press, 1927.

"Graham Harvey" (pseud.). *See* Flack, Isaac Harvey.

GRIFFIN, W. H. "The Murder of Pompilia" (translation of the Casanatense MS.). *Monthly Review,* Nov. 1900.

HODELL, C. W. *The Old Yellow Book.* Everyman edition.

IMBERT, G. *Seicento fiorentino.* Milan: Athena, 1930.

LASSELS, R. *The Voyage of Italy.* London, 1686.

MONTAIGNE, M. *The Diary of Montaigne's Journey to Italy in 1580 and 1581.* Translated by E. J. Trechmann. London: Hogarth Press, 1929.

MOORE, J. *A View of Society and Manners in Italy.* London, 1781.

MOSCHINI, V. *S. Giovanni Decollato.* In series "Le Chiese di Roma illustrate." Rome: Danesi, 1926.

NIBBY, ANTONIO. *Roma nell'anno* MDCCCXXXVIII. Rome, 1839.

PASTOR, L. VON. *The History of the Popes.* London: Kegan Paul, 1898–1953.

RAYMOND, W. O. *The Infinite Moment.* Toronto: University of Toronto Press, 1950.

RICCI, C. *Anime dannate.* Milan: Treves, 1919.

——— *Beatrice Cenci.* London: Heinemann, 1926.

SHAW, J. E. "The 'Donna Angelicata' in *The Ring and the Book.*" *Publications of the Modern Language Association,* March, 1926.

SPRETI, U. *Enciclopedia storico-nobiliare italiana.* Milan, 1932.

TREVES, SIR FREDERICK. *The Country of "The Ring and the Book."* London: Cassell, 1913.

YARRILL, E. H. "Browning's 'Roman Murder Story' as Recorded in a Hitherto Unknown Italian Contemporary Manuscript" (translation of the Baylor MS.). *Baylor Bulletin,* Dec., 1939.